millennial *Fandom*

LOUISA ELLEN STEIN

millennial
Fandom

Television Audiences in the Transmedia Age

UNIVERSITY OF IOWA PRESS *Iowa City*

University of Iowa Press, Iowa City 52242
Copyright © 2015 by the
University of Iowa Press
www.uiowapress.org

Printed in the United States of America

Design by Richard Hendel

The University of Iowa Press is a member of Green Press Initiative and is committed to preserving natural resources.

Printed on acid-free paper

The following earlier versions of sections have been reworked and reprinted with permission from the publishers.

"#Bowdown to Your New God: Misha Collins and Decentered Authorship in the Digital Age." In *Companion to Media Authorship*, edited by Jonathan Gray and Derek Johnson, 403–425. Malden: Blackwell-Wiley, 2013.

"*Gossip Girl*: Transmedia Technologies." In *How to Watch Television*, edited by Ethan Thompson and Jason Mittell, 338–346. New York: New York University Press, 2013.

" 'Word of Mouth on Steroids': Interpellating the Millennial as Media Fan." In *Flow TV: Television in the Age of Media Convergence*, edited by Michael Kackman et al., 128–143. New York: Routledge, 2010.

Library of Congress
Cataloging-in-Publication Data
Stein, Louisa Ellen.
Millennial fandom : television audiences in the transmedia age / Louisa Ellen Stein.
pages   cm
Includes bibliographical references and index.
ISBN 978-1-60938-355-8 (pbk)
ISBN 978-1-60938-356-5 (ebk)
1. Television viewers—Social aspects.
2. Fans (Persons)—Social aspects.
3. Generation Y.   I. Title.
PN1992.55.S74   2015
302.23′45—dc23   2015005561

To Penny and Jude

Contents

Acknowledgments

I am greatly indebted to those who read drafts and helped me talk through ideas over the four years of this book's inception: Kristina Busse, Natalie Hennessy, Melanie Kohnen, Allison McCracken, Jason Mittell, and Sharon Ross.

Thank you to my colleagues in the Film and Media Culture department at Middlebury College, and to my students, especially in my Gender/Sexuality/Media, Millennial Media, Remix, and Theories of Spectatorship courses, all of who helped me work through these ideas. I am also grateful to my editor, Catherine Cocks, my copyeditor, Karen Hellekson, and to everyone at the University of Iowa Press.

Thank you to fandom for never, ever being boring. Fan creativity is endlessly inspiring, and at any time when I felt less than excited about my work, all I had to do was go online to be awed, impressed, and reinvigorated. A special shout-out to my absnosome Gishwhes team for inspiring me to leave self-consciousness behind.

Special thanks to my husband, Ben, who was sounding board, draft reader, *Pretty Little Liars* and *Gossip Girl* fellow viewer, and overall support throughout; to my daughter, Penny, who is always pointing me to new things to love (from *My Little Pony* to *Barbie Life in the Dreamhouse* to Stampylongnose); to Jude, who incubated along with this book; and finally to my parents, for instilling in me at a very young age the belief that I would one day author a book.

Introduction

On July 13, 2013, I uncharacteristically took a break from my digitally mediated world. My Internet hiatus wasn't really driven by any conscious decision. For some reason, I just didn't log on to Twitter, Tumblr, Dreamwidth, or Live-Journal that day, that evening, or the morning after. As a result, I was in a bit of a fandom news vacuum. So it was my husband who asked me, on the way to a small-town event on Sunday, if I had heard about Cory Monteith. What about Cory Monteith, I asked? I hadn't heard any news of the actor who played Finn, Glee's innocent and sometimes pigheaded football star turned singer. What I hadn't heard would permanently change my feelings about Cory, Finn, and Glee as a whole: Cory Monteith was dead, of unknown circumstances, found in a hotel room after having gotten out of rehab a month before. I stole moments during our town picnic to look at Tumblr on my phone, where I saw the first of many images picturing the whole cast in mourning. They were going about their business, but I and many other fans read shock, loss, and disbelief on their faces.

I'd been a latecomer to Glee. I had stormed my way through it, deeply ambivalent yet deeply enamored with some of it, and completely taken by its fandom and fan energy. Glee is the focus of three chapters in this book (and now this opening) because I feel that, perhaps more than any other show, it encapsulates the hopeful discourses surrounding the millennial generation, a mind-set I discuss as millennial hope. But that seemed to change with Cory's death. Now, at the time of writing, in this in-between moment after Cory's death and before the start of the series' fifth season, *Glee* represents a collision of millennial hope and what I've termed millennial noir—the darker narratives that circulate about millennials, and the difficult issues faced by millennials but often obscured by the more prevalent hopeful narratives. As a friend said to me right after the announcement of Cory's death, "How do you maintain a show called *Glee* when one of the primary actors dies?" How do you represent a generation's outlook as gleeful, hopeful, and forward moving in the face of unexpected and illogical tragedy—tragedy that speaks to individual isolation and struggle, if not to generational struggle and desperation?

As timing would have it, I'm (re)writing this book introduction in the summer of 2013, in the precipice before we see how *Glee* handles Cory's death in the coming season. I think it's somehow important to capture this in-between moment—this moment in which *Glee* no longer means hope, no longer seems so clearly to herald the sense that "it gets better," but hasn't yet become something else either—hasn't been recuperated into a safe, hopeful narrative. Cory's death has not yet been assimilated into a story line about mourning that will no doubt be both troubling and important for its millennial viewers, who are struggling with the contradictions inherent in all the narratives circulating about their generation. I'll have more to say once those episodes air and no doubt do things with all these issues that I can't predict (as *Glee* is wont to do), but I do think there is something important about this in-between, messy moment where our media narratives can't address, redress, or even attempt to contain the strong feelings resulting from Cory's death.

Some Notes on Method

This book is about millennials—that is, members of the so-called millennial generation—and it is also about media fans. However, these are amorphous, contested categories. Who gets to say who is a millennial or who is a fan? And what would it mean to be a millennial fan? Both terms are used to label others in order to try to define and quantify particular ways of being in culture, and both are also terms that have become self-nomers—calling cards indicating one's own particular cultural outlook, experiences, interests, practices, or pleasures. I identify as a fan, and I have done so since my early twenties (though if I look back on my own personal history I can see the fan in me

[handwritten margin notes:] Unfinished + unknown — I'm between — irony of a lovate about pop culture fandom

for as long as I can remember). I'm too old to feel that I can also call myself a millennial (more on those generational delineations shortly), but I find that I'm drawn to millennial culture and millennial media, and, despite my birth year of 1975 (making me a late Gen X-er), I do feel my own interests and life experiences reflected in much of millennial media. There are moments where all this research on millennials has made me feel rather old, as I realize the distance between myself and some parts of the culture I've been studying; but for the most part, I've found that the issues being worked through in millennial media still resonate with my thirty-something outlook. I argue that this expansive resonance is key to the potency of the very notion of millennial, and thus to its acceptance as a generational label.

Many words float through our cultural lexicon in attempts to label and define the current generation of teens and young adults—terms such as Gen Y, Generation Next, Generation Me, and the Digital Generation, to name just a few. William Howe and Neil Strauss's term "millennial" came to the fore in 2000, initially popularized in their book, *Millennials Rising*, with help from a significant amount of endorsement and publicity by the Pew Research center.[1] In *Millennials Rising*, Howe and Strauss argue that the generation coming of age in 2000 would not be disenchanted and cynical like their Gen X predecessors but instead would be goal-oriented pragmatists with a positive, family-oriented outlook, intent on solving the world's problems. Central to this positive vision is the sense that millennials combine traditional family values with immersion in digital popular and commercial culture. Howe and Strauss identify millennials as simultaneously hopeful and savvy, and as digitally skilled but willing to accept a corporate claim on their lives. As the term has spread and gained traction, mentions of the millennial generation conjure visions of Facebook-dwelling, iPhone-buying Obama supporters and college students who return home to be with their families on weekends. The millennial concept has become more than simply a generational group. It now also refers to a vision of the ideal multiplatform cultural participant.

Popular discourse envisions millennials to be active participants in, rather than passive recipients of, the media culture that surrounds them. This image of the young, media-savvy millennial reworks popular perceptions of a cultural figure with a much longer history: the media fan. Like millennials, media fans have come to be known as digitally resourceful (and/or overdependent) and community oriented. Inspired by their love of a specific media text or of media culture in general, fans use digital networks like LiveJournal, You-

Tube, Tumblr, and Polyvore to build communities and to share and respond to their creative work. Fans often use digital tools in unexpected and unintended ways, creating interactive narratives via linked online journals or constructing fannish narrative worlds out of unaffiliated world-building games such as The Sims.[2] Fans also coordinate with each other to raise charity, to campaign for canceled shows, or to increase the visibility of their favorite series.[3] Although media fans may make up only a small percentage of film and TV viewers, fan modes of engagement have become increasingly visible. Simple Google searches offer entrance into fan activity; the not-for-profit, fan-run Organization for Transformative Works represents fandom as creative culture; academic work on fandom brings fans to the fore in the field of media studies; and industry discourse hypes the potential and promise of fan dedication.

However, precisely because of their proactive engagement with a franchise or concept across platforms, and because of their potential visibility (a potential that's there whether a corporate interest wants it or not), media fans are not necessarily ideal audiences in the eyes of media conglomerates. Fans may be (perceived as) too outspoken, too focused, too obsessive, or too transgressive.[4] Industry and popular discourse often present fans as excessive figures who may be convenient to depend on as core audience members but who are too demanding and unruly to be desirable consumers. Popular representations often posit fans as too niche—as cult figures with unusual tastes and obsessive practices who are not representative of the majority audience.

But even with their potential unruliness, the modes of engagement that fans model certainly appeal to the media industry. At the least, fans represent viewers who will come back for more—and who may be convinced to invest money in affiliated merchandise.[5] Enter the millennials. The popular vision of the millennial offers a modified version of the media fan, retaining some commercially friendly fannish qualities like expectations of engagement, willing consumerism, and technological savvy, while downplaying others such as subcultural status and the potential for political or social transgression. Millennial discourse (at least, as represented by Howe and Strauss and as spun by corporate interests) seems purged of many of the negative connotations of media fandom; for example, millennials can be social online without necessarily triggering taboos of obsession or inadequacy, or the inability to discern reality from fantasy. — where is the boundary btwn stereotype/stigma &

In this book, we'll examine the evolving relationship between fan and mil- really
lennial, keeping in mind that both exist as constructs formed at the juncture here?
This
all seems like other
people's children,

of academic, popular, and commercial discourse. The picture I paint here will certainly not be a totalizing portrait of either millennials or fans. Both are slippery concepts that shift depending on who is doing the defining, and both are highly multifaceted cultures that I, or anyone else, could only ever know in part. The case studies that I offer here are shaped by my particular experiences, both personally and through my research, with millennial representations, cultures, and fandom. As you read, you may think of comparisons that resonate with the pictures I paint here, based on your own experience of millennial media culture, fandom, or both; or you may think of counterexamples that no doubt would enrich our understanding of these two intersecting categories and cultural experiences.

As a significant part of this project, I explore commercial media texts that represent millennials and that are directed at a millennial market. However, exploring only commercial representations of millennials would result in too limited a picture, in part because many of those creating the representations of millennials in film and television would not be considered millennials themselves but rather part of the Gen X or boomer generations. This book thus moves beyond commercial millennial representations to look at millennial self-representation, examining texts created by and circulated among millennials such as blog posts, tweets, remix videos, YouTube posts, and image-sharing streams. When we turn to millennial self-representation, what we find expands and confounds the commercial narratives that circulate about millennials. Looking at what millennials do with digital technology as they represent themselves or as they respond to representations of themselves demonstrates the molding impact of commercial representations, while revealing how millennials undermine, negotiate, and alter those narratives.

In this book, we'll explore millennial self-representation and the modes of digital authorship and media engagement emerging from within millennial culture. As we look at how millennials represent themselves and their engagement with media, we'll find that not only do millennials recreate and rework long-standing fannish behaviors, but also that some—perhaps even many—identify as fans themselves. We'll follow threads that link representations of fan culture and millennial culture, and we'll consider the intersection of the two in millennial fan culture.

This book's examination of millennial media traverses a decidedly transmedia landscape. In *Show Sold Separately*, Jonathan Gray illustrates the way in which today's media texts—and indeed past media texts—cross platforms, with significant meaning making taking place beyond the core film or television series, in industry discourse, advertising, and digital paratexts. This book explores all of these sites, often within a single chapter. The multiplatform cultural life of a media text includes audience engagement and fan authorship, and we will look at all of these elements as part of an interdependent, dynamic transmedia system.[6]

This project is not a sociological or ethnographic attempt to define millennials. Rather, it is a discursive analysis; through textual analysis of press coverage, industry promotions, televisual texts, official digital paratexts, and online viewer participation, I map an emerging picture of millennials and millennial fans that is created in part by the industries that seek to court them and in part by millennial self-representation and self-initiated online engagement.[7] The digital technologies, platforms, and interfaces that host millennial and fan culture inform the shape of both and their intersection. My examination of millennial fan culture thus consistently takes into account the limitations and affordances offered by the interfaces used by industry, fans, and millennials.[8]

The term "millennial" connotes a member of a digitally connected youth culture that rises above national boundaries. Likewise, the affordances of digital tools supposedly enable cultural participants to connect across national boundaries. However, this is only the case insofar as economic, cultural, and political restrictions allow. Online fan and millennial cultures are international to varying, limited degrees. The most commercially visible images of millennials come from US and British media texts. Most online English-language millennial and fan communities, while potentially international in theory, focus predominantly, if not in totally, on American- or British-based media and culture. In its examination of commercial representations of millennials, this book focuses predominantly on these more visible English language texts, but the digital millennial cultures that engage with these texts do cross national boundaries to limited degrees.

One problem that remains at the heart of this project is whether there is even a category "millennial," whether we can even use the term, and, more broadly, whether the logic of generations actually holds cultural weight or valid insight. I argue that generational concepts are discursively constructed rather than essentially true. Yet while writing this book, I have found that I need language to talk about the agency and creative culture of the people within the age group identified as millennials. I use the term "millennial" with an awareness of its status as problematic construct, as a shorthand term to refer to those who fall within its construct and are affected by it. In the end, even the digital media practices that we might identify as millennial are not practiced just by millennials. As with so many questions of identity online, ascertaining people's real age is a complex, elusive, and potentially misguided project. Perhaps the best way I have found to think of my use of the term "millennial" is that I am examining millennial as construct and as evolving, self-defined culture.

One final note: this book focuses primarily on television and digital media. I do reference key millennial film texts such as the *Harry Potter* and *Twilight* franchises, especially to the extent that these series have found a life online. Overall, however, I would argue that serial media texts and spaces fostered by television and digital media serve as the core landscapes for millennial articulation in the current cultural moment.

Defining Millennials

As originally defined by Howe and Strauss in *Millennials Rising*, the millennial generation purportedly spans across two decades, encompassing those born between 1982 and 2004. This wide age range merges two desirable markets, teens and young adults, both of whom are thought to have significant disposable income. This compounded demographic positions millennials as a highly desirable target audience for advertisers and TV networks alike.

Digital technologies figure largely in popular notions of the millennial generation and in representations of millennials. Marketers desire millennials in part because of their supposed comfort with technology and with the corporatized digital world. According to popular narratives, because millennials grew up with digital technologies, they feel more innately comfortable with, and thus dependent on, Web 2.0 and emerging Web 3.0 media technologies and the new ways of being social those technologies foster. This theme of embedded digital dependence runs through discourses surrounding millennials, be it commentaries that celebrate millennial technological skill put to good use or that condemn millennial social isolation and ethical depravity.[9]

In 2001, Mark Prensky distinguished between digital natives and digital immigrants, arguing that the generation raised into digital technology moves with significantly greater ease through the digital landscape then do their parents because they were raised with digital expectations.[10] Such generational portraits depict young people using media technologies in the constant patterns of their lives to form a social tapestry built on ongoing digital conversations. Thus imagined, this generational construct (whether labeled millennial or digital) offers an antidote to long-standing fears of technology. Rather than technology signaling the breakdown of human society via social alienation, here we have a vision of a developing generation (and by extension a society) that intuitively uses technology (and specifically, commercialized technology) to build community. Where past and continuing visions of media fans hold more tightly to the anxieties around technology replacing human sociality, millennials' use of technology does not necessarily suggest social deficiency. Rather, it calls up notions of social prowess or even social power.

Industry discourse describes millennials as not only technologically savvy but also ideologically unique, and thus both commercially and socially significant. For example, a piece in *Advertising Age* about millennial-focused cable network ABC Family describes—and thus constructs—their target audience as technologically skilled multitaskers who seek "relevance in their media."[11] The article describes millennials as a generation with an ethical core, armed with technological skill, ready to take over from their parents and to solve society's most difficult challenges from their own perspective. Regardless of how millennials perceive themselves (if they even recognize themselves as a coherent generational group), industry discourse such as this—and to a degree academic discourse as well—projects onto millennials the technological, ethical, and social skills seen as key to future cultural, economic, and political success. Public discourse hails millennials as a generation of hope—hopeful in and of themselves, and offering hope to older generations unable to adapt to the complexities of the digital world.

This is not to say that prevailing visions of millennials wholly celebrate this new generation's potential. Accompanying the visions of millennial hope is the murkier imagery of millennial noir, which features millennials who are morally challenged, alluring but trapped in their own digital excesses. This more negative discourse reframes millennial technological skill as overdependence, critiquing the heavy mediation of millennials' social experience and their lack of self-censorship in online publics. Taken in full—hope and noir combined—popular discourse about millennials represents them as a curious combination of idealist and corporate. For example, Bazaar.com's "Millennials Are Socially Conscious Consumers" describes millennials as a "growing generation of the most educated, jaded, rich, and socially conscious consumers ever."[12] Blog posts like this construct a vision of millennials as innocent yet knowing, individually minded yet corporate bred, socially aware yet welcoming of their roles as consumers.

To return to the interrelationship between millennials and media fans: even the more ambiguous noiresque picture of millennials remains distinct from the harsher stereotypes of the fan. Indeed, it is as if the mainstreaming of a millennial identity depends on the existence of the separate, more taboo, and excessive form of media engagement relegated to the fan. However, the fan imprint can be seen clearly in the practices assumed to characterize the millennial generation, including the use of technology to engage with media in what fans have termed affirmational and transformational ways.[13] Millennial media practices simultaneously reject notions of fannishness and recreate modified fannish modes of media engagement.[14]

These attempts to modify the fan into the more mainstream millennial are highly gendered. Understandings of fandom have always been heavily shaped by gendered assumptions, be it the incoherent, screaming, excessive Beatles fans of Beatlemania, the seemingly failed masculinity of Trekkies, or, in more recent years, the recognition of media fandom as primarily female collective and as space for articulation of female and queer desire.[15] Both the fangirl and the fanboy, seen as taboo and compromised individual figures and as threatening outspoken collective, have troubled media producers in pursuit of the magic combination of cult buzz and ratings success. The perceived mainstreaming of the fan position into the millennial generation seems to offer TV networks the opportunity to defuse the (gendered) fan threat. Yet as the years pass, the celebration of high emotion, or "feels," in millennial spaces and in the spaces of millennial fandom suggest a larger cultural shift, one that perhaps moves beyond these gendered taboos. Millennials have made fan practices more socially acceptable by action, word, and image, if not name, and I would suggest that many of the perceived divisions between millennial and fandom will soon dissolve—or that we're seeing them dissolve already.

Mainstreaming Fandom . . . Studies?

In *Convergence Culture*, Henry Jenkins (author of the formative work in fan studies, *Textual Poachers*) argues that commercial media producers, for better or worse, must contend with the expectations of participatory culture, much of which he sees as having roots in fandom.[16] Jenkins's more recent *Spreadable Media* (coauthored with Sam Ford and Joshua Green) takes this argument further, providing a picture of participatory culture, including but not limited to fandom, that industrial producers might (the book seems to suggest) be wise to at least work with, if not emulate.[17] *Convergence Culture* and *Spreadable Media* both ask us to consider fandom as significant beyond itself—as offering a vital model for present and future media culture en large.

Likewise, in *Digital Fandom*, Paul Booth argues that fandom past and especially present holds insight into contemporary digital culture more broadly.[18] Booth also contends that contemporary digital fandom maps out necessary directions for the broader field of media studies, prodding us to consider a new media studies that is dynamic, multiplatform, and collectively authored. I agree, and a similar impetus drives this project. However, I want to stress here that as we open the door to drawing analogies and parallels between fan culture and broader digital culture, we cannot lose sight of the fact that both of these categories—fan culture and digital culture—exist as discursive constructions with specific and ideologically loaded histories. Fan culture and millennial mainstream digital cultures are, to a degree, discursive fictions that in any given moment break down into a diversity of specific experiences, We must be wary of equating the two or assuming causal relationships of influence between the two. Karen Hellekson and Kristina Busse's edited collection *Fan Fiction and Fan Communities in the Age of the Internet* offers various perspectives on fandom's evolution in digital contexts; such a multiauthored diversity of perspectives helps resist singular narratives that might put too narrow a point on fandom or its relationship to digital culture. Most specifically, Francesca Coppa's "A Brief History of Media Fandom," included in *Fan Fiction and Fan Communities*, asserts the specifics of media fan history and reminds us to question easy conflations between mainstream digital culture and fan culture and practices.[19]

In their introduction to *Fandom: Identities and Communities in a Mediated World*, Jonathan Gray, Cornell Sandvoss, and C. Lee Harrington argue that contemporary fan studies no longer only (or perhaps even primarily) serves to offer insight into the more limited worlds of particular fan cultures but rather offers "an investigation of fandom as part of the fabric of our everyday lives." Gray, Sandvoss, and Harrington term this movement third wave fan studies and suggest that for this wave, "fandom is no longer only an object of study in and for itself. Instead, through the investigation of fandom as part of the fabric of our everyday lives, third wave work aims to capture fundamental insights into modern life."[20] I like the label of third wave fan studies precisely because it insists on locating fandom within the fabric of the everyday. The concept usefully highlights interconnections between fan studies and the projects of third wave feminism, most significantly including a determined unsettling of divides between the political and the personal, as well as questioning the notion that academic knowledge can and should be objective. In addition, research on media fan communities, from *Textual Poachers* to the growing field of scholarship published in the journal *Transformative Works and Cultures*, points to fandom as a space for predominantly female audience communities and for queer identification.[21] Issues of gender and sexuality are key to fan traditions of media production, including understandings of fan fiction as pornography written by and for women, the ever-evolving traditions of slash fan fiction as queer critique, and fan vidding as a forum for unmasking gender tropes in popular media.[22] However, these femalecentric fan communities and fan authorship traditions have been predominantly perceived as cult practices with only minority participation. It seems to me that a third wave of fandom studies could potentially insist on the presence and centrality of these dimensions of fandom as beyond niche and beyond cult. Furthermore, as corporate media producers modify notions of the fan and fandom to meet their needs, gender and sexuality become central points of conflict, affecting whom commercial media producers will address and acknowledge as their audiences. This book explores the gendered politics at play in the perceived transition from fandom as cult activity to defining feature of the mainstream millennial audience. Indeed, as I've suggested above, the millennial construct is in many ways not only a modification of the fan position but also a modification that is highly (and purposefully) gendered to defuse the (again, gendered) fan threat.

The call for a third wave of fan studies can be both a call to recognize the deepening relationship between fandom and mainstream culture and a call to be aware of the cultural, historical, political, and personal negotiations that color that relationship. As we necessarily search for "fundamental insights into modern life" through fandom, it is crucial that we acknowledge and map the nuanced relationships between the wide range of modes of contemporary media engagement, be they labeled fan, millennial, both, or neither. Matt Hills warns in *Fan Cultures* that scholars of fandom must be wary of seeking out similarities between academia and fandom and ignoring significant differences.[23] Likewise, I would call for increased attention to the distinctions between fan and millennial culture even as we explore the relationship and potential affinity between the two. As this book maps the relationship between fan and millennial, the tensions and negotiations between the two must always be at the forefront of our thinking. It is my intent that this book build on the vibrant work published in fan studies over the past two decades, but that in its focus on the nuanced and shifting relationship between fan and millennial, it also offers a model for moving forward into the third wave of fan studies.

Summary

The remainder of this introduction considers ABC Family's industry discourse during its network redefinition in 2007, including its television programming, transmedia extensions, and audience engagement. Specifically, I turn to ABC Family's network rebranding and website redesign in 2007, in which the network used notions of the millennial generation to help juggle the competing logics of a niche, young adult–oriented television network with the demands of the more conservative Disney brand. I examine the digital extensions built for the network flagship series *Kyle XY* (ABC Family, 2006–2009) to explore how ABC Family used its redesigned website to court a millennial audience that they constructed in the image of a cleaned-up fandom. By integrating alternate reality game–like elements into its online material, not to mention constructing a fake fan figure, the website simultaneously courted already digitally interactive fans and educated viewers on how to engage with prescribed fannish behaviors. *Kyle XY* paratexts shaped and modified the image of millennial fan behavior to fit the understanding of millennial touted by ABC Family as a key part of its network redefinition.

After the introduction, the book is split into three conceptual sections, each including several chapters with more concrete foci. Part 1, "Millennial Hope," examines the celebratory discourse that surrounds the millennial generation and that characterizes much of its media representation. I consider how the image of millennial as modified fan allows for a consumer youth figure that media producers, advertisers, and politicians alike feel comfortable embracing. I explore the relationship between Howe and Strauss's reframing of Gen Y as millennial in *Millennials Rising* and Henry Jenkins's reframing of fans as active, critically minded media participants in *Textual Poachers*. As a case study that stretches across three chapters, this section examines the Fox network's attempt to court and construct its millennial audience with the musical television series *Glee* (2009–present). Millennial hope is a pervasive discourse that we can observe in a range of series, including ABC Family series like *Kyle XY* and more recently *The Fosters* (2013–present); the WB and CW prototypical millennial series *Buffy the Vampire Slayer* (WB/UPN, 1997–2003), *Roswell* (WB, 1999–2002), and *Smallville* (WB/CW, 2001–2011); network series *Heroes* (NBC, 2006–2010) and *Friday Night Lights* (NBC, 2006–2011); and even season 4 of *The Wire* (HBO, 2002–2008). I choose a sustained focus on *Glee* because the series offers a particularly rich and expansive view of millennial hope discourse (and its contradictions) in narrative construction, genre revision, paratexts, and fandom. Where ABC Family constructed an individual, ideal fan, Fox provided an entire alternative terminology, popularizing the term "Gleek" rather than "fan."[24] *Glee* positions itself as a politically progressive show, speaking to millennials through its liberal approach to issues of sexuality, gender, race, and disability while heralding the importance of the collective, hopeful community. Fox offers a vision of Gleeks as an underdog collective, a group composed of diverse individuals who come together (like the characters on the series) to celebrate the hopeful power of community rather than individual or subcultural dissent. *Glee* draws on the toolbox of the movie musical to manage these ideological contradictions, usually by concluding episodes with a celebratory collective musical number that assuages any individual dissatisfaction. Moreover, these collective moments frequently revolve around a heteronormative paired performance. However, *Glee*'s millennial fan audiences often reject these moments of superficial collective resolution, pushing back at what they perceive as the series' ideological shortcomings. In the case of *Glee*, gender and sexuality become clear tension points in the push and pull between commercial representations of millennials and millennial self-authorship. The first chapter in this section examines *Glee*'s construction of the hopeful millennial collective, the second chapter looks at how *Glee*'s genre mixing and serial structure continually destabilize the series' more conservative ideological tendencies, and the third chapter looks at how fans use *Glee*'s ideological stew to create their own revised version of millennial hope.

Part 2, also consisting of three chapters, examines television programs that offer an alternative take on millennials: not millennial hope but millennial noir. In contrast to part 1's extended case study, here I offer a snapshot of millennial noir discourses across a cluster of associated series. I consider *Gossip Girl*'s televisual text and paratextual campaigns (CW, 2007–2012), alongside ABC Family's *Pretty Little Liars* (2010–present), the WB/CW's *Veronica Mars* (2004–2007), and ABC's *Revenge* (2011–present) to explore the emerging construct of millennial noir. More specifically, I examine the gender-inverted trope of the digitally empowered female private investigator as well as the merger of the infamous femme fatale with the private investigator into a single threatening, empowered, yet sympathetic female lead. The characters featured in these series use digital tools to fight corruption, both personal and political. They also use digital technology to attain power, at times becoming sympathetic terrorizers themselves. These series feature and celebrate the power of the female collective as a version of the digital network. In turn, millennial audiences celebrate and emulate the power of these characters in their own digital networks and digital authorship. In certain instances, they even take these darker narratives and turn them on the more hopeful ones discussed in the previous section—for example, writing fan fiction in which a terrorizing anonymous blogger (borrowed from *Gossip Girl* and *Pretty Little Liars*) wreaks terror on the innocent kids of *Glee*. The first chapter of part 2 examines the noiresque discourses that surround millennials and that counter the narratives of millennial hope put forward by Howe and Strauss et al. The second chapter of this section explores the genre and gender revision at work in four millennial television series that feature digitally empowered girls— *Veronica Mars*, *Gossip Girl*, *Pretty Little Liars*, and *Revenge*—and the third chapter examines millennial noir in fan engagement and production.

Part 3, "Millennial Transformation," looks at transformations in notions and processes of authorship in millennial culture. I consider how the increased options for audience authorship and audience–producer interaction change our understanding of audiences, authorship, and media more broadly. In the first chapter of this section, I focus on the rise to fame of the character actor Misha Collins, who used his small but fan-favored role on the CW series *Supernatural* (2005–present) to build a significant following on Twitter. Together, Collins and his fans have created a sense of shared subversive culture. They deploy their digital community to organize various projects, including web series, charity work, and a transmedia scavenger hunt. The models of shared authorship enacted by Collins and his fans build on and transform traditions of collective authorship that have evolved in predominantly female fan communities over the past two decades.

The concluding chapter of part 3 considers the extent to which millennial culture celebrates the transformative possibilities of collective affect (or, in fannish terminology, "feels"). While much of millennial fan culture touts the values of collective energy and emotion, discourses of professionalism still hold power. I look at the possibilities of transmedia storytelling within this fraught landscape. Specifically, I examine the emerging form of the web series, in which independent producers use YouTube, along with social-media tools like Tumblr and Twitter, to tell ongoing stories that inhabit the spaces and experiences of millennial culture and the traditions of fandom. Transmedia web series such as *The Lizzie Bennet Diaries* (Pemberley Digital, 2012–2013) and *Squaresville* (Wonderly, 2012–present) situate themselves squarely within fandom and work to achieve a sense of shared culture and community while still cultivating discourses of professional authorship and artistry. These web series reveal a millennial media landscape in which creators embrace a do-it-yourself collective ethos tempered with indicators of professionalism. Step by step, we are moving to a millennial media landscape no longer dominated by fears of the excesses of the unruly fan, one that instead embraces personal investment, performativity, emotion, and excess within the context of shared digital creativity.

Constructing Fandom

KYLE XY—A NEW KIND OF FAMILY

In 2007, the niche cable network ABC Family launched *Kyle XY*, a TV series that tells the story of a teenage boy who wakes up with no memory and no belly button, and yet who has an instinctive aptitude for harnessing technology and for building deep friendships. The series offers a vision of technologically savvy millennials who use digital media to construct value-oriented life experiences and social networks—very much the picture painted by Howe and Strauss in *Millennials Rising* seven years earlier.

Kyle XY follows the quest of its title character to discover his identity, ending (spoiler alert!) in the revelation that he was created as a corporate lab experiment. Over the course of its two seasons, the series explores issues of coming of age as a contemporary teen while being pursued by corporate interests. Kyle and friends seem to spend half of their time evading the reach of the corporation that created Kyle and the other half breaking into the company's headquarters to wrest corporate power for themselves. With its focus on teens finding themselves (in all senses) within corporatized systems, *Kyle XY* serves as a fitting opening text for us to consider as we think through the relationship between grassroots and corporately produced audience engagement, and between fan and millennial culture.

Kyle XY was the flagship show representing cable television network ABC Family's rebranding project. ABC Family's makeover also included a new logo and tagline—the open-ended and potentially provocative phrase "a new kind of family."[25] The framing of "a new kind of family" signified a strategic shift on the part of ABC Family to address the demographic of teens and young adults. Disney–ABC had purchased Fox Family in July 2001 and launched ABC Family in November 2001.[26] The rebranding was intended to signify the niche network's individuation from ABC and from its Fox Family past. The network originally attempted to signify this complex relationship by changing its name to XYZ. This name would have suggested that the niche network embodied the inverse of the ABC television network while also gesturing to the network's desired demographic: a merger of Generation X, Generation Y, and the future Generation Z. However, because of a contractual stipulation to keep the word "family" in their network title (dating back to the network's 1977 origins as a branch of Pat Robertson's Christian Broadcast Network), the network found itself having to give up the XYZ name in favor of ABC Family.[27]

To guide its redesign, the network turned to consultancy group Magid International, which advised the network to base its new image on the insights of (you guessed it!) *Millennials Rising* authors Neil Howe and William Strauss. Guided by Magid International, ABC Family pitched itself as the go-to destination for an audience that seemed to merge the safety of family values with the edginess of youth culture—the millennials.[28] As part of this network rebranding, ABC Family ran a special "branded content" section in *Advertising Age* entitled "Getting to Know the Millennials."[29] This piece served to educate potential advertisers as to the age range, core values, and behaviors of the network's new generational target. The very existence of this advertising piece suggests that "millennial" was still only on its way to becoming a recognizable category in the industry and commercial sphere, and that ABC Family had a vested role to play in that process.

In "Getting to Know the Millennials," John Rood, then senior vice president of marketing for ABC Family, explains that through research conducted by Magid International, ABC Family had discovered that millennials "seek relevance in their media" yet at the same time "value their family."[30] According to Rood, this meant that Disney-owned ABC Family was ideally positioned to capture the millennial audience: "As a network called ABC Family, that was music to our ears. We realized through our research that it wasn't that America's young adults had a problem with family; it is that they had a problem with family television—specifically the stereotypical conservative, boring or insincere aspects of family television."[31] The network's revised modus operandi would thus be to update family values for the new generation, making traditional family values relevant in a contemporary context. However, ABC Family had to walk a fine line, actively seeking out an audience immersed in contemporary cultural change while maintaining the more traditional qualities associated with its Disney and ABC corporate frame. To court the highly digital (according to Howe and Strauss, at least) millennials, ABC Family emphasized digital extensions, including gamelike transmedia elements, social networking, and digital authorship.

Paul Lee, president of ABC Family Channel from 2004 to 2010, pronounced the network's audience "a new generation" that was "changing the way people watch TV or use other technology."[32] According to Lee, the combination of digital technology and TV programming functioned like "word of mouth on steroids," and could, if handled correctly, be harnessed for network success.[33] Lee offered a vision of a network website that would connect viewers to programming and to each other via social networking. He described the ABC Family website—newly redesigned in 2007—as a "a full-scale online community that will allow our viewers to not only constantly connect with our shows and games, but also with each other."[34] Rather than seeing viewers networking with each other as only marginally important or potentially problematic, Lee argued that community building offered a route to brand loyalty. In his words, "We're confident that this enhanced interaction will only help to strengthen our Channel's relationship with viewers."[35] Lee emphasized the centrality of user-generated content to the network's new identity, describing the revamped ABC Family website as a "safe haven where ABC Family fans can upload their videos and share their stories about friends and family—two things we know our audience is deeply passionate about."[36]

While this notion of a safe haven seemed to embrace and encourage viewer/ fan authorship and the sharing of fan-authored texts, it also contained and limited authorship to that encouraged by the official interface, as is evident in Lee's comment: not just any stories were welcomed, but stories specifically about friends and family—stories that resonated with the network's "new kind of family" tagline. Lee presented these limits as being put in place in service of viewers, offering them a safe space for sharing, apparently somehow safer than the wilds of non-corporate-guided social networking.

The bigger picture painted was thus: while ABC Family may welcome and even go to great lengths to cultivate fannish behavior, it does so on its own terms. By recreating something akin to fannish modes of engagement, ABC

Family's digital extensions interpellated potential viewers (whether they perceived themselves to be media fans, millennials, both, or neither) into an industrial interpretation of fannishness. ABC Family promoted a corporate-sponsored and guided version of fannishness, packaged as contemporary youth identity, thus sidestepping negative associations of fans as excessive, obsessive, or antisocial. In this way, the network appropriated fannishness to bolster viewer brand loyalty and to strengthen advertiser faith in ABC Family as a viable venue with a compelling demographic reach.[37]

ABC Family thus etched out its brand identity by attempting to conflate fan and millennial viewing positions, constructing millennials as a desirable audience that would embody just the right amount of active engagement—engaged enough to strengthen the ABC Family brand but not disrupt it. In its simultaneous construction of and address to the millennial audience across media platforms, ABC Family interpellated an ideal viewer who was liminal yet poised to be mainstream, expert at media yet potentially malleable for advertisers, willing to go the extra mile in terms of textual investment yet happy to play within the officially demarcated lines.

A NEW KIND OF FAN

While *Kyle XY* represents the ideal millennial in televisual form, its digital extensions demonstrate how (and at what cost) industrial logics translate fan modes of engagement into industrially constructed viewing positions. The network-demarcated digital extensions for *Kyle XY* worked to ignite fan participation and the dedication that comes with it while attempting to mitigate the threat of unruly transgression that fans can be seen to pose. The digital options offered by ABC Family carefully guided the ways viewers could create and participate. Divided into a five-part rubric—Share, Play, Go, Celebrate, and Watch—the ABC Family website cultivated a sense of positive, playful community while reminding the viewer to return to view the television show itself.[38]

The ABC Family site wooed potential *Kyle XY* millennial viewers by combining community-oriented social networking with video game–like explorative play, but both of these elements were designed to feed back into the ABC Family brand, and most crucially to the television series at the center of the brand. A visitor to the ABC Family site in 2007 in search of *Kyle XY* online material would have first encountered the Clue Tracker area.[39] Upon entering Clue Tracker, an image of a futuristic metal door prompted visitors to enter a password. Entering any password revealed a room containing a bookshelf, a climbing wall, and a desk with a computer on it. *Kyle XY* viewers recognized the climbing wall as a challenge that Kyle has to overcome with the guidance of his mentor in order to come closer to the secrets of his identity. This was the first of many challenges within Clue Tracker, each of which, when completed, displayed a partial clue; when put together, these clues offered insight into the mysteries posed by the *Kyle XY* series. Completing the subgames in Clue Tracker (a project that took a fair amount of time and dedication) yielded access to a video clip containing a significant clue to *Kyle XY*'s larger televisual mystery. Fans used the ABC Family–hosted bulletin boards to collaborate as they worked through the Clue Tracker challenges in hopes of unlocking the mysteries of the *Kyle XY* narrative.

In addition to Clue Tracker, ABC Family also offered fake, alternate reality game–style websites designed for fictional entities featured on *Kyle XY*, playing with the line between fiction and "reality." For example, the site Madacorp .com (no longer available online) represented itself as the official corporate site of the company that created Kyle, with password-protected areas contributing to its sense of verisimilitude. (In addition, the TV series played fake commercials for Madacorp during commercial breaks.) Fans pooling information on ABC Family bulletin boards discovered hidden layers to the Madacorp site, including a Madacorp intranet that, once broken into, revealed further clues to the mysteries of the *Kyle XY* TV series.

These transmedia storytelling experiments may sound familiar; the fake commercials and fake Madacorp site shared much with the more famous transmedia experimentation affiliated with ABC's *Lost* and *Lost*'s fake corporation, the Hanso Foundation, which also had a website and fake commercials.[40] What was distinct about ABC Family's forays into the land of transmedia storytelling was the network's attempts to guide its millennial viewers through their digital extensions, teaching them to play within the networks' desired participatory paths. These paths always returned to the TV series itself rather than spinning outward into fan realms beyond the network's control.

ABC Family went to significant (and admittedly quite creative) lengths to guide fan engagement with the *Kyle XY* transmedia extensions. In January 2008, visitors to the ABC Family Insider Blog (an official online offering not specific to *Kyle XY*) noticed something strange.[41] Flickering images broke up the usual combination of text and promotional images. What looked like a girl crying for help flashed across the page's mise-en-scène, intermittently punctuated with broken, pixilated text. Enterprising fans in the site's forums brainstormed together about what these images could be. Fans quickly dismissed notions of a real hacker hijacking the ABC Family website, especially when similar images disrupted the diegetic transmedia extension Madacorp .com. Fans concluded that these were embedded narrative clues to *Kyle XY*. One fan suggested layering the broken text that had appeared at the different sites. With the help of screen-capture software, multiple fans shared their results: a plea for help to somebody named Cooper. The fans hypothesized that the SOS came from yet another test tube baby like Kyle, soon to be featured in later television episodes.

But there was something more at play here than a transmedia mystery for its own sake. At around the same time that fans began to notice and analyze the strange flickering images on the various ABC Family sites, the ABC Family Insider Blog drew attention to the "coolest new website by a *Kyle XY* fan": Coop's Scoop. Coop's Scoop presented itself as the blog of a young adult (millennial), Cooper.[42] In his blog, Cooper professed his love of *Kyle XY* and devoted his posts to unraveling the mysteries posed by the various *Kyle XY* websites. He offered an extensive walk through Clue Tracker and provided hints about how to locate and interpret the many clues embedded in Clue Tracker's game play. The banner at the top of Coop's Scoop was a clickable image of his bedroom, on the walls of which he had plastered images of the various mysteries posed at the *Kyle XY* official website. Like Clue Tracker, Cooper's banner offered a space of explorative play and mystery solving, but it also served to help fans navigate *Kyle XY*'s transmedia extensions.

Coop's Scoop presented itself as a fan website dedicated to unpacking the various paratextual story elements offered at the ABC Family site. Cooper never broke character, but after his website was hyped in such a direct and unusual way at the official Insider Blog, fans quickly searched his site for clues, much as they would Madacorp.com or Clue Tracker, and discovered that it was copyrighted by ABC Family. Soon thereafter, a character entered the *Kyle XY* TV episodes who looked very much like Cooper. Fans on the ABC Family forums debated among themselves whether these two characters were played by the same actor. At the same time, they interacted with Cooper as a fan construct and possible character on his own (ABC Family–copyrighted) blog. Cooper's artificial construction suggests the difficulties a network may face when attempting to shape fan engagement and to reach more potential fans. Cooper seems to have been introduced as a tool to make sure that fans

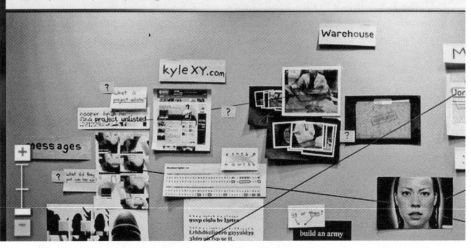

Figure 1. Coop's Scoop was a fake fan bulletin board (since taken down) guiding fan participation in *Kyle XY*'s transmedia extensions.

were being hailed effectively by *Kyle XY*'s transmedia efforts and were responding properly. Cooper himself was the site of producer discourse about what they believed millennial fans to be, and how to corral them in order to ensure that they respond appropriately and in significant numbers.[43]

Cooper also sets into relief the way millennial viewers engage in playful and personal ways with transmedia stories, often blurring the lines between fiction and their own experience of reality. First, fans applied their collective research skills in ways unintended by the network to discover Cooper's corporate origins as a fictional creation of ABC Family. Once they knew that Cooper was a corporate construct, fans interacted him as a fictional character, but one that had entered their "real" digital world. Cooper seemed to exist to fans as a liminal figure between producer and character, simultaneously a "person" they could interact with and a text to mine for clues. Cooper was quite the millennial contradiction: he seemed to emanate from the program's story world, he spoke with the authority of a commercial media producer, and yet he performed as a millennial fan.

In the end, perhaps what is most telling about Cooper is how untroubled fans were by his constructed nature and obvious corporate performance. The blurring of real and fictional characterizes much of fan engagement, whether in role-playing games or pseudonymous online interaction.[44] However, the clear corporate origin of Cooper changes the stakes of such identity play, implicating it overtly in consumerist frameworks, calling to mind Howe and Strauss's vision of millennials at ease with the omnipresence of corporate branding in their lives. Cooper thus offers a fascinating instance of the corporate appropriation of fandom into a millennial context. Masking the official capacity of his authorship, Cooper invited fans into his digital bedroom, which itself became a corporate-authored space for exploration.[45] A young corporately constructed fanboy encouraged his audience to explore his performance of millennial fan engagement, and millennial fans responded to his call. We could read this corporate construction of a fan and fan bedroom as a harbinger of things to come, suggesting that more independent fan spaces (and fans!) may be eradicated in the face of industry transmedia strategies, or we could see it as an industrial move of desperation, seeking control within a culture that is clearly no longer within corporate control.

Cooper's potential double meaning exemplifies the central tension Henry Jenkins talks about in his work on convergence culture—the tension between, on the one hand, digital technologies' democratic empowering of a wide range of users, and on the other hand, corporate consolidation of power across the contemporary media landscape. As digital media markets grow, corporate conglomerates (like Disney, ABC Family's parent company) deploy franchises across multiple media platforms, including digital media, to control and shape viewer engagement with their product. Yet at the same time, the increased ubiquity of digital technologies turns viewers into users, "viewsers," or "prosumers," demanding varying levels of viewer participation and co-creation, and transforming media engagement into an overtly interactive process.[46]

The tensions that emerge in the millennial media landscape between increased corporate consolidation and more democratized opportunities for digital authorship affect our understandings of the ideological work of millennial media and the possibilities of audience engagement and authorship.[47] Once we thought of the remote control as a site of resistance and self-authorship; viewers' control lay in their ability to change channels or to turn the TV off, or perhaps to scribble in the margins after the fact.[48] In

convergence culture, media texts and franchises flow across multiple platforms, giving viewers multiple avenues for control in more nuanced ways than
just turning a program off.[49] This transmedia flow (or what Will Brooker has
called overflow) is sometimes driven by corporate planning and sometime
by fan creativity.[50] As story worlds manifest in interfaces that allow for more
direct modes of audience engagement and community interaction, they invite
audience participation in their very creation. Fans and millennials now not
only consume but author ideological meanings in online spaces. Thus, millennials, like fans, spread and at times revise the value systems created in commercial media. Even when corporate media producers invite and encourage
audience authorship, they cannot be sure that viewers will engage and author
in the ways intended. The landscape of millennial media and millennial fandom is necessarily a volatile one, a constantly shifting process of negotiation.
It is such negotiations that we will explore throughout the following chapters, starting with an in-depth look at the text, context, and reception of the
Fox TV series *Glee*.

Millennial Hope

1

A shaky camera captures the scene: eight young adults, sitting on two couches, face away from the camera and toward a television, where on the screen two young men in private school blazers engage in heartfelt conversation. The young adults on the couch tap their feet and jitter in anticipation as on the television screen one of the young men declares his feelings for the other. As the two TV characters, Glee's Kurt Hummel and Blaine Anderson, lean in to kiss, the room of TV viewers erupts. The viewers jump up and down and hug one another, partially blocking the TV screen, where the kiss between Kurt and Blaine is still occurring. Finally the viewers shush themselves as the dialogue begins again—and thus the two minute and three second video concludes.

This video was posted on YouTube on March 15, 2011, later on the same night that the Glee episode featured within it aired on Fox. The video bears the title "Gleek Freak Out: Kurt & Blaine Kiss Reaction," and at the time of this writing, it has 295,668 views, with 3,772 likes and fifty-seven dislikes.[1] Two of its top-rated comments read:

> Best 9 second fangirlmoment ever!
> Videos like this give me hope for humanity_:)☺ & ♥[2]

These two comments celebrate the video as a representation of fandom and fan engagement (specifically gendered as fangirl engagement) and as a sign of broader cultural

▶ ◀) 1:26 / 2:02   ⓘ ⚙ ▢ ⌄

Gleek Freak Out: Kurt & Blaine Kiss Reaction

**Figure 2. In the "Gleek Freak Out" video, available on YouTube,
fans celebrate *Glee*'s featuring of a gay kiss.**

change, or "hope for humanity." However, as the fifty-seven dislikes suggest, deeper within the 1,597 comments, arguments bubble. One commenter,
clearly trying to drum up a flame war (a hostile online argument of the sort
that often flourishes in YouTube comments), posts homophobic comments
and receives many reprimands from fellow YouTubers. The presence of so
many defensive and celebratory responses further highlights this YouTube
video as a site for celebratory discourse around *Glee* and *Glee* fandom. The video
and comments together posit *Glee* fandom as a place of open-minded and progressive, enlightened support in the face of homophobia and discrimination.[3]

This self-depiction of Gleek fandom echoes the representation of community and identity on the series itself: *Glee* tells the story of a school glee club
that connects an unlikely alliance of outsiders, bridging race, ethnicity, gender, class, and sexual orientation. Through narrative development and musical numbers, the series celebrates the power of the outsider turned insider,

encouraging people to accept and celebrate their differences within a collective community. Yet by defining which outsiders get to be celebrated and in what ways, and by privileging the containing community over the individual, the series also embodies some of the more conservative values projected onto the millennial generation in public discourse, such as an emphasis on so-called traditional family values and an erasing of difference within a supposedly postracial, postsexist culture.

Glee depicts a hopeful teen community, with teens working together with adults to be there for each other. At times *Glee* also entertains more negative visions of millennials, showcasing cultural anxieties about sexual activity, drug use, and overdependence on digital technology. However, *Glee* presents these perceived negative dimensions of contemporary youth culture as obstacles to be overcome in order to achieve narrative resolution and personal growth. Through seriality, narrative-stopping collective performance numbers, and transmedia paratexts, *Glee* contributes to the prevailing positive vision of millennials as networked individuals working together for personal and community betterment.

In the first chapter of this section, we will look closely at the hopeful ideology set forth by Howe and Strauss in *Millennials Rising*, considering it in relation to perceptions of fandom and fans. We will explore the text of *Glee* to see how this hopeful vision manifests. Discourses of millennial hope run through *Glee*, but a close look at the text of *Glee* reveals these discourses to be pregnant with contradictions. In the second chapter, we will consider those revealing moments in which millennial hope's contradictions come to the fore. In the third chapter, we will examine how *Glee* fans negotiate and rework millennial hope's ideological contradictions in discourse, community activism, and authorship—in millennial-authored texts such as the "Gleek Freak Out Video" and its comments, as well as in fan fiction and fan activist campaigns. *Glee* offers a complex set of representations of millennial identity and millennial community, and millennial engagement often exceeds what one might read as the limits of the TV series proper.

ONE

Glee and the Hopeful Collective

Glee embraces many positive narratives about millennials, embodying the hopeful vision of millennials distilled in the work of Howe and Strauss. In *Millennials Rising*, Howe and Strauss herald the millennial generation as cultural saviors:

> Over the coming decade, the Oh-Ohs, this rising generation will introduce itself to the nation and push the nation into a new era. Once this new youth persona begins to focus on convention, community, and civic renewal, America will be on the brink of becoming someplace very new, very "millennial" in the fullest sense of the word. That's when the "end of history" stops, and the beginning of a new history, their Millennial history, starts.[1]

Howe and Strauss argue that they are setting the record straight, correcting misconceptions about present day-young people.[2] However, in making this argument, they have established a new set of assumptions that have shaped discourse about millennials at the corporate, popular, and even academic level. Where many expected millennials to be even more disenchanted and apathetic than their Gen X predecessors, Howe and Strauss contend that millennials care; they embrace civic responsibility and expect to change the world:

The Millennial Generation will entirely recast the image of youth from downbeat and alienated to upbeat and engaged. . . . As a group millennials are unlike any other generation in living memory. They are more numerous, more affluent, better educated, and more ethnically diverse. More important, they are beginning to manifest a wide array of positive social habits that older Americans no longer associate with youth, including a new focus on teamwork, achievement, modesty, and good conduct.[3]

As part of their positive spin on millennials, Howe and Strauss stress that millennials use digital technologies in meaningful rather than destructive ways. They also argue that millennials look for positive, community-affirming meaning in their media, including in their television-consumption and on-line activities. This perspective counters popular narratives that purport that young adults are obsessed and addicted to digital technology and media, and that these addictions cause them to become antisocial and narcissistic.[4] In contrast, Howe and Strauss posit that millennials are not only socially and civically minded, the "next great generation," but that this greatness is due in large part to their digitally networked nature, which lends them a multivalent agency and a tendency toward successful collective social action.[5]

Millennials Rising builds its argument out of a combination of selective statistics, quotes from millennials, and quotes from popular press and media "experts."[6] Because of the limited nature of the book's central survey source and the way in which the authors build their argument by juxtaposing selective quotes, it is quite easy (and justified) to critique their findings as biased, self-fulfilling, and limited in scope. Certainly *Millennials Rising* is rife with selective cultural interpretation and overly simplistic predictions. The book's positive take on the current generation creates a highly partial and exclusionary picture. One particularly vital critique argues that Howe and Strauss's study focuses only on economically well-off, predominantly white American young adults and thus does not address the diverse range of millennial experiences across class, culture, and race.[7]

The often unacknowledged narrowness of Howe and Strauss's take on millennials is especially problematic given the reach and influence of their perspective. Propelled by a network of consulting firms and self-help books, Howe and Strauss's vision of millennials has impacted popular views of millennials across the board. Various experts convey the Howe and Strauss–ian take on millennials and together form an echo chamber of sorts, instilling further self-fulfilling prophecies about millennial in education, politics, the workplace, and the consumer market. Howe's consulting agency, LifeCourse Associates, states on its website, "Our clients have included hundreds of community colleges, liberal arts colleges, state colleges, and brand-name universities."[8] Consulting company Magid and Associates executive Michael Hais, together with coauthor Morley Winograd (once a senior policy advisor to Al Gore), draw on Howe and Strauss to claim in *Millennial Makeover* that "millennials are more positive than older generations, both about the present and future state of their own lives and about the future of their country."[9] Even the Pew Research Forum, labeled a "nonpartisan think tank," seems to reiterate, almost word for word, Howe and Strauss's take on generational cycles and millennials: "Generations, like people, have personalities, and Millennials—the American teens and twenty-somethings who are making the passage into adulthood at the start of a new millennium—have begun to forge theirs: confident, self-expressive, liberal, upbeat and open to change."[10] In turn, this narrative of positive millennials changing the world for the better reverberates in political discussions, with both parties staking claim over millennial allegiance. The prevailing opinion seems to be that millennials lean toward a liberal and progressive mind-set, and were responsible for Obama's win in the 2008 presidential election.[11] In the 2012 American presidential elections, blog posts like Henrik Temp's "With Apologies to Mitt Romney: 3 Reasons Millennials Vote Democrat" continue to assert millennial allegiance to the Democratic Party, proclaiming that "millennials are significantly more liberal than older Americans on issues of the family, homosexuality, and civil liberties."[12]

However, Howe and Strauss's work has been successful in part because it allows room for both conservative and progressive views of millennials. Howe and Strauss argue that contrary to popular belief, millennials are actually returning to religion as part of their overall positive, value-oriented outlook. They assert that millennials "think and talk more about faith, and do more with it, than older people realize. It matters to them."[13] Further, "millennials see church as a way to cut through the clutter of contemporary life, to find relief from the pop culture, to meet like-minded members of the opposite sex, and to do good civic deeds."[14] With statements such as these, Howe and Strauss encourage a vision of millennials as a generation returning to traditional values, including heteronormative family, religious tradition, and civic responsibility.

Howe and Strauss also emphasize millennials' willingness to be consumers, to value capitalist gains, and to identify with brands, providing that those brands cater to the traditional turn of their millennial leanings: "What's returning among teens is a more conventional look. . . . Mass fads, big brands, group focus, and a lower-profile commercial style are ready for a comeback."[15] They cite the 1998 Gap ad campaign in which freshly scrubbed, khaki-attired young adults dance to swing music as getting the tone right: "Still loud, but bright and happy."[16] According to Howe and Strauss, this return to convention even includes a return to gender divides in fashion, with masculine and feminine clothing supplanting androgynous styling. In their words, "Gender distinctions are widening."[17] They cite Wall Street Journal Market Watch reporter Lisa Bannon, who writes that "after two decades of adopting a 'gender-neutral' tone and carefully avoiding boy girl stereotypes . . . many markets have decided that it is once again safe to emphasize gender differences in products and pitches aimed at children."[18] As Howe and Strauss envision it, this return to gender difference resonates with the millennial ethos; they cite the response to the Toys"R"Us launch of "boy's world" and "girl's world" as proof, reporting that the change "prompt[ed] complaints from parents, but not from kids," as if children could or would complain to Toys"R"Us about gendered store structure.[19] Rather than place the (attempted) return to a traditional gender divide on corporate strategy, Howe and Strauss suggest that these marketing choices reflect already existing millennial preferences. In moments like this, we see the corporate logic underpinning Howe and Strauss's argument as they contend that conservative corporate values are already millennial values. The reintroduction of traditional values into what Howe and Strauss claim is organic millennial culture allows for the folding together of two markets—teen and adult—planting the seeds for the millennial generations' function as an expansive marketing category in the eyes of contemporary corporate brand marketing. In Howe and Strauss's words: "Millennials are beginning to *reverse* the separation of youth and adult markets."[20] This newly understood expansive category becomes a highly desirable marketing segment, with all of the positives of a teen market (expendable income, longevity of brand commitment) without the limited niche status.

The conservative bent and commercial logic suffusing Howe and Strauss's picture of the millennial generation helps explain why Disney-owned ABC Family chose the Howe and Strauss take on millennials (as channeled through Magid and Associates) to rebrand their network (as I discussed in the introduction), and also why *Glee*'s version of millennial representation has found a home (if at times an uncomfortable one) within the conservative-leaning Fox Entertainment Group.[21] Whether heralding millennials as the Democratic Party's saving grace, corporate interests' dream come true, or the foundational audience of a new family values television, these celebratory narratives cast millennials as the conveyers of a potentially positive future, a generation of people who will wield their (digital, social, and economic) power adeptly and who could mean significant success to whomever manages to capture their allegiance.

As I noted in the introduction, this view of millennials as digitally and socially active and productive is in some ways analogous to the ways in which fandom has been understood over the last two decades, both in academia and in fandom itself. Earlier (and continuing) work on fan culture, starting with Henry Jenkins's *Textual Poachers*, arguably paved the way for positive visions of millennials. While Howe and Strauss do not take up Jenkins's argument wholesale, or even directly, we can recognize threads connecting the two different books. Howe and Strauss's vision of millennials emphasizes community-evolved ethics as well as active engagement with media. In *Textual Poachers* we can see the seeds of at least part of the narrative of millennial hope—most centrally the notion that hands-on, proactive engagement with media on the part of audiences can be considered of value not only for the texts produced and ideological processes resisted but also for the development of creative, networked communities.[22]

Both *Millennials Rising* and *Textual Poachers* work to recuperate and celebrate previously devalued cultural work, in the former case that of young people and in the latter case that of fans. Howe and Strauss make it a point to emphasize that they're proffering their positive view of millennials in reaction to and as a corrective for the negative portrayals of young adults at the time; they argue that they are intervening in problematic negative assumptions about young people. Likewise, *Textual Poachers* strategically introduces the notion that long-devalued fannish practices and objects actually have cultural worth. In the moment of its original publication in 1992, *Textual Poachers* offered a necessary counter to dominant perceptions of fandom, intervening in both academic and pop cultural assumptions about fans as passive or excessive viewers.[23]

Textual Poachers' legacy is thus in part the recognition that fan engagement may not be taboo, excessive, or passive. In 1992, when fandom was still predominantly driven by in-person meetings at conventions (what Jenkins called "a weekend only world"), *Textual Poachers* foregrounded trends of communal creativity and resistance to dominant ideological meanings in mainstream media and in fan practices such as writing slash fan fiction, creating art, and vidding.[24] These practices came to characterize much of fandom online in the intervening years, and they laid the groundwork for the major thrusts of fandom today, including, of course, *Glee* fandom.

Thus, like *Millennials Rising*, *Textual Poachers* has had a significant impact on broader popular understandings of the value of fan practice and the possibilities of fan communities and fan identity. The ideas put forth in *Textual Poachers* have long since been disseminated into fan culture and into industrial as well as pop cultural perceptions of fan culture.[25] These two positive visions of the possibilities of contemporary cultural engagement (millennials on the one hand and fandom on the other) have come together in a range of iterations of the millennial fan or millennial fandom—as defined by the industry and as self-defined by contemporary fan communities. As a TV program and transmedia (and partially fan-authored) text, *Glee* brings together these two discourses: one celebrating the networked collectivity of civic-minded millennials in the face of negative assumptions about today's young adults, and the other celebrating the collective power and creativity of fan communities in the face of taboos against fan engagement.

The Uneven Text of *Glee* and the Limits of Millennial Diversity

The discourses of millennial hope set into motion by Howe and Strauss encompass charged cultural contradictions: millennials must be progressive, inclusive, and representative of positive change, yet they must also represent a future that older generations can be comfortable with, a conservative return to civic responsibility, family values, and culturally safe consumerism. This contradiction is embodied in the concept of the hopeful, networked millennial community, one that encompasses but at the same time manages diversity. This notion of the diverse yet unthreatening, hopeful community is at the heart of Fox's hit series, *Glee*.

Glee depicts high school misfits and outsiders joining with cheerleaders and football players to face the struggles of adolescence together. They are connected in this unexpected alliance by their membership in their school's glee club (a glee club being a school choir that dances while singing, and that competes with other similar groups). The original members of the glee club in the first season include a diverse range of types—or, one could argue, stereotypes—including Rachel, the Broadway-dreaming Jewish girl with two gay dads; Mercedes, the at times angry (or sassy, as the character herself terms it) African American girl with a killer voice; wheelchair-bound Artie with the soulful voice; Brittany, the blonde bimbo cheerleader who can't tell her left hand from her right (literally); Finn, the clueless football player with a heart of gold; Quinn, the pregnant cheerleader and president of the chastity club; Puck, the misunderstood and underestimated delinquent bad boy; and Kurt, the flamboyant gay kid who loves Broadway and fashion and can hit a high F. Thus, Glee simultaneously enacts a range of culturally defined stereotypes and brings them together in an unlikely array of diversity.

Much of the press surrounding the show describes it as a progressive and risk-taking series that pushes an agenda of diversity and acceptance, with story lines that address such issues as (dis)abilism, sex education, racism, interracial dating, coming out, and bullying. A *Huffington Post* article described Glee as "the most progressive, boundary-pushing show on network primetime, with particular emphasis on pushing head-on the reality of high school sex, both hetero and homosexual."[26] An *Independent* article suggests that "from its launch, Glee has embraced homosexuality, explored the consequences of teen pregnancy and placed at centre-stage characters who might be outsiders in other series."[27] These and many other popular assessments of the series celebrate its incorporation of diverse characters and its choice to give attention to social issues rarely addressed on television. Show runner and cocreator Ryan Murphy talks frequently about his intention to make a social impact through Glee. Discussing the plot point in which Kurt comes out to his father, Murphy says, "I thought so you can do entertainment and maybe do something responsible and socially relevant. That's when I got interested in looking at the impact that we possibly can have and what can we do with that."[28] The *Huffington Post* article cited above describes Glee as a "haven" for its viewers, "an hour a week to which they can relate in an otherwise lonely world."[29] Production discourse surrounding the show (including commentary about the show in its spinoff reality series, *The Glee Project* [The Oxygen Network, 2011–2012]) continually emphasizes Glee's social agenda, its intent to teach social acceptance and empathy and to provide a positive resource for teens who feel isolated and alienated for any reason.

However, the series' text does not live up to all of this positive press, especially regarding its representation of issues of race.[30] Glee ricochets between engaging substantively with millennial issues of identity and whitewashing difference. The series does foreground identity issues rarely given prolonged attention on television. Nevertheless, episodic and serial narrative structures primarily revolve around heteronormative romance and the interiority of white, able-bodied, heterosexual leads.[31] Indeed, if there's one thing you can expect of Glee, it's for it to be ideologically uneven. The series repeatedly probes at and then reasserts hierarchical values of race, gender, class, ability, and sexuality, although not all to the same degree. In this unsettling and resettling of cultural norms, we can see the series' embodiment of contradictory millennial discourses. Glee's very unevenness reveals the tensions between the progressive and conservative dimensions of millennial discourse as set out by Howe and Strauss and magnified outward. The series makes more progress in some arenas than others; over its five-plus seasons (at the time of writing), it has only paid periodic and usually insubstantial attention to issues of race, class, and disability, while it has engaged in a more prolonged way with issues of gender and sexuality. However, even its engagement with gender and sexuality remains uneven, held in uneasy tension with its celebration of the hopeful millennial collective. The series reasserts hegemonic norms frequently, but it does so precisely because it also obsessively unsettles those norms on a regular basis, resulting in rampant ideological unevenness.

Narrative Complexity and Ideology in *Glee*

Glee's ideological unevenness plays out through its serial narrative composition. Glee draws on a particular version of televisual seriality familiar from such formative teen TV shows as *Buffy the Vampire Slayer*, *Dawson's Creek* (WB, 1998–2003), and *Beverly Hills 90210* (Fox, 1990–2000). These series feature the story lines of multiple individual teens who together form a teen community. Sharon Ross describes the multipronged focus of teen television as part of an "aesthetics of multiplicity."[32] Because millennial-focused television programs like Glee intertwine narratives about multiple characters and relationships, their seriality depends on a juggling act between different characters' story lines, with various stories rising to prominence in a narrative ebb and flow, a dance (pun intended) for dominance between different characters and story arcs.

We can understand Glee's rendition of this "aesthetics of multiplicity" as a form of what Jason Mittell terms televisual narrative complexity.[33] Glee weaves its multiple character-focused story lines into an intricate narrative web, in which individual story lines advance separately but at moments come together to inform and influence one another. Mittell describes the way contemporary TV programs such as *The Wire* (HBO, 2002–2008) and *Lost* (ABC, 2004–2010) intertwine different serial arcs to create a complexly paced, integrated whole.[34] It may be more obvious to recognize narrative complexity within programming framed by the industry as "quality" and associated with adult audiences, but much of millennial-focused television also intertwines multiple serial story lines in complex ways, both thematically and narratively.

For a show like *Glee* that is so invested in negotiating teen identity and in having a social impact, the negotiations of narrative complexity and seriality matter. They matter in terms of whose identity is given primacy, whose perspectives are shown to matter, and who falls into the background at key moments. The interweaving of multiple story lines guides the narrative focus, privileging some stories over others, and integrating individual threads into larger ideological frameworks. Each of *Glee*'s characters represents a particular identity position on an intersectional graph of race, gender, and sexuality, and each in a sense vies for narrative dominance, with their various story lines assembling and reassembling to temporarily assert ideological hierarchies. This narrative interplay carries ideological weight and communicates ideological meanings about millennial identity and community. *Glee* juxtaposes various romantic pairings and personal struggles, but it privileges some over others, returning without fail at episode's conclusion to the larger group, thus asserting the importance of the hopeful, diverse collective as the series' overarching ideological payoff.

Production and press discourse suggests that the producers of *Glee* are very much aware of the ideological significance of narrative construction. Speaking of a story line in season 3 that focuses on teen sex, Ryan Murphy notes, "Everybody has seen a straight couple losing their virginity, but has anyone dovetailed the gay and straight stories together and given them equal weight? That seemed like an exciting choice and a new thing."[35] In this way, Murphy celebrates *Glee*'s narrative and ideological innovation and thus claims *Glee*'s structural choices as part of the series' social agenda. *Glee*'s ideological acrobats do offer possibilities we could read (and that fans do read) as significant, progressive, and liberating. Yet at the same time, *Glee*'s structural choices also function to tame the series' potential transgressions or to defuse perceptions of *Glee* as an overly radical social threat.

The Singing and Dancing Collective

Millennial media's narrative architecture integrates a generous mix of different genres, each of which bring with it specific sets of narrative elements and ideological associations. For Glee, teen drama mixes with the movie musical; this mix is then tinged with comedy and satire, arguably inherited from both the movie musical and teen genre traditions.[36] Glee's musical numbers serve as outlets for the millennial characters' frustration with the hegemonic structures in which they find themselves trapped; solos, duets, and group numbers interrupt the narrative flow for moments of affective self-expression. Through song and dance, the characters convey their adolescent struggles to each other and to the television audience. Glee's solos emphasize individual interiority and the experience of difference; duets explore the parallel or distinct experiences felt by different individuals within the Glee collective; group numbers provide climactic moments of communal celebration, unification, and closure. These different pieces slot together within Glee's larger ideological work, with the series' moments of collective spectacle entering into conversation with the individual and paired performances that lead up to them. In the ideological mess that is Glee's narrative development, musical numbers rein in any possibly transgressive elements, subsuming them into a harmonious, in-sync collective—a utopian vision of the millennial community joined in song. Yet those same musical numbers also often (and sometimes simultaneously) let transgressive meanings loose, resulting in a much more unstable but compelling representation of millennial identity.

The movie musical elements at work in Glee bring to the table particular aesthetic and narrative traditions and histories of ideological work. As Richard Dyer argues so influentially in "Entertainment and Utopia," the movie musical offers "the image of 'something better' to escape into . . . alternatives, hopes, wishes."[37] Jane Feuer suggests that the movie musicals of the 1930s to 1950s work to valorize community and to break down the divide between performer and audience, production and consumption, through the seeming spontaneity and transparency of movie musical performance.[38] With these associations in mind, we can see how the movie musical genre offers a resonant fit for the contradictions of millennial ideology. Movie musicals and millennial hope both emphasize collective community and strive to blur the boundaries between producer and consumer. Both also channel traditional values and yet at the same time break down hegemonies in favor of a celebration of collectivity.

Likewise, recall Howe and Strauss's insistence that millennial culture includes a return to traditional gender dichotomies. The movie musical also offers tools to this end. In his influential *American Film Musical*, Rick Altman argues that movie musicals revolve around a "principle of duality" rather than the more traditional narrative structure of "cause and effect."[39] Specifically, musicals convey a (normative) gendered duality that emphasizes gender difference by paralleling male and female perspectives and performance, while making sure that these perspectives remain distinct from one another. *Glee* uses what Altman terms paired sequences, juxtaposing male and female experiences to progress character development and heteronormative romantic pairings. However, *Glee* also uses paired sequences to juxtapose other types of pairings, including a range of masculinities and femininities and nonstraight romantic developments, thus fueling yet at times destabilizing any traditional hierarchies, gendered and otherwise, that might take hold in *Glee*'s establishing of the collective teen community.[40]

Performing Authenticity

Throughout *Glee*, musical numbers function as tools for characters' seemingly raw self-expression, offering us access to their individual perspectives.[41] Solos sung to specific characters or duets sung in conversation help characters communicate truths they are not able to share in everyday life. These moments of personal connection allow characters to overcome difference and build a sense of the collective, which is in turn expressed through group numbers. Most *Glee* episodes move from a focus on multiple, diverse individuals (via solos and duets) to a celebration of the collective, ending in a group performance.

Glee drives home its particular version of millennial ideologies by emphasizing the necessity of the collective: diverse individual perspectives must be fostered but must also be collected and contained within the networked whole, usually through the group musical performances that close each episode. *Glee*'s group numbers provide the means for diverse characters' story lines to unite, conveying a sense of ideological union and hopeful positivity while erasing any seemingly irresolvable conflicts between too-diverse perspectives. For example, early in the series' first episode, we see the teen characters auditioning for the glee club, singing songs that shorthand their individual personalities. Mercedes sings Aretha Franklin's "Respect," quickly signposting her character as a talented black diva with attitude and the desire to be taken seriously. Kurt sings "Mr. Cellophane" from *Chicago*, emphasizing his sense of social invisibility and exclusion as well as his love of high drama. Rachel sings the highly sentimental high school audition favorite, "On My Own," from *Les Misérables*, simultaneously showcasing her egotism, talent, and vulnerable outsider status. Dressed in pseudogoth clothes, Tina sings an aggressive version of Katie Perry's "I Kissed a Girl," suggesting her character's function as representative of the uncomfortable uncertainty of adolescent self. All of these numbers shorthand stereotypes while opening up individual character interiority that will spur long serial arcs and character development. However, the pilot ends with a collective performance of Journey's "Don't Stop Believing" (also infamous for its place as the soundtrack for the final moments of the controversial *The Sopranos* finale, bastion of narrative complexity that it is). The *Glee* kids' collective rendition of "Don't Stop Believing" functions to prove that the sum of the parts is larger than the whole: they gather on stage in front of an empty audience to practice the group number that they have organized, staged, and choreographed themselves. As they sing, their to-be glee teacher and other to-be members of the glee club enter the auditorium to watch, united in the collective of the performing moment without overt narrative explanation. The performance is inexplicably professional, with full stage lights and a highly skilled accompanying jazz band appearing out of nowhere. Driven by the nonnarrative logic of musical performance, the community collective overrides the narrative pacing of the season even as it provides faith in the narrative, bolstering our belief that this glee club actually could ascend in the ranks of show choir competitions to reach a satisfying season conclusion.

Often *Glee*'s need to affirm the value of the collective over the individual seems to border on obsessive. Another example demonstrates how the collective whole subsumes the individual plights of the series' diverse characters: slightly further along in season 1, in an episode in which cheerleader Quinn's parents find out that she is pregnant and throw her out of the house, the glee club abandons an "individual ballad" assignment to sing "Lean on Me" as a group number to Quinn and Finn. The group ode to the teen parents-to-be asserts the power of the millennial collective over more traditionally assumed values like biological family as well as over the needs of the individual. Indeed, the number, and thus the episode, cannot conclude before the full community performs together: the group pulls Quinn and Finn out of their seats to dance with them before the end credits roll. In "Don't Stop Believing" and "Stand by Me," as well as countless other *Glee* group numbers, editing and staging help synthesize individual story lines into a collective whole. Any given group number intercuts between stage performance, rehearsal, private performance, and visual moments from narrative scenes that gain added meaning by being juxtaposed with the musical soundtrack. Via this intercutting, individual story lines intertwine into the collective, televisual whole.

These heavily intercut numbers function as moments of what Jason Mittell calls "narrative special effect," moments in which "a show flexes its storytelling muscles" and in which we are called upon as viewers to assess the value and meaning of the spectacular synthesis.[42] In these moments, editing and narrative come together to "call attention to the constructed nature of narration" in order to celebrate the art of narration itself as spectacle.[43] Now, the movie musical tradition already emphasizes spectacle and is known for breaking the fourth wall, and so *Glee*'s integration of the movie musical into its genre mix already brings with it a tendency to highlight the "constructed nature of the narration."[44] Because of this, it perhaps should not come as a great surprise that many of the musical numbers within *Glee* serve as examples of narrative special effect, with baroque intercutting that requires the audience to make self-conscious interpretive connections between various story lines and between individual and collective performances.[45] What is even more of interest here is the ideological work performed by these moments of narrative special effect. *Glee*'s spectacular group numbers not only integrate multiple story lines but also sluice away any ideological discomfort that may have been released in the series' focus on the diverse experiences of individual characters, subsuming any discomfort into a spectacular celebration of the networked collective.

The conclusion of season 1 offers a striking example of how, through carefully intercut group numbers, *Glee* integrates individual diversity into the hopeful collective, mitigating any potential ideological threat—in this case, teen pregnancy and the perspective of a teen mother. McKinley's glee club, New Directions, have just performed at the Show Choir Regionals competition when pregnant cheerleader Quinn goes into labor. We see images of Quinn being rushed to the labor and delivery, intercut with another glee club's performance of Queen's "Bohemian Rhapsody," complete with sound overlay of Quinn calling to her estranged mother as the competing glee club sings the famous line, "Mama . . . (I just killed a man)." The intercutting between the performance of "Bohemian Rhapsody" and Quinn's labor transforms this very personal moment into a heartfelt collective performance. The entire McKinley glee club surrounds Quinn at the hospital as she goes into labor. Through editing, even the competing glee club becomes part of the collective for this "very special" narrative moment.

This sequence unites individual story lines into the community collective, yet with its primary focus on Quinn, it is cathartic but not fully climactic. In *Glee*, climaxes are usually reserved for numbers whose prime purpose is to unite the collective and not to progress an individual character's story line. For season 1, this climax takes the form of two parallel group numbers (a paired set), one a group dedication to the glee teacher, Mr. Schuester, in which the various members of the glee club sing individual lines before joining together, and another in which Mr. Schuester sings (in harmony with a student) a dedication to the group as a whole, with the performance intercut with interactions between various members. This closing song? "Somewhere Over the Rainbow," an anthem of shared millennial hope (and entertainment as utopia) if ever there was one. These and many other episode- and arc-closing group numbers work to connect individual story lines into a whole and to celebrate those connections, at least temporarily erasing any instability that might come from the multiple perspectives being featured, merging them all into a hopeful, utopian celebration of the millennial collective.

For theorists of the interplay between narrative and ideology in film and television, the question of closure is key. Closure is understood to have the potential to affix meaning and reify value systems, to dole out punishment and reward. Television may be a serial medium, but its seriality does not completely foreclose the ideological work promised by closure. In her study of soap operas, Laura Mumford argues that "closure asserts an especially powerful force by drawing stories to a conclusion with events that reinforce the essential rightness of the program's moral and ideological rules, that lend a sense of inevitability to the status quo and suggest that certain outcomes necessarily follow certain behaviors."[46] *Glee*'s obsession with sewing individuals into the collective through narrative special effect and with closing episodes with fully collective group numbers demonstrates its overriding impulse to establish the hopeful millennial collective as a dominant value.

T W O

Destabilizing the Millennial Collective

A strong closing group number may quite effectively sell a safe and heartwarming vision of the millennial collective—for the moment of performance, at least. It's hard to deny the satisfying thrill when the *Glee* kids gather to sing "Don't Stop Believing" at the end of the series' pilot episode. However, in serial television, closure is not all. As Laura Mumford puts it, serial narratives can result in an "excess of resolving gestures," a seeming obsession with closure, even as new plots are opened up and old ones are reopened.[1] This constant almost closing—or closing and reopening—unsettles the ideological work that closure may be seen to perform. As we saw in the previous chapter, *Glee*'s episodic closing numbers may celebrate and reaffirm the containing millennial collective, but they work in continual counterpoint with solos and duets that remind us of the diverse perspectives of the individuals who make up the collective. Together, *Glee*'s multiplicitous serial plot and musical numbers play out in an uneven mix of containing collective synthesis, diverse perspectives, and individual felt emotion. Sometimes even *Glee*'s group numbers offer a vision of the collective that is more ideologically unsettling than not. For the movie musical's utopian spectacle, adapted here in *Glee*, does more than enforce community norms and remove discomfort; perhaps more fundamentally, it also exceeds narrative—and the ideological status quo—in moments of excess. Glee's most spectacular, performative moments often release the Glee characters, and Glee itself, from normative ideological constraints in moments of sublime excess and performative transgression.[2]

I'd like us now to dig deeper into the ideological stakes and muddiness that result from the interplay between plot and musical number, between narrative and spectacle, and among solos, duets, and collective group numbers in Glee. Specifically, we'll focus on one of the characters most beloved by fans, Kurt Hummel, and the narrative and musical numbers that lead to the kiss between Kurt and Blaine featured in the YouTube video with which part 1 opened. Kurt's story line introduces alternative modes of performance and spectacle that unsettle Glee's more hegemonic tendencies.

Resisting Containment: Representing Queer Teen Experience

Kurt's first season story arc follows his coming out to his family and friends, his struggle with bullying at school, and his eventual choice to leave McKinley High after a fellow student threatens to kill him. At times Kurt's struggle with homophobia advances in only a scene or two an episode, or none at all; at other times, his story line takes up a more privileged position. Kurt's character arc in season 2 introduces a new narrative space and vision of an alternative set of teen experiences and codes of musical performance. He decides to attend the prestigious Dalton Academy to escape the bullying he faces at public school. At Dalton, Kurt discovers a world of uniforms and wealthy teenage boys, but also a school with a no-bullying policy and with students who can be open and unafraid about their sexual orientation. Kurt takes on the role of the viewer, both discomfited and awed by the combination of conformity and acceptance that Dalton appears to offer. The musical numbers at Dalton highlight this combination of containment and release, from the first impromptu performance that Kurt witnesses when spying on Dalton's glee club, the Warblers, to his own tenuous inclusion in the numbers once he himself becomes a member of the Warblers.

The Warblers and Dalton introduce a different performance aesthetic to Glee, one that offers a mode of collective community not focused on outsider identity and yet inclusive of a more flexible sense of masculinity and gender performance. The Warblers depend on rhythmic group movements, school uniforms, and collective accompaniment of their solo featured performer, crooner Blaine Anderson (also Kurt's love interest). Allison McCracken argues that the Dalton space and musical numbers represent a significant shift in the norms of televisual masculine performance.[3] She writes of the scene in which Kurt first witnesses a Warblers' performance (in which Blaine sings "Teenage Dream" to Kurt): "From the very first moment Kurt is introduced to Blaine and the Warblers, as they perform a cover of Katy Perry's 'Teenage Dream' to a group of equally enthusiastic young men, we know we're not in Kansas anymore."[4] And indeed, we're not in Kansas—or McKinley High—anymore. The Warblers' aesthetic represents a new option for imagining male performance (and performance in general) in Glee, one that includes a more flexible sense of gender identity, and one in which a young male singer can sing a song from a female perspective to another man.[5]

Dalton Academy offers an alternative mode of spectacle and gender performance, as well as an alternative vision of millennial community—but one that the larger narrative of Glee does not fully embrace. The episode "Original Song" (season 2, episode 16) brings head to head the two developing visions of millennial collective musical aesthetics when McKinley High's New Directions and the Dalton Warblers compete at Show Choir Regionals. In this episode, Glee most clearly presents its ambivalence to the vision of millennial identity offered by the Warblers. The episode celebrates the Warblers' spectacular synchronized performance style but also critiques the group's uniformity. Kurt becomes the voice of this critique, complaining that, in comparison to New Directions, the Warblers fail to celebrate individual difference. He complains that all of the Warblers' numbers center on lead singer Blaine, with the rest of the members performing as an overly unified group; in his words, "Sometimes I don't feel like we're the Warblers. I feel like we're Blaine and the Pips." We might go so far as to read this dimension of the Warblers as a satiric commentary on the conservative potential of millennial generational identity. During an argument over uniforms, in which the Warblers resist changing the color of the piping on their suit jackets for the Regionals competition, the Warblers' members reveal themselves to be deeply invested in the traditional social rules of the school, with one of the members declaring in dismay, "This is a kangaroo court!"

Into this moment of satiric conformity, Kurt interrupts with a display of authentic emotion that proves to be transformative in multiple ways. He bursts through the door, dressed not in uniform but in a striking black suit and an Alexander McQueen–esque skull pin, to announce the death of his canary. He requests the opportunity to sing in mourning, and, with permission granted, he sings a heartfelt rendition of the Beatles' "Blackbird," compelling the attention and respect of all the Warblers. Kurt's performance is intercut with shots of Blaine watching him, in a revision of the traditionally gendered male gaze at female spectacle. Where Laura Mulvey and many who have followed her argue that classic, heteronormative film language situates the male character as the active gazer and the female as a to-be-looked-at passive spectacle, here instead we have the male gaze at a male performance of spectacle—and not just a passive spectacle but the spectacle of authentic interiority, performed millennial style.[6]

Moreover, this sequence does not simply replace the female spectacle with the male. While Kurt sings, we see Blaine listening, looking, and feeling. The very gaze structure of cinema is thus temporarily dismantled in favor of the dual examination of character interiority. Later in the episode, Blaine describes this moment to Kurt with language that merges their journeys of self-discovery and romanticizes that merger: "Kurt, there is a moment when you say to yourself, oh, there you are. I've been looking for you forever. Watching you do 'Blackbird' this week, that was a moment for me, about you. You move me, Kurt." Here we have a two-for-one expression of emotional interiority through performance, with Kurt's emotional spectacle also representing Blaine's emotional transformation. Out of the synthesis comes the next step in Glee's representation of gay teen romance and, to a limited degree, the ideological breakdown of the Warblers' collective conformity. Most obviously, this is the speech that leads into Blaine and Kurt's first kiss (the one featured in the Gleek Freak Out YouTube video). In addition, Blaine's emotional transformation paves the way for the series' assessment of the different configurations of the millennial collective; convinced by Kurt's performance of "Blackbird," Blaine announces that he doesn't want to "silence any other voices" by continuing to always sing lead. However, he doesn't suggest that all members should have a chance to sing; rather, he proposes that he and Kurt should perform a duet together for Regionals. Kurt has spoken up for the performance of collective diversity, but Blaine's response uses performance to propel the romance between himself and Kurt.

Given that the Warblers are pitted against the New Directions at Regionals, this means that narratively, Kurt and Blaine's queer romance must face off with The New Direction's networked millennial collective. As per Blaine's plan, Kurt and Blaine sing a love song together: Hey Monday's "Candles." Originally a solo meant for a female vocalist (with lyrics that emphasize the singer's isolation), here the song is reimagined as a romantic duet between

Kurt and Blaine, again blurring the line between individual and dual interiority. Where many of the series' duets are sung in the manner of a paired number, with two characters singing together but not necessarily to each other, here Kurt and Blaine sing directly to one another. The song expresses their feelings for one another while performing their romance to the audience as an authentic expression of dual self.

However, there are some limits placed on this representation of queer romance. The intercutting logic of *Glee* means that Kurt and Blaine's duet becomes an affective musical backdrop for lead characters Rachel and Finn's more heteronormative romantic story line. As Kurt and Blaine sing, we see a shot/reverse shot of Rachel and Finn looking sadly at one another, Finn having broken up with Rachel for cheating on him. Kurt and Blaine's moment of musical performance becomes the emotional landscape advancing resolution in Rachel and Finn's relationship.

Although Kurt and Blaine's duet may serve as the climax of their romantic story line up to that point, it does not serve as the climax of the episode, or even of the Warblers' performance, and it is certainly not deemed the winning number valued by the episode's closure or the season's episodic development. The Warblers follow Kurt and Blaine's performance with an enactment of almost but not quite *Glee*-style networked collectivity. They sing a rendition of Pink's "Raise Your Glass," a song that celebrates the shared experience of underdogs and freaks. Even this performance, however, does not fully inhabit the millennial collectivity of individual difference celebrated by *Glee*, as it falls back into the (supposed) overfocus on Blaine and the conformity of the uniformed, private school Warblers that Kurt has previously critiqued. Blaine darts in and out of the mass of rhythmically moving boys as he sings, and while the lyrics may celebrate shared underdog identity, the performance aesthetic lacks the celebration of the diverse collective at the heart of *Glee*. Thus the episode's narrative pacing and staging undercuts Kurt and Blaine's romantic duet with the Warblers' group performance, and then undercuts both performances with the ideological work embedded in the episode's closure. Both Warblers' performances must be necessarily upstaged by the following New Directions performances in order to uphold the series' celebration of the diverse collective as embodied in McKinley High's glee club.

Like "Raise Your Glass," the New Direction's big group number, "Loser Like Me" celebrates the underdog, and specifically the underdog narratives of *Glee*, as the song was supposedly written by New Directions members themselves (hence the episode's title, "Original Song"). This emphasis on originality sits strangely as an ideological enforcer in a series that is all about newly interpreting and performing existing music. The narrative drafts Kurt to support this (temporary) ideological shift. Kurt whispers to Blaine in awe, "My god, they're singing original music," then corrals all the Warblers to dance along to the wonder that is the New Directions' originality. Yet the New Directions original collective anthem of underdogness is in many ways more traditional than the Warblers' performance. While the choreography appears to put less emphasis on conformity of movement and costume, in truth, the visual element of difference introduced is gender difference. Instead of the singular Dalton blazers, the New Directions girls wear blue dresses and the boys black suits. Instead of single lead singer Blaine, New Directions features two lead singers: the heteronormative pairing of the series, Rachel and Finn. From this context, the return to valuing originality rather than remix seems to be a heavy hand enforcing New Directions' heteronormative dominance.

Predictably, New Directions wins Regionals, meaning that only New Directions will advance to Nationals, which in turn paves the way for Kurt's return to McKinley and reintegration into the glee club collective (and this in turn means a partial phasing out of the Dalton story line). The narrative structure renders Kurt and Blaine's plotline and performance secondary, subsumed within the larger framework of collective millennial hope. The conclusion of this arc pushes forward the series' perceived social and cultural progressiveness, yet maintains its more conservative hegemony of the diverse, but safe and hopeful, collective. What is most ironic here—and perhaps most frustrating to those of us invested in the progressive potential of Glee's ideological project—is that Glee's moments of celebration of the diverse collective often function as a veneer masking a heteronormative core, yet the series still sells these moments as risk taking and socially significant.

Millennial Multiplicity and Ideological Instability

All of these ideological negotiations and any temporary affirmations of more conservative millennial ideals take place within the ever-undulating multiplicity of Glee's serial narrative structure. The multiplicity and seriality of Glee is both boon and limitation to its representational politics. Because of the multiplicity of characters, no one character remains alone in representing a particular identity category or stereotype for long. At the same time, however, if a character's story line or performance has the potential to become too transgressive, other characters can step in to tame potential meanings, or the collective as a whole can subsume the individual. For example, Kurt and Blaine are not the only representation of queer identity or queer romance on the series, and one might argue that many of their representational short-comings are addressed in the characters of Brittany and Santana. Where Kurt and Blaine's story line emphasizes a narrative of coming out and of productive progress in "it gets better" form, Brittany and Santana's narrative explores more fluid notions of sexual identity. Both Brittany and Santana resist labeling their sexual identity, where Kurt and Blaine resist only temporarily and quickly reaffirm their identity as specifically gay rather than something more fluid.[7] Likewise, Kurt and Blaine's representation of queer identity plays out against what Melanie Kohnen might call a "screen of whiteness": the series highlights their sexual identity while their whiteness functions as a normative base, hypothetically offsetting potential viewer discomfort with the explicitly queer narrative.[8] In contrast, the representation of Brittany and Santana offers cross-cultural as well as queer romance. Specific episodes directly address Santana's Latina identity and the way it intersects with her sexuality. In "I Kissed a Girl" (season 3, episode 7), the series acknowledges the way in which race and sexuality can intersect and also problematizes the notion that coming out is always a positive move forward. Santana comes out to her grandmother, and her grandmother rejects her and tells her it would have been better if she kept her sexuality a secret. This episode depicts Santana accepting a label that she had previously resisted, and it relies on easy stereotypes of resistant older generations from other cultures to displace homophobia. However, it also fights against notions of easy closure won by expressing authentic self. For the closing number of the episode, Santana sings a song that in its very title, "Constant Craving," rejects closure.[9] Her performance morphs from a solo into a shared number through associative intercutting, with various characters shown singing lines as they move beyond the rehearsal room. The song unites these multiple characters in the emotions of uncertainty and desire rather than collective celebration. Such moments of collective uncertainty recur from time to time in Glee, but they are not norm; more often, the collective serves to unify, to erase difference, and to resolve the conflicts borne of diverse perspectives.

The series' address of teen sexual activity in the third season also demonstrates its delicate ideological acrobatics as it attempts to be simultaneously progressive and conservative, embodying the contradictions inherent in notions of millennials and millennial hope. In this case, the result was unstable enough to result in censure from the family television advocacy group, the Parents Television Council.[10] In what seems like a standard teen TV cliché, Rachel and Blaine consider having sex with their partners, Finn and Kurt, to achieve authenticity in their performances in *West Side Story*. Both Finn and Kurt reject their partners' misguided advances, but the episode concludes with both couples deciding to have sex because they love each other. In another of *Glee*'s more self-conscious moments of narrative special effect, both "sex" scenes are intercut with Rachel and Blaine's performance of *West Side Story*'s epic love song between Tony and Maria, "Tonight." I put quotes around the word "sex" because the depiction does not even suggest any sexual act and is more intimate than erotic, with characters still clothed—at least as much as we can see of them, since the shots are short and show only parts of faces. The only characters we can make out clearly are Rachel and Blaine performing Tony and Maria's tragic love.

The series received a significant amount of criticism for depicting (or rather for overtly suggesting) gay sex on broadcast television. Fans observed that in following episodes, the scenes featuring Kurt and Blaine being intimate were significantly reduced. These scenes seemed to be replaced with scenes of Santana and Brittany kissing, the traditional filmic televisual language of female sexual spectacle more easily accepted than male spectacle, even if its result is a nonwhite and more fluid depiction of queerness. Both sets of queer representations continued to be significantly limited within the series' overall flow, a point that did not escape viewer notice. Yet the fact that the series did allow Kurt and Blaine to be sexually active (and continues to do so), at least off screen, remains significant to viewers and provides opportunities for viewers to make visible in fan authorship that which the series suggests but stops short of showing. We will return to viewers' expansive and critical responses in the following chapter, when we examine fan engagement with *Glee*.

Nostalgia beyond Narrative: Millennial Affect

As these multiple examples have, I hope, made clear, nothing about any episode of *Glee* is ideologically simple. Musical spectacle is key to *Glee*'s ideological unevenness (we could call it ideological complexity if we're feeling generous), often unsettling the ideological work of the narrative. Theorists of movie musicals have argued that musical numbers have the potential to interrupt the ideological work of film narrative, to confound reified norms, and to elicit cultural change in the form of self-reflexive spectacle.[11] Spectacle can exceed the boundaries and limits of narrative, setting loose meanings that cannot necessarily be recontained by narrative work.

The tension between spectacle and narrative has been a sore point since Glee's conception. Creator Ryan Murphy made it clear that he (and Fox) wanted to distinguish Glee from the obvious comparison to movie franchise High School Musical by basing Glee's musicality in realism rather than spectacle. In an article in the New York Times, Murphy was quoted as saying, "Fox was not interested, and neither was I, in doing a show where people burst into song."[12] The glee club premise allows narrative explanations for why characters express themselves through song, be it a rehearsal or a performance, or in some cases a character's fantasy sequence. This emphasis on realism is meant to facilitate the show's earnest look at the high school experience. However, Murphy's insistence that Glee is not fanciful musical fare overlooks the fact that Glee more often than not muddies the line between realism and spectacle.[13] Moreover, while production discourse may tie the series' realism to its social purpose, its moments of spectacle — the moments where its narrative special effect exceeds the bounds of clear realist logic — are the very moments when its progressive ideologies burst beyond the restrictions of millennial hope, when the contradictions that are part and parcel of the hopeful millennial collective implode, setting loose more complex and potentially transgressive meanings.

We've already looked at a few instances where one could argue that spectacle transcended narrative ideological work, rupturing it. Many of the Dalton numbers could be considered to interfere with Glee's dominant ideological projects because while on screen, the Warblers' visual and performative spectacle offers an alternative aesthetic, an alternative vision of millennial community and the possibilities of millennial masculinities, gender performance, and gender identity. But perhaps the most confusing and fascinating example is the Glee third season Christmas special, "Extraordinary Merry Christmas" (season 3, episode 9), in which the local public TV station drafts the McKinley glee club to create a live-airing TV holiday special. Glee club member and aspiring director Artie rejects his fellow Glee members' call for a more somber tone in favor of nostalgic but upbeat holiday celebration, a black-and-white homage to the 1963 "Judy Garland Christmas Special." Glee recreates the Judy Garland Show's holiday special (CBS, 1963) very closely in set, pacing, and style, as a sort of episode within the episode. Kurt and Blaine share the role of host, with Kurt especially filling Garland's role through styling and staging.

This nostalgic retrofitting may seem unmillennial, as it is apparently rooted in a traditional past rather than a progressive future, but I would argue that is very millennial indeed.[14] The episode's emphasis on a playful yet heartfelt nostalgia allows for the exploration of experimental liberalism and simultaneously a return to traditional values, thus embodying the contradictory discourses of millennial hope articulated by Howe and Strauss. The nostalgic framing (including the black-and-white filter and the careful construction of sets and costumes evocative of the Garland special) allows for the positive, celebratory, and traditional elements of millennial discourse to be embedded within the mise-en-scène rather than in a hegemonic narrative.

Within this black-and-white, nostalgic millennial frame, Kurt and Blaine welcome the viewer into their "bachelor chalet," with Kurt introducing Blaine as his "best friend and holiday roommate." Normally a series that prides itself in making strides in queer visibility, this episode of Glee instead reclaims the closet as nostalgic parody, one not confined by the series' usual ideological restrictions but also not impacting the series' larger narrative. What Melanie Kohnen calls the pastness of the representation—its location in a removed and safe time period—contains its queer vision and at the same time facilitates it.[15] The black and white imagery and periodesque clothing distance the viewer from the sequence's depiction of a queer domestic space even as the spectacular performance transcends this distancing. The nostalgic closet as parody becomes an opportunity for an extended focus on Kurt and Blaine's queer space and performance—a focus normally denied them, especially after the sex episode earlier that season. For twenty minutes, we are inside the black-and-white nostalgic world of Kurt and Blaine's holiday chalet, with the other characters entering into their world instead of the other way around. Gone are the negotiations of different plotlines and their attendant ideologies. Within that chalet, spectacle and performance (of authentic and performative self simultaneously) reign supreme.

Kurt and Blaine's performance in this sequence uses the inherited language of classic movie musicals to offer an alternative vision of masculinity than that usually valued in the series. Building on scholarship on the movie musical and on the gendered structures of film language, Steve Cohan argues that for the "exemplary male [movie] musical performer," Fred Astaire, a performance could simultaneously "sustain his power as dominant male in the narrative" and interrupt "the linearity of the story with . . . musical performance," thus "insist[ing] on his own ability to signify 'to-be-looked-at-ness,'" a quality traditionally reserved for female stars.[16] Cohan suggests that by undermining traditional gaze structures, Fred Astaire as male musical star offered a revised masculinity to contemporaneous audiences of the 1930s, 1940s, and 1950s.[17] We can see a similar process at work, millennial style, in the Christmas special. In the opening, just as Garland did, Kurt addresses the audience/camera and invites them/us into his "holiday chalet," thus embodying Garland's performance and, in Cohan's words, "insist[ing] upon his own ability to signify 'to-be-looked-at-ness.'" The series at times seems uncertain as to the stability of the male as spectacle, and especially of nontraditional masculinity as erotic spectacle, but the Christmas special bypasses these uncertainties by nostalgically recreating the language and traditions of the male movie musical star.[18]

Within this nostalgic recreation, Kurt does not shoulder the weight of redefining masculinity alone. The opening song, "Let It Snow," features Kurt and Blaine in a parallel dance number with heavy emphasis on duality of movement. The staging of this number echoes Liza Minnelli's performance of "Steam Heat" with her then boyfriend, Tracy Everett, in the original Judy Garland special. Minnelli and Everett's performance of "Steam Heat" was in itself a self-conscious nostalgic recreation of Judy Garland's own parallel performances with Fred Astaire. Cohan argues that these parallel male/female performances emphasize the egalitarian star value of the paired male and female performers.[19] But in the Glee version, the two actors performing collective movement are two young men who both, if differently, confound gender norms. Kurt and Blaine's paired dancing is thus multiply queer, as is arguably befitting the multiplicity of millennial media.

Cohan argues that Fred Astaire's revision of masculinity in musical spectacle was part of a wider scale revision of masculinity at the time and could be seen in other concurrent film genres, including in the figure of the film noir private eye. Likewise, Glee's play with the integrated musical and its foregrounding of multiple male performers is part of a redefinition of millennial masculinity that is simultaneously finding its expression in other genres, including a millennial rebirth/reworking of noir (the topic of later chapters). Male musical performance such as those of the all-male Warblers, Kurt and Blaine's "Candles" duet, or their Christmas performance demand an interruption or interference of Glee's narrative economy and even the series' preferred ideology. In the end, it may be the very instability of this interplay between narrative and spectacle that is the most millennial dimension of Glee.

But does this push and pull of meanings matter? How much of these ideological acrobatics do audiences engage with? These questions bring us back the notion of narrative structure, and more specifically narrative complexity. Series that ask viewers to make affective and intellectual associations and assumptions depend on a form of televisual media literacy, which includes the viewer's understanding that some story lines are marked as more important than others, depending in part on how much time they are given or how they are situated within the larger narrative structure. This understanding means that viewers can (and do) critique the ideological work performed by series' narrative structure. Moreover, when narrative ideological structures become incoherent or fold under the demands of spectacle, uncontained progressive or transgressive meanings spin outward, fueled by the interpretive communities and transformative productions of fans. If one were to dismiss *Glee* as fluffy musical programming or mindless teen TV, then it might be easy to assume that these subtleties of ideological negotiation, incoherence, or implosion are lost on viewers. As we will see in the next chapter, *Glee* viewers are very much aware of and invested in the ideological subtleties, stakes, and potential of the series, and they turn this same attention to their own production as well. While *Glee*'s representational limits and shortcomings may be many, the program offers raw material that lends itself to the cultural critiques and transformative productions of fan practices. Millennial fan engagement with *Glee* exposes the limits of discourses of millennial hope, reshaping *Glee* in the millennial fan image rather than vice versa.

THREE

From Fandom to Gleekdom

Glee's basic premise puts at its center outsiders and geeks, celebrating talent and perspectives not recognized within the mainstream. *Glee* reframes those outsider perspectives as part of a new norm, a new center. At least on its surface, the series celebrates the niche made mainstream, the uncool made cool, imagining that everyone is and should want to be a "loser like me." It declares to audiences that its stars are outsiders just like them, creating a world in which the marginal is the center and the center is the margin.

Glee's ideological emphasis on millennial hope as found in the diverse, networked collective extends beyond the series' narrative and textual representation to its figuring of its own production and its audience in the series' many official paratexts. The series attempts to merge teen niche and broadcast family through the slippery concept of the millennial audience, which can stretch to encompass both markets. Where ABC Family defines its network brand more narrowly, reworking the teen show to a millennial mold, *Glee* constructs a more broadly pitched representation of millennials within broadcast network Fox, directed at a multigenerational audience. While they differ in degrees, the two networks share their use of the millennial concept (if not the term itself) to create a brand that appears both expansive and of the moment.

Something for Everybody

Glee reframes the traditional elements of teen television in a multigenerational context, weaving adults into its narratives and performances. Many a number illogically feature the talents of glee club faculty sponsor Will Schuester, played by Broadway star Matthew Morrison. The same musical numbers that bring together (and smooth over) the diverse perspectives of race, gender, sexuality, and class also merge generations. In so doing, they expand the potential age demographic of *Glee*'s audience, allowing the series to bypass the niche teen identity for a more mainstream family umbrella. In show runner Ryan Murphy's words, "It's not a kid show. The adult leads are equal in part to kid leads . . . it is designed for families to watch together. It's sweet, but it will appeal to both kids and adults, it's written for both of them."[1] *Glee*'s claim to family TV is in part based in its musical choices and inclusion of the spectacle of multigenerational musical performance that assumedly the whole proverbial family can enjoy. *Glee*'s musical choices construct a vision of a diverse audience that bridges generations and taste cultures. Production discourse around the series' use of music emphasizes the way in which it purposefully straddles cultural realms including niche and mainstream, teen and adult, and Broadway and pop hits. Murphy states, "I spend hours and hours listening to songs and picking songs that I like or that I think will be great. . . . I want there to be something for everybody in every episode. That's a tricky mix, but that's very important—the balancing of that."[2]

In its pursuit of something for everybody, the series showcases music from a range of decades, musical styles, and genres. *Glee* includes contemporary and classic rock, musical theater, and heavy metal, and sometimes even mashes together music from different eras or genres. This diversity of music aligns with Howe and Strauss's vision, in *Millennials Rising*, of the increasing diversity of the millennial generation. Not incidentally, the diversity of music also supports Fox's demographic needs as a broadcast network. Just as Howe and Strauss's expansive millennial definition brings with it ideological contradictions that are in turn reflected in the *Glee* text, so too does *Glee*'s paratextual discourse reveal fissures and contradictions inherent in the Fox broadcast "something for everybody" framework.

This "something for everybody" approach could be read as an attempt to narrowcast *Glee*'s audience in multiple directions at once, with different audiences drawn to the Broadway, top 40, indie, country, and past and present music. However, the series' ideological obsession with collective unification suggests instead a smoothing over of differences, a mashing into a new millennial vision of family—to borrow the phrase from ABC Family's marketing, "a new kind of family." *Glee*'s integration of music from diverse decades contributes to the series' efforts to expand the boundaries of the millennial collective and demographic, from teen niche to millennial mainstream. From this perspective, *Glee* has served Fox doubly—as a hip show bringing in young viewers and as a family-friendly show connecting generations. Fox has positioned *Glee* as the mixer that can unite these purposes and audiences, mashing them into one money-making phenomenon.

The Remix Machine

At the heart of *Glee*'s something-for-everybody co-optation of niche culture is its appropriation of the logics and aesthetics of remix culture. Broadly speaking, remix can be understood as the transformative recombination of already existing cultural materials, including reversioned music, mashed-up music, and combinations of video and music. In his work on remix culture, copyright lawyer Lawrence Lessig argues that remix is a fundamental dynamic of our contemporary culture and vital to the continued health of a thriving public sphere.[3] He describes our contemporary culture as a "read/write" culture in which we do not only passively consume but rather rework and transform the cultural material we encounter.[4] Lessig poses culture as the property of all, as raw material with which we form new creative expression. He argues that all culture builds on and with the culture that came before, and that our copyright laws have been twisted by corporate interests to overlook this fact.[5] In its own way, *Glee* is a child of the logic of remix and read/write culture. *Glee*'s narratives are based on its characters' rehabilitation of music both old and new. *Glee* depicts its millennial characters performing reinterpretations of music from past and present—music that means something to them personally because of their engagement with popular culture. When their teacher pushes them to sing music from his generation, they frequently argue for the validity of using "their" music, although they often eventually realize that past music can have contemporary resonance if the glee club members connect to the music through their own performance. *Glee* features the characters performing mash-ups of past and present songs such as a combination of Rihanna's "Umbrella" and the movie musical classic "Singin' in the Rain," with the added bonus that such a mash-up will appeal to two demographics of potential consumers at once. It might even cross-pollinate interest, inviting young viewers in via nostalgia and older viewers via the promise of inclusion in millennial culture. *Glee* thus embraces the cultural value of remix and mash-up as transformation — and conveniently gets to widen and shape its demographic reach as a result.

Remix is a fraught concept, seen as a battleground between generations and between corporations and audiences/consumers. According to Murphy, *Glee* overcomes concerns about copyright infringement through its positivist millennial frame. As he tells it,

> So when we wrote the pilot, we wrote those songs in. Then in the process of getting them cleared, we were shocked that after a lot of these big artists and their companies read the script, they approved it . . . I think the key to it is they loved the tone of it. . . . They loved that this show was about optimism and young kids, for the most part, reinterpreting their classics for a new audience.[6]

As Murphy stresses here, *Glee*'s positive tone makes its version of remix marketable, so that even artists and labels that initially resisted having their music used in *Glee* have for the most part eventually given permission (or at least so the narrative goes). For example, Coldplay initially refused to have their music featured on *Glee*, but they later gave the series access to their full discography.

This perceived marketability of *Glee*'s version of remix culture defuses one of the central perceived threats of the millennial generation: that millennials' dedication to collective sharing will cause traditional media industries to lose control of their product and thus to become irrelevant in the face of file-sharing millennial (sub)culture. *Glee*'s covering and remixing invites millennial viewers to get in line as converged consumers, buying cast versions of songs on iTunes and attending live *Glee* concerts, or purchasing *Karaoke Revolution Glee* to perform their own versions of songs, buying their way into the collective authorship of an industry-condoned (and -driven) cover machine. Thus, *Glee*'s celebratory stance — collapsing difference into a collective millennial whole — fuels and is fueled by the commercial logics underpinning the ideologies of millennial hope. *Glee*'s version of millennial culture allows remix practices and values to be folded back into commercial media culture, in part because *Glee* legally pays for most songs (even if it is highly unlikely that diegetically New Directions does). Indeed, *Glee* takes the energies of remix culture and channels them into profit for the media industries.[7]

Project *Glee*

If remix culture is all about audiences becoming authors of culture in their own right, and if *Glee* is all about making an industry-friendly version of remix, then it stands to reason that *Glee* would strive to support the blurring of the line between producer and audience while controlling that blurring. *Glee* found a home on Fox as an extension of the wildly successful *American Idol* (2002–present), which also focuses on amateur performances of popular music and on blurring the line between real people and celebrities, and between amateur and professional, while functioning as a visible conduit through which real people can hypothetically become stars. The *Glee* phenomenon came full circle with its spin-off series, *The Glee Project* (the Oxygen Network, 2011–2013), which, like *American Idol*, negotiates the blurry boundary between audience and star. *The Glee Project* is a reality/competition show cut to the mold of *Project Runway* (Bravo, 2004–present) and *Top Chef* (Bravo, 2006–present), in which *Glee* fans respond to an open call and are eventually whittled down to fourteen contestants, all vying to earn a spot on *Glee* itself. *The Glee Project* is thus a television program in its own right, performing its own ideological work, as well as a paratext of *Glee*, supporting and contributing to the *Glee* phenomenon and its attendant ideologies of millennial hope.

Where series like *Project Runway* and *Top Chef* often emphasize competition over any sense of community, in *The Glee Project* the ideology of the networked diverse community prevails. Participants mourn rather than celebrate when a fellow member doesn't make the callback list (*The Glee Project*'s version of getting voted out of the competition). *The Glee Project* offers a carefully structured look inside the production of *Glee*; *Glee*'s casting director and choreographer serve as the series' main on-screen coordinators, and Ryan Murphy makes the final decision as to who does or doesn't make the callback list. The series both reinforces and reveals the mechanics of *Glee*'s ideological work, with contestants being informed on a regular basis that they must be able to connect with the group as an underdog and stand out within group numbers as individuals. Contestants don't make the callback list if they don't work well with others or if they don't have enough personality. When contestants are asked to leave, the request is made with much regret. Each episode of *The Glee Project* ends with a different version (a re-reversioning) of the same group number, "Keep Holding On," a song featured on *Glee* itself. In each episode, the departing member sings the number's solo, conveying their authenticity and performative worth even though they did not advance further in the competition. In a sense, *The Glee Project* has to overcompensate because the casting and contest format do not mesh naturally with *Glee*'s emphasis on collective diversity. *The Glee Project* repeatedly, almost obsessively, drives home the power of community and the individual's place within the community while still policing who gets to stay in that community—whose difference is the right kind of difference to fit in the new diverse collective norm.

Cast members/contestants in *The Glee Project* receive training in not only singing and dancing but also in ideology. In the course of an episode, contestants are frequently given notes such as, "On *Glee* you're going to need to stand out in a group, but at the same time be able to move with everyone," and "If it's real for you, it's going to be real for the audience"—guidance offered in *The Glee Project*'s first and third episodes, respectively. The first quotation emphasizes the codependent relationship between individual and collective, and the second urges authentic performance, two themes key to *Glee*'s millennial ideology. *The Glee Project* thus exposes the manufacturing of ideology while driving that ideology home

The Glee Project cast members profess themselves to be fans of *Glee*, and they regularly perform/portray their fan knowledge and enthusiasm. Various actors from *Glee* serve as mentors and judges each week, and a portion of every episode is spent with *The Glee Project* cast ogling the *Glee* cast and speaking of them as role models and inspirations. In addition, the series' opening episodes (of both seasons) put *Glee*'s millennial fandom in front of the camera. These opening episodes feature the series' open call, with masses of *Glee Project* hopefuls gathering in hallways and cafeterias, waiting for the opportunity to audition. As they wait, they declare their love for *Glee* and their belief in its social significance, echoing much of the producer discourse about *Glee*'s import. Rather than behaving like cutthroat competitors, auditioners join together to sing hopeful *Glee* anthems like "Don't Stop Believing" and "Keep Holding On."

The Glee Project depicts millennial fandom in the form of Gleekdom (more on that term shortly) as an organic embodiment of *Glee*'s ideology of the outsider turned insider turned member of the hopeful collective. The Internet Movie Database description of *The Glee Project* echoes the core messages of *Glee*: "From thousands of entries, and an exhaustive nationwide talent search, the series uncovers a unique group of artists from both pro and amateur backgrounds proving every underdog has a fighting chance at stardom."[8] Yet at the same time *The Glee Project* works to delimit what *Glee*'s fandom can look like by depicting fans who fit a prescribed mold, who meet with the producers' approval because they are neither too transgressive nor too mainstream. For example, *Glee Project* second-season contestant Tyler Ford was the first female-to-male transitioning participant on the series, but he was eliminated because his performances were not traditionally sexy enough, while the winner of *The Glee Project*'s second season chose to recite a poem in the final contest to emphasize that he was more different than he appeared. The poem included the line, "I'm the guy who's the whitest half-Cuban ever," thus attesting to his appropriateness for *Glee*'s millennial collective diversity. To be a *Glee Project* success story, a contestant must strike the perfect balance of niche and mainstream, individual and everyperson. If they fit that mold, contestants move from online or in-person auditions to the niche cable Oxygen network to, for the lucky winner or winners, broadcast network Fox. In this way, *The Glee Project* defines what a good *Glee* (and millennial) fan should look like and be like, and it sets TV—*Glee* in particular and broadcast TV more generally—as the ultimate goal.

Manufacturing Gleeks

In *The Glee Project* and in *Glee*'s various other paratexts (including, for example, the *Glee Live Tour* movie), *Glee* represents its audience as a united whole of like-minded folk who share perspectives not only with each other but also with the show's producers and actors. Both *Glee* and *The Glee Project* take advantage of the movie musical's preoccupation with themes of community and collective creative production, integrating backstage musical elements into their millennial musical TV blend, suggesting that anyone can join the *Glee* community and potentially be a star. Jane Feuer argues that the Hollywood movie musical strives to erase the divide between performer and audience, through the frequent depiction of the community process of "putting on a show."[9] Feuer describes the movie musical as "mass art which aspires to the condition of a folk art: produced and consumed by the same integrated community."[10] The backstage movie musical in particular (of which *Glee* and *The Glee Project* are both televisual variations) encourages its audience to imagine that they too could come together on the stage to put on a successful performance.

"Mass art which aspires to folk art"—no description could be more apropos for a consideration of how millennial identity is marketed to millennials as if it were already produced by them, and more specifically for this chapter how the transmedia empire that is *Glee* seeks to label itself as folk art and become integrated into the folk (read fan) culture. The series hails its fans as "Gleeks," a portmanteau of *Glee* and geek, thus envisioning a merger of the series and its imagined audience. Gleek discourse depicts fandom as a community identity formed through an industry-initiated proclamation of shared outsider-hood, a mainstreamed invitation to join the fan collective—at least the fan collective wished for by the media industry. Gleek as an identity label suggests an industry-driven redefinition of fandom, but more than that, it is a cooptation and commercial transformation of fandom norms, into an (at least perceived) industry/audience merger. Gleekdom is *Kyle XY*'s fabricated fan, Cooper of Coop's Scoop, writ large as imagined fan community and projected onto fandom.

The term "Gleek" suggests a charged union between the series and its audience, yet it is a term also meant to unite a shared but private community. Fans often define communities within fandom by made-up names and terms, often combining two names to signify allegiance to a particular romantic pairing. These fan-made terms function to create fan-specific codes or language, further facilitating a sense of enclosed community—a subcultural group not necessarily fully legible to the industry and official commercial producers. Fans create portmanteaus to use as code for romantic or sexual pairings, often for slash pairings not officially recognized or condoned by a series' producers. For example, *Smallville*'s Clark Kent and Lex Luthor became Clex, a code widely legible (as signifying the pairing's romantic and/or erotic entanglement) within slash fandom but largely indecipherable beyond it. By creating the term and category "Gleek," *Glee* moves from mashing up two songs or even two demographics to mashing show and audience, producer and consumer, into one commercially desirable category.

Like "Clex," "Gleek" synthesizes two words to create a community-specific language and identifier. However, the two merged words are not two characters but the name of the series, *Glee*, and the word "geek," the term for a form of cultural identification through knowledge of media and technology. The term "geek" has been recuperated over the last two decades to claim media savvy as an empowered position—think geek chic—as well as a site for negotiation of diverse subcultural identities (as in the Geek Hierarchy).[11] Because it bypasses "fan" for "geek" (though "glan" is not really an appealing option), the term "Gleek" creates a label that is nominally not fandom yet calls upon the affect of fandom. The dominance of the word "glee" in the portmanteau suggests the happy and goofy aspects of fannish affect, and not the angry or erotic parts. Moreover, "Gleek" is a community-defining term not broken down by gender (like fanboy or fangirl) or by particular pairings. Fans of course have created their own terms for fandoms within *Glee* and Gleekdom: Faberry, Britanna, Klaine, Kurtsies. These coexist alongside the officially sanctioned Gleek identity in a sort of symbiosis between industry-defined fandom and audience-defined fandom, a merger of commercial product and audience culture. Again like Cooper, the industry-created fanboy of *Kyle XY*, the modified fan image of the Gleek allows for a consumer youth figure that media producers, advertisers, and politicians alike could potentially feel comfortable embracing.

Audience and Reception
THE SELECTIVE ECONOMY

In the previous chapter, as we considered how *Glee* communicates millennial ideology, we relied on a textual reading, and more specifically on a textual reading that assumed that narrative and seriality progressed with linear intent and impact. While we acknowledged that spectacle may temporarily interrupt the narrative, for the most part we took for granted that one musical number would follow the next in ideological battle. However, within the convergence transmedia sphere, this linear process cannot be assumed. Songs circulate from *Glee* before an episode is released. They circulate in spaces sanctioned and unsanctioned; they are released as additional products that viewers consume in different orders and repeatedly. The various ideological meanings and aesthetic moments set in motion by a millennial television series and its paratexts enter a stew of swirling meanings that coexist online in network-condoned spaces and in spaces beyond network control. This means that elements may hold different values on different platforms to different viewers, or even to the same viewer at a different moment.

For example, for the period of Kurt's stay at Dalton Academy (discussed in the previous chapter), the Dalton plots were clearly secondary or tertiary story lines, often warranting only a few minutes per episode, arguably because they risked upsetting *Glee*'s ideological balance by offering a different vision of millennial community. However, those moments were among the more hyped of the *Glee* paratextual machine and often the most celebrated by fans in terms of musical performance. As we saw in the previous chapter, the Warblers represented an aesthetic and ideological departure for *Glee*, offering a new boy band style of performance that merged synchronized male dance with gender fluidity and queer romantic narratives into an amalgam of queer conformity—another bundle of contradictions emerging from the simultaneously conservative and progressive discourses of millennial hope. Along with the regular *Glee* musical releases in 2011, Fox released an album entitled *Meet the Warblers*.[12] The Warblers also played a key role in the live show and a 2011 live show movie (*Glee: The 3D Concert Movie*), which depicts many fans in attendance wearing Dalton ties as a show of allegiance to Dalton's queer collective. Where *Glee* may have limited the Warblers' queer conformity to a few scenes, one can purchase the Warblers CD and listen to it many times over, prolonging the Warblers' queer aural landscape. This process of nonlinear preferential selection, while shifting the ideological meanings at work in *Glee*, does not necessarily subvert the series' larger commercial or industrial logics. In fact, it's the opposite; this process of selective emphasis through consumerism is exactly what allowed *Glee* to thrive as a media franchise. We can think of this as a selective economy, where fans pick and choose their priorities out of the uneven multiplicity on offer. The convergence market facilitates this selective consumption, so that fans can buy the Warblers CD, buy particular musical numbers on iTunes, purchase a Warblers tie or a Gleek T-shirt, or buy the karaoke Wii *Glee* game and microphone.

However, this selection economy also facilitates its less obviously commercialized (if not illegal) counterpart. With all of these separate elements circulating online, fans can, if they choose, attempt to access particular portions by noncommercial and noncondoned means. Fans can choose to torrent rather than purchase *Meet the Warblers* or the *Glee Christmas Album*. Or, rather than buying the Christmas album, a fan might choose to put the season 3 Christmas special-within-the-special on repeat during the holiday season, decontextualized from its larger narrative frame and commercial context. The fact that this sequence was already a twenty-minute spectacle separated from the ongoing narrative, as discussed in the previous chapter, encourages this process of selection and removal.

Indeed, audiences do not always play along the industry-prescribed paths of convergence culture. Beneath the veneer of officially sanctioned selectivity lies a more negotiative if not antagonistic relationship between the series and its viewers. Fans can, and do, ignore the already perforated lines, preferring to break *Glee* down as they see fit. This process of active selection can be rigorous and even aggressive. Here's a clear example. In the previous chapter, I mentioned that Kurt and Blaine's story line advances in season 2 for the most part in only a couple of scenes per episode. These scenes are integrated into the multiple advancing narratives that play off one another and merge in moments of narrative special effect, and thus they are situated within episodic collective logic as well as serial logic. However, fans have dismantled this progression and imposed a singular serial narrative focused only on Kurt and Blaine, unseating the ideologies of the diverse millennial collective that *Glee* works so hard to continually reassert. In 2012, those who knew their way around the social-networking interface of Tumblr and had the desire could find a video that compiles all of the Kurt and Blaine scenes from season 2 into an hour-and-forty-five-minute movielike experience. This video removes the collective and the serial; it includes brief moments from group numbers only if they feature Kurt and/or Blaine's response. This edit decenters the collective entirely, prioritizing Kurt and Blaine's narrative. This practice of altering narrative focus is by no means unique to *Glee* or Klaine fandom. Fans of other series, characters, and pairings often do the same thing if a character or pairing of special interest to fans is given minimal screen time. This is a basic method of poaching (as Henry Jenkins originally conceived it) as well as of remix, where fans select what has priority meaning for them and do what they will with it.[13] Though no completely new narratives per se may come into being, new narrative structures and ideological priorities emerge through the process of selection and recombination.[14]

THE CRITICAL ECONOMY

On top of and motivating the selective economy, we have the critical economy, where fans' selections result from dissatisfaction or critical engagement with the source text. Here fans engage in a comprehensive but nonlinear way with the *Glee* text and its paratexts to critique its narrative structure or politics, or its featured performers or performances. Fans may assert their selective preference and reject the larger whole, as in, for example, the *Jezebel* post entitled "Glee Does Original Songs, We Only Care About Kurt & Blaine's Duet."[15] Likewise, at a Tumblr dedicated to releasing only Kurt and Blaine–focused video sequences from each episode, notes include sentiments such as, "Honestly, Klaine is the only reason I'm still watching these days. To the point that when that ends, there's a good chance I'll stop watching."[16] Or, in response to the third season Christmas special, a fan posted selected moving-image GIFs of Kurt and Blaine's performance together with the following selectively celebratory commentary:

Chris Colfer, doing Kurt, doing Judy Garland. It's so perfect. >_O He's got the Judy Garland voice going on and I was laughing so hard when he flung himself into the couch. XDDD. . . . This episode had so many little tiny homage jokes and really, that made it fantastic even if there was a lot of GLEE going on. It's so weird that this show that does such a great job with its music and has such really outstanding actors and storylines still manages to screw up things in their writing, directing, and editing that make the show less appealing. . . . So much potential you guys. O_O You can get it back! I believe in you![17]

This quote embraces *Glee*'s nostalgia, homages, remix, and spectacle as positive but removes these elements from the domain of the series. The name of the series becomes synonymous with its failings ("even if there was a lot of GLEE going on"), yet at the same time the poster expresses faith in the show's past greatness and future potential. In this way, fans assert their power to select as a form of critique.

Fan critiques may evolve out of fannish affect—fans love one character more, or hate one character more, or love what a show was but not what it is becoming—but often fan critique may also come out of ideological dissatisfaction, where fans are unhappy with the values and value systems being upheld by a given narrative or aesthetic choice. In these moments of critique, fans often showcase their media literacy and their ability to engage with the complex dance of narrative and ideology at work in much contemporary TV.

THE TRANSFORMATIVE ECONOMY

All of these intersecting modes of engagement are forms of transformative authorship, but it is important to emphasize the way in which both selection and criticism (and criticism via selection) mobilize the creation of new, fan-authored texts. I'd like to look at several instances to consider how fan authorship functions as transformation, and more specifically how fan texts transform the ideologies of millennial hope at work in *Glee* and in *Glee*'s official paratexts. Fans of the relationship between Kurt and Blaine—Klaine—offer one dynamic example of what this engagement can look like, where selection, criticism, and transformation meet.

In the previous chapter, I mentioned that after the sex episode, Fox received many complaints regarding their depiction of teen sex, and especially gay teen sex. Fox seemed to dial back the representation of Kurt and Blaine's intimacy and sexuality in the following episodes of season 3. Fans were highly critical of this perceived self-censorship. When photos circulated of what looked like Blaine proposing to Kurt in the Christmas episode, fan excitement grew with hope that the series would rectify its recent wrongs, but the scene (known as the box scene) never appeared in the episode. Word leaked that the scene had not been a proposal but rather that Blaine gifted Kurt a promise ring made of gum wrappers. Fans then organized to buy the episode script as part of a charity drive to raise money for Project Angel Food, a nonprofit organization dedicated to providing food for the sick.[18] Fans raised $13,606 on Tumblr and then coordinated a live stream event in which they "aired" a YouTube video featuring the missing scene and arguing for the significance of *Glee*'s representation of Kurt and Blaine.[19] This video celebrated the fan ability to reclaim a narrative moment that had been removed from the advancing serial plot. "The Klaine Box Scene Script Livestream 5/29/12" has gone on to have an afterlife on YouTube. At the time of writing, the video has 64,243 hits, 1,585 likes, eleven dislikes, and multiple pages of comments, making it a site of significant discourse around the potential of *Glee* and the extent and limits of the series' representational liberalism.[20]

The Klaine Box Live Stream features the script of the missing scene, combined with still images so that viewers can imagine what the scene would have looked like. It also includes an overview of the controversies spawned by the series and a self-reflexive narrative of the fan coordination that led to the live stream video's release. The video opens with the key romantic scenes between Kurt and Blaine on the show, from their first meeting to their first kiss. Like the season 2 Kurt/Blaine compilation I mentioned earlier, through the power of selection, this video removes the multiplicity of *Glee*, focusing on the Kurt/Blaine story line. It intercuts and overlays these scenes with positive press coverage of the series. Via audiovisual remix, Ellen DeGeneres, known for her character's coming out in her sitcom, *Ellen*, narrates and affirms *Glee*'s social significance, thus passing the baton of representing gayness on TV.[21] After DeGeneres's introduction, the actors who play Kurt and Blaine (Chris Colfer and Darren Criss) talk about their sense of the series' significance and their experiences with the series' fans. This section concludes with imagery of fan affect, including footage from the Gleek Freak Out/Klaine Kiss response video, depicting fans jumping up and down and spinning in joy as they watch Kurt and Blaine kiss.

The video then moves into a compilation of the negative press *Glee* has received, leading off with a story from Headline News (CNN's secondary cable news channel) entitled "Glee Kiss Outrage." A commentator proclaims, "It's stealing the innocence away from this whole generation," as we see an image of Kurt looking lovingly at Blaine. Next, we see a Fox and Friends commentator (notable here because of the Fox association) protest, "Now I have to explain this to my eight-year-old, if I just want her to see a nice family show with some nice music?" as Fox News–chosen imagery plays in the background featuring Kurt wearing a T-shirt that reads "Likes Boys."

On their own, these quotes and images, taken directly from news programs, reveal the tensions emerging from Glee's contradictory claims to be simultaneously mainstream and niche, escapist and progressive. Placed within the context of this video, especially given the assumed fan audience, the clips read as closed-minded bigotry and thus attest to the power of fan remix to transform meaning and to communicate cultural critique. The first few clips stand on their own with the original sound and image aired on Headline News and Fox News. But soon the vidder intervenes, aligning the audio of the clips with imagery from Glee for additional affective impact. We briefly see, under the headline of "Is TV Too Gay?" a continuation of the Fox News clip with the spinning Fox logo emblazoned clearly on the screen; Brian Fischer of the American Family Association proclaims, "Because what these television programs are doing is glamorizing homosexuality." On the word "glamorizing," the image cuts from the Fox News story to an image of a bully throwing a slushie onto Kurt. As we hear Fischer continue to speak against homosexuality, we see various images of Kurt being bullied. The alignment of sound and image strongly suggests that Fischer and others like him are not only condoning bullying but are the cause of it, are supporting it, and are themselves verbal bullies—and not only that but are on some narrative level the cause of Kurt's fictional bullying. The video also includes voice-overs of the counterperspective, also from the Fox News piece, such as "it's time people start to be honest together with their sexuality," intercut with images of Kurt and Blaine overcoming the odds and attending prom together. Other images include a brief moment from actor Chris Colfer's "It Gets Better" video and the multiple performances of the fan-beloved kiss between Kurt and Blaine that was part of the Glee Live Tour. This section of the video reaches its climax with a brief intercutting of Kurt and Blaine's key romantic moments in season 3, including the sex scene, interwoven with images of fan video responses and actor discussion of the significance of the sex story line. Overall, the video up

The Klaine Box Scene Script Livestream 5/29/12

Figure 3. The "Klaine Box Scene Script Livestream 5/29/12" video critiques the limits of *Glee*'s queer representation.

to this point follows a narrative that starts with a celebration of the series' braveness, then engages with and condemns the series' declaimers, and then returns to celebrate the series' continued social significance and progressiveness in season 3.

At this point, the video shifts into a critique of *Glee* itself, again using selection. It begins with the intertitle "and here's what you missed on *Glee*," an appropriation of the *Glee* tagline that opens every episode to catch viewers up on the ongoing serial plots. But the video's context shifts the meaning of the tagline: rather than referring to what a viewer might have missed by skipping an episode, here it means that which was not shown on the series itself, that which was not represented, not allowed to fit in, not narrated. The following sequence intercuts various hugs between Kurt and Blaine, but rather than accelerating into an affective combination suggesting the couple's affection for one another, as might be expected in a relationship-focused fan vid, the video instead invites the viewer to think of these images as the absence that they represent—the absence of more visible intimacy or sexuality between the two characters. The layering of text makes this critique explicit: images of multiple hugs in public spaces with onlookers are accompanied by the repeated phrase "cockblockd," and scenes when the two lean in as if to kiss and instead hug are framed by the phrases "kiss??" and "nvm"—in fannish/millennial texting netspeak, "nevermind." The layered netspeak text makes visible the fan dissatisfaction with the limitations of representing a queer relationship on a TV show that is touted as so socially progressive and risk taking. This sequence thus critiques Glee itself, and by inference the institutional contexts that lead to such repeated representational patterns.

This sequence of critique of the series' representational failings leads into the video's positive story of fan activism. The video presents fandom as the saving grace that has the potential to undo the silences, absences, and failings perpetrated by Glee. This depiction of fandom as (millennial hopeful) savior is communicated through an intertitle that reads, "For all those missing moments, today the fandom will finally be able to take back a piece of what was originally ours." While the video critiques Fox and Glee as only superficially inclusive, at the same time it is full of the language of millennial positivity that suffuses Glee. The video suggests that originally there was shared ground between viewer preference and producer intent, but that the relationship between the two has steered off course. Images from the missing scene are interspersed with the narrative of fan coordination and activism that led to fans' procuring the script and raising money for Project Angel Food. As the video reaches its positive climax, celebrating the fan activism that resulted in the script's release, background music plays: the song is "Keep Holding On," the same song used at the end of every Glee Project episode when they send a failed contestant on his or her way. Even while critiquing Glee, the video relies on the series' ideological message of millennial hope and perseverance against odds to lend emotional import to its narrative of fan success. Like The Glee Project, the video works to erase any divides between the video's producers and its viewers, using the language of family values to affirm the positive millennial fan narrative, concluding with a direct thanks to viewers: "And lastly, a special thanks to you: If you offered to help in any way, or simply read and reblogged our promos, or told a friend. Those 'small' acts are the threads that weave us together as a community and make us not just a fandom, but a family."

More than seven minutes into the video, and only after the full fan success story is told, the box scene script runs. We see images of the script dialogue layered over the still images that had originally leaked from the scene. Even in only script and still image form, the cut scene highlights the way in which millennial discourse transforms conservative notions of appropriate youth behavior. In the cut scene, Blaine gives Kurt a promise ring made of gum wrappers. But where promise rings traditionally promise virginity, Blaine instead promises "to always love you. To defend you even if I know you're wrong. To surprise you. To always pick up your call no matter what I'm doing. To bake you cookies at least twice a year and to kiss you whenever and wherever you want. Mostly to make sure you always remember how perfectly imperfect you are." This scene uses the language of the conservative promise ring to put forward a more nuanced vision of (nonstraight) relationships but still a highly romantic one. The phrase "perfectly imperfect" sums up the contradictions that the ideologies of millennial hope thrive on. This scene draws on yet complicates the conservative dimensions of millennial discourse. If its vision of queer romance upset millennial hope's delicate ideological balance, then it was precisely that overflow that encouraged fans to rescue the narrative and to give it new life online.[22]

"The Klaine Box Scene Live Stream" video, when taken in full, mixes critique with Gleekesque celebration. However, in some *Glee* fan communities, criticism is more overt, taking the form of protest launched at the modes of production. For example, the Glee Equality Project organized a postcard-writing campaign critiquing the lack of representation of intimacy and sexuality between queer characters on the series. A Glee Equality Project–affiliated video, the "Glee Equality Project—Season 3 Kiss Compilation," tallies the ratio of gay versus straight kisses in season 3, with a final count of 51:6.[23] But even this video uses the language of the series to make its criticism, closing with Santana offering a critique from within the show itself: "I'm sorry too, because all I want to be able to do is kiss my girlfriend, but I guess no one can see that because there's such an insane double standard at this school." Thus, the writers of *Glee* wrote the words that fans use to sum up their coordinated critique of the series in order to mobilize for change.

In all of these efforts—selection, critique, activism, and production—participants may position themselves in opposition to the Fox network or the creators of *Glee*, but in many cases they are working with the raw materials offered to them by *Glee*, often with the support of some *Glee* producers, if not of Fox itself. Although it is not clear who put the box scene script up for auction, it is likely that someone from *Glee*'s production staff must have been involved, and Ryan Murphy finally did post the cut scene on YouTube after it was excluded from the deleted-scene extras on the season's DVDs.[24] The series thus to some degree invites fan activism, at least regarding issues of gender and sexuality; however, it does not so consistently model a critical stance for issues of race, class, and disability—and notably the more visible fan campaigns do not focus on these issues either. Indeed, in its own uneven way, *Glee* seems to invite some modes of fan critical engagement over others.

Fan Fiction and Millennial Ideology

"The Klaine Box Scene Live Stream" and the Glee Equality Project serve as examples of fan activist movements designed to purposefully critique *Glee*'s ideological failings as fans see them. However, fan reworkings of *Glee*'s ideology do not always take the form of overt activism. For example, the immensely popular fan fiction series "Dalton," as the title suggests, sets *Glee*'s narrative at Dalton Academy, picking up at the point when Kurt decides to transfer, and never returning Kurt or the central narrative to McKinley.[25] The queer/conformity space of Dalton, rather than being limited to select scenes and secondary narrative arcs, becomes the full narrative space. More than that, "Dalton," initially written by C. P. Coulter, has become a multiauthored transmedia playground in which fans congregate to expand on this vision of Dalton while leaving behind McKinley High and its attendant ideologies.

Other stories more directly critique *Glee*'s ideological failings. For example, "Steal a Heart," by mochacappucino, not only confines *Glee*'s main McKinley High–focused narratives to the margins but takes playful pleasure in shutting them down. The fan fiction overturns seasonal conflicts at the whim of Kurt or Blaine, with attention instead given to Kurt and Blaine–focused dramatic plots—for example, Kurt's house is burned down in a hate crime.[26] In addition, extensive sex scenes make up the bulk of the series; narrative advancement is arguably secondary to the written spectacle of sex—all the sex and intimacy denied in *Glee* itself, if we recall the critiques of The Box Project ("cockblockd!") and the Glee Equality Project. Finally, SugarKane_01's fan fiction series, "Come Here Boy," veers toward social activism as it intertwines its dramatic narrative with corrective plots and educational information, giving readers the information about, for example, PFLAG, that *Glee* rushes over, and critiquing *Glee*'s failure to fully punish the homophobic behavior of key characters on the series.[27]

Even as these fan fiction series shift the ideological work of the series, they also channel millennial hope discourse. In addition, a fair number of these popular fan works recreate the limits of millennial liberalism, retreating away from issues of race and class in favor of a romantic vision of white able-bodied queerness.[28] For example, millennial hope ideologies seep into C. P. Coulter's "Dalton" and its fandom. Just as in *Glee*, in "Dalton," Kurt must teach the Warblers to embrace the networked diverse collective rather than fetishizing the alpha performer that is Blaine. In "Steal a Heart," millennial consumerism and brand identification actually plays a more visible role than in *Glee* itself; the series devotes a novel-sized volume to the New Directions' and the Warblers' trip to Disney World, with Blaine professing how much Disney meant to him as a child and continues to mean to him as an adult. The story details each ride, meal, and extravagant hotel stay, and concludes with Blaine proposing to Kurt within the walls of Disney. Such branded lifestyle immersion echoes Howe and Strauss's belief in millennials' willingness to identify with brands in pervasive ways. However, "Steal a Heart" suggests that millennials' acceptance of corporate branding in their lives does not extend to all brands equally or to blind allegiance. Thus, the series simultaneously critiques and reworks fundamentals of the *Glee* brand while celebrating Disney's centrality to millennial identity.[29]

Acknowledging Millennial Hope's Contradictions

Glee sets into motion the contradictory ideologies of millennial hope, a mix of willing consumerism, embrace of diversity, and celebration of the redefined, nontraditional family. Because *Glee* and its fandom are an aggressively transmedia phenomenon, audiences negotiate these values online, entering into conversation (or struggle) with the text of *Glee* and with each other as well. This negotiation is especially evident in viewer reactions to the "Gleek Freak Out: Kurt & Blaine Kiss Reaction" video. Responses to this video celebrate its depiction of the Gleek viewing experience, but at the same time they question its representational limits.

This video and its comments cannot be fully considered without taking into account the YouTube context that shapes and frames them. In the introduction, I spoke about how transmediated experience means that the flow of texts and ideologies extend from television, where only official producers have the ability to write on screen and shape the text, to digital media, where audiences have the ability and even expectation themselves to become authors and shape new texts, and thus to affect the ideological work of the larger fan-text. These moments of interpretive and expansive (or even resistive) author-ship are shaped by the digital tools audiences use as well as by the affordances and limitations of the interfaces at play. YouTube reaction videos like "Gleek Freak Out: Kurt & Blaine Kiss Reaction" are shaped by the technology avail-able to record (most likely a camera on a laptop, or perhaps a cell phone cam-era); YouTube's video hosting service; its tagging function, which allows visi-tors to find videos; its automated takedown system, which blocks videos that appear to have misused copyrighted material; its embed codes, which allow viewers to share videos on other sites while providing a route back to YouTube; its commenting function; and its thumbs-up/thumbs-down rating system, which allows for a visibility of collective approval and disapproval.

Alex Juhasz argues that YouTube's ability to foster a creative community is deeply flawed. She contends that rather than transcending cultural divides, YouTube illuminates them, in part because of the specifics of its interface and in part because of the way industry and amateur users deploy it in dif-ferent ways.[30] In Juhasz's words, "By reifying the distinctions between the amateur and the professional, the personal and the social, in both form and content, YouTube maintains (not democratizes) operating distinctions about who owns culture seriously."[31]

However, YouTube also functions as a cultural community, with cultur-ally enforced norms and expectations that at times (indeed, even often) ex-ceed the industry/amateur hierarchy Juhasz rightly observes.[32] In looking at the "Gleek Freak Out" response video, we must take into account the way in which YouTube as a cultural forum intersects with the other cultural forums at play in the video—fandom more broadly, Glee fandom more specifically, and fandom (Glee and otherwise) on YouTube more specifically yet. The "Gleek Freak Out" video was made possible and legible within an already existing cul-ture of sharing viewing/response videos to significant moments of television, as well as the already existing presence of Glee fandom on YouTube where view-ers become authors and distributors by sharing favorite Glee performances, fan-created vids, verbal responses to Glee episodes, and their own renditions of Glee songs.

Within this context of already evolving culture on YouTube and in fandom, the "Gleek Freak Out" response video becomes a site of audience negotiation with the televisual text and with each other regarding what it means to be a fan of Glee. The comments posted in response to the video reiterate and reaffirm the values of millennial hope, but also convey a sense of disparity, limitation, and restriction. For example, the following comment invokes the millennial redefinition of family and family values:

> It's really nice to see a whole family sitting in front of the TV and watching a show without anyone squabbling to change the channel! But really? Dancing in front of the TV when they are in the middle of kissing scene, no matter how happy u r is just rude, those poor guys who can't watch the beautiful way Darren's and Chris's lips work during a kiss![33]

This quote draws on the millennial redefinition of family and conjures up the long-standing vision of television as the (re)uniter of family—a narrative present from the earliest days of TV and TV advertising.[34] The commenter playfully rebukes the dancing, celebrating together family as not being sufficiently attentive to the material on the TV screen. Of course the material that they are being rebuked for not watching (or blocking other people's view of) is not a traditional evocation of family values but rather the physical details of an eroticized kiss between two young men. This comment thus celebrates fan community, envisioning it as a uniting of family, but it also playfully polices the extent to which this community becomes the spectacle in its own right, taking attention away from the original televisual object.

The majority of comments on this video unequivocally celebrate both Glee and Gleekdom, and they echo the series' positive discourses of millennial hope, celebrating the power of the diverse millennial collective.[35] The following remark is fairly representative of the comments' overarchingly positive tone:

> [I] was watching these reactions from different people for a while. And this is so much important and inspiring for some people out there— for every person who feels that everybody has the right to be happy . . . and I am so happy to see that society one by one is moving in the right direction and being more acceptable, tolerant and respectful . . . I believe one day we all will be treated equal and will not be judged based on our sexual orientation . . . these videos give so much hope and honesty.[36]

This quote seems to reaffirm millennial hope's somewhat monolithic, forward-looking positivity; but in other comments, millennial realities and contradictions bleed through. For example, the following two comments introduce the specifics (and specific limitations) of localized reception, acknowledge an international context, and recognize the ideological differences that can exist and be irreconcilable within families:

> I so envy you guys . . . I was screaming even before the kiss because of excitement and then all of a sudden the local channel that i was watching it from cut the scene. And I was sooo damn disappointed. It could have been epic for my country. We don't get to see gay relationships on mainstream television and I was just hoping that maybe they could set an example that nothing about gay relationships is wrong and there is acceptance. It could have been a real uplifting moment for gay kids out here.[37]

> I would've screamed and cheered if i had not been watching it with my super conservative dad, who looked at me and said my name with disgust as this happened. I had to wait until I got to my room and shut the door to start cheering and freaking out about it. I almost couldn't get to sleep last night over it! lol:D I'm so happy they're together.[38]

Although these comments take their place within the larger flow of positive, progressive millennial discourse, they also acknowledge the way in which Glee's and Glee fandom's preferred ideologies come into conflict with personal, national, and familial contexts. Glee itself attempts — if unevenly — to mobilize millennials' desire to become producers and to help shape meanings across media platforms. The YouTube comments to the "Gleek Freak Out" video represent this notion made reality. In these comments, we see the positive dimensions of millennial ideologies simultaneously writ large and confounded by the realities of a multiauthored millennial landscape.

Millennial Noir

2

Thus far, we have focused on positive narratives that circulate around millennials — millennial hope — but a significant portion of millennial-directed media takes a different tack, embracing more negative visions of millennials, or at least their ambiguities. These millennial media texts build up, revel in, and capitalize on ambivalent visions of millennials. While these narratives are certainly less than positive, they are not necessarily unappealing depictions of millennials. They paint millennials as illicit, powerful, sympathetic, dangerous, erotic, and alluring, and they sell them as such. Such representations negotiate anxieties about millennials, including anxieties about how millennials' excessive digital know-how may take them out of adult (and industry) control. Millennial noir makes these anxieties a place of desire and celebration, turning a perceived threat into a marketable commodity.

The move from celebration of positive values to an embrace of immorality and excess occurs in part through a shift in genre. I call this construct millennial noir because these more ambivalent depictions of millennials often rework the cinematic tradition of film noir, sometimes taking the form of self-conscious homage and sometimes surfacing in more incidental recreations of noir themes and aesthetics. Millennial noir texts do not necessarily heed the rules and regulations of classic film noir as laid out by film scholars. Rather, they pick and choose and transform to serve contemporary purposes.

Millennial noir media texts depict millennials as morally ambiguous, as adult before their time, and as digital pirates with no respect for institutions—unless they themselves own those institutions. They show millennials as simultaneously perpetrators and victims of modern cultures' excesses, at once digital terrorizers and digital captives. They also depict millennials who push at gendered boundaries, paying special attention to technologically empowered young women whose desire, curiosity, and quest for control drive the narrative. These darker representations take on the emotional, ethical, and social experiences of young adults engaged with the production and consumption of contemporary digital culture, and in so doing, they intersect with perceptions of the value and threat of fannishness and fandom—specifically with the problem of the digitally empowered, producing female fan.

Noiresque visions of millennials such as the TV series *Gossip Girl* and *Veronica Mars* hail a female millennial audience as a key desired demographic, and they are thus rife with issues of gender negotiation. Media texts directed at female millennials must engage with a set of confused ideas about what it means to be female and millennial—a strange mix of cultural policing, emotional excess, willing consumerism, power through technology, and acknowledgment of female sexual desire. This weighty process of gender negotiation and redefinition finds apt expression in the codes of film noir, a generic tradition that in its heyday celebrated the allure of the illicit, the criminal, and the dangerous femme fatale, only sometimes concealed in the guise of a morality tale.[1] The moral ambiguity of film noir, combined with its long history of pushing at gender roles, provides a ripe tradition of visual and narrative language that may be used to depict the alluring, darker side of millennials and the complexities of gendered experience in the millennial generation. Powerful young women populate millennial noir texts, cast as filles fatales (a younger twist on the infamous film noir femme fatale), as (private) investigators, or as both. The young male characters in these series also present a significant noir gender revision, as they fall into the roles of hommes fatales, serving as either obstacles or ambiguous allies to our young female leads.

The conflicted vision of millennial female subjectivity and of shifting gender roles in the millennial generation is perhaps nowhere more clearly expressed than in the unlikely site of the piracy warning on the season 1 DVDs of *Gossip Girl*. While this piracy warning appears on a range of other DVDs as

THE WOMAN HE LOVES
IS PIRATING DVDS

Figure 4. Viewers posted and critiqued the Warner Bros. *Casablanca* antipiracy warning on YouTube.

well, its inclusion on the *Gossip Girl* DVDs seems especially apt, as *Gossip Girl's* audience has been infamous for watching the series in less than legal ways, sharing episodes on social-networking sites and on peer-to-peer file-sharing forums.[2] Even more striking is this particular piracy warning's mode of approach: it tells of the evils of piracy through the language of video remix. The sequence reedits that ultimate film noir, *Casablanca*, to make it seem like the archetypal Rick (Humphrey Bogart) is rejecting Ilsa (Ingrid Bergman) because she pirates DVDs. Teary eyes wide, Ilsa begs Rick to forgive her, but Rick is staunch in his moral high ground: pirating DVDs is wrong.

The underlying logic of this antipiracy warning is heartbreakingly and hilariously ironic. It relies on remix to make its point, but its point is that while this type of media remixing may speak to audience members, they had better not try to get access to the raw materials of media culture necessary to make their own similarly remixed creative expressions. Compounding this irony, the remix warning is highly gendered, as macho Rick must stand for his moral code and turn away emotive Ilsa, who loves her illegal downloads. Is this trailer truly meant to guide its viewers away from the evils of downloading? Could this piece really work for its stated purpose as a piracy deterrent on a DVD set that is no match for DVD-ripping software, as fans, vidders, and remixers can attest? How exactly does this warning function as an introduction to *Gossip Girl*, a series that is all about embracing and celebrating the nostalgic, emotive, and transgressive passion that Ilsa represents?

The vision of millennials constructed in this warning—millennials as pirates who need to be policed, or as emotive (fangirl) Ilsas who need Rick to put them in their place—certainly doesn't sound like the hopeful collective considered in the previous chapter. Instead, we can recognize in Ilsa the outlines of millennial noir. She—and the antipiracy warning in full—distills fears that the industry will lose control of its media product and its viewers in the face of millennial technological power. By mapping this negative vision of millennials onto the emotive and romantic figure of Ilsa/Ingrid Bergman, intentionally or not, this warning colors anxieties about uncontrollable millennials with a strange glamour of illicit nostalgia. Such is the paradox of millennial noir.

From this perspective, Ilsa/Ingrid becomes one of the many representations of morally ambiguous (if not compromised and depraved) young women in millennial noir who wield power through a combination of emotion, sexuality, and technology. These powerful and emotional millennial noir filles fatales build on long-standing gendered visions of fandom—notions of fans as emotionally excessive and buried in affect, as the figureheads for incoherent feminine desire, misplaced devotion, and obsession. At the same time, millennial noir representations distance themselves from other negative perceptions of fans, especially the concept of fans as infantile dupes. Millennial noir representations transform the negative associations of feminized fandom (for example, emotional affect as dangerous and desexualizing, and obsession as a social problem) into positives. In millennial noir television series, affect meets savvy and coheres into self-aware transgression. The heroines of these millennial series may be depicted as obsessive and obsessed, but more often than not, their obsession signifies a determination to revenge wrongs, to expose corruption, or simply to succeed and be powerful in the world. This reclamation of elements associated with fandom extends from the representation of characters within the series to the construction of the imagined viewer for these series. These programs often celebrate savvy and playful excess in their narrative construction and in their transmedial address to audiences. The three chapters that comprise this section will explore the flow from powerful but excessive televisual heroine to the acknowledged power of excess in fandom.

Furthermore, millennial noir transforms the gendered problems of fandom—where female fans are seen to be excessive, dangerous, and incoherent in their desire, and where male fans are seen to be emasculated and compromised in their dedication to fannish details—into a celebration of gender ambiguity. These programs feature alluring characters whose gender play becomes something to be desired and celebrated rather than condemned. Not only are filles fatales allowed to survive, even thrive, as serial heroines who continually challenge gender binaries, but these series also depict sympathetically ambiguous male characters, antiheroes trapped within the confines of societal restrictions of masculinity. The male characters celebrated within these series also challenge gender assumptions and cross gender lines as they serve as the heroines' muse, inspiration, supporter, victim, or duplicitous homme fatale.

From within this context, the *Gossip Girl* DVD set's opening warning against millennial pirating fails in everything from casting to concept—assuming that the warning is actually trying to dissuade *Gossip Girl* viewers from ripping DVDs, that is. It's the emotive, pirating Ilsa who would read as the primary celebrated figure within the context of millennial noir, and certainly within *Gossip Girl* in particular. If a millennial series were to unfold from this *Casablanca* piracy warning, I predict that Rick would be drawn into Ilsa's web, and soon they would be running a downloading empire together, with Ilsa at the helm.

FOUR

Mapping and Marketing Millennial Noir

Part 1 explored the construct of millennial hope through the *Glee* phenomenon, demonstrating the contradictory ways in which, for a (supposedly) singular television text, millennial hope threads through production discourse, paratexts, marketing structure, fan reception, and fan creativity. These narratives of millennial hope are certainly not limited to *Glee*; one could also consider the work of millennial hope in ABC Family's branding (discussed in the introduction), the Harry Potter franchise, or even the 2008 Obama presidential campaign, famous both for its "hope" tagline and its engendering of enthusiasm in the younger generation.

However, positive narratives about millennials do not always exist in such undiluted form as in *Glee*—and even *Glee* has its darker side, usually channeled through satire, and also emerging in the wake of actor Cory Monteith's death. Many of the sites that assert notions of millennial hope also embrace darker narratives about millennials. Both the Harry Potter franchise and ABC Family (especially with its later hit, *Pretty Little Liars*) are simultaneously sites of positive discourse and of millennial media's darker turn. As I described in the introduction to part 2, millennial texts draw on elements of film noir to represent the (perceived) darker dimensions of the millennial generation, recuperating—with a noir sheen—millennials' supposed technological dependence, sexual transgression, rampant consumerism, and collective immorality. All these fears come to the fore in the *Casablanca* anti-piracy "public service announcement" video that opens the *Gossip Girl* DVD set.

Before we discuss the specific ways in which millennial noir programming reworks tropes of classic noir, we need to understand how the television industry—and specifically the CW television network—capitalizes on the anxieties surrounding millennials in development, marketing, and promotional campaigns. Industry discourse negotiates the threat and allure of the millennial generation, turning what could be seen as pitfalls into marketing and branding strategy. As we will see, even the negatives of millennial noir narratives can be drafted into the larger commercial projects of millennial hope, if not into a similarly conservative-friendly picture of upright, traditional millennial citizens.

Millennial Threat and Allure

The millennials offer an expansive yet elusive generational fantasy, holding promise and threat in their mystery and otherness. Narratives of millennial hope may put a positive spin on millennials' technological prowess, but the media industry also struggles with millennials' supposed digital media immersion. Millennials' digital savvy means that they know how to sidestep traditional methods of media consumption. Not only do they know how to rip DVDs and use peer-to-peer networks to share video files, but they also teach each other to do so, spreading the skills necessary to file share, remix, and recirculate.[1] Millennial online viewing cannot be presumed to be legal. Yes, millennials may legally download digital files via iTunes, but they also participate in peer-to-peer file-sharing networks, and they hide copyrighted material within YouTube as well as within other, lesser-known video streaming sites. Such elusive audience patterns mean that traditional methods of measuring viewership may miss millennials. Moreover, many of the viewing methods supposedly favored by millennials—for example, unofficial streaming, file sharing, and DVRing—avoid sponsors' advertisements and thus potentially bypass the very commercial structures of television.[2] Thus, it is not clear whether millennial viewers "count," that is, whether they should be counted when assessing a media product's commercial viability. A television program successful in attracting millennials might not be legible as a standard commercial success because the normal modes of assessing success (the Nielsen ratings) would not register the results.

Various consulting companies and panels of so-called media experts have attempted to ease fears about millennials by promising that millennials can be known, controlled, and tamed. A 2010 article by Nielsen states, "In the US, young people's media usage is markedly different from that of older generations but is likely to converge with their elders as they themselves grow older."[3] This article quells anxieties by arguing that while millennials' modes of media engagement may be "markedly different" in the present, in the future their behaviors will become more traditional.[4] A panel at the South by Southwest Interactive Conference in 2013 sported the title, "How Do You Solve A Problem Like Millennials?"[5] This title alone suggests that millennials are a problem, but one with a solution available to a panel of experts. Taking a slightly different tack, many blog posts highlight millennials' return to traditional cultural practices such as crafting, cooking, and reading as proof that this younger generation isn't such a different breed after all, even if these cultural practices are finding new life online.[6] One might even suggest that Lawrence Lessig makes a similar move in his book Remix; his vision of digital read/write culture as a return to folk traditions adds a nostalgic balm to his legal argument for remix.

However, not all coverage of millennials attempts to contain the millennial threat by underplaying the change they represent. The CW's Gossip Girl serves as a good counterexample. After the series' initial success, New York Magazine ran an article entitled "The Genius of Gossip Girl," the tagline of which read, "How a wunderkind producer, seven tabloid-ready stars, an army of bloggers, and a nation of texting tweenagers are changing the way we watch television." A Wired magazine article declared that "Gossip Girl's online success is a preview of TV 3.0."[7] These articles painted a picture of television on a precipice, with the future to be seen in those programs and networks that cater directly to the preferences, interests, and practices of millennials as epitomized in Gossip Girl. As the New York Magazine article put it, "Even executives at Nielsen threw up their hands and admitted that Gossip Girl appeared to be speaking to an audience so young and tech-savvy they hadn't really figured it out just yet."[8] In the words of then–CW president of entertainment, Dawn Ostroff, "Nielsen doesn't have a great grasp on measuring younger viewers. You couldn't go anywhere in the country without finding people obsessed with the show. Where Gossip Girl ranked No. 100 on the Nielsen list, it was No. 13 when you looked at the power-content ratings—a combination of Nielsen ratings, traffic online and buzz."[9] While Ostroff bemoaned the Nielsen's ability to assess Gossip Girl's success, she also positioned Gossip Girl (and the CW) as having successfully figured out the problem that is millennials. With a target age demographic of eighteen to forty-nine, we can understand why Ostroff would have wanted the CW to be seen as the network getting it right, the model of the future TV revolution.

The CW has gone back and forth regarding whether to endorse or police online viewing. As a broadcast network serving a niche audience, the CW found itself caught somewhere between the promise and threat of millennials. In 2008, the CW removed *Gossip Girl*'s streaming episodes from the official CW site, but in 2010, it reinstated streaming with double the advertisements. Although millennials may be seen as threatening, elusive, and excessive, that same excess holds commercial promise. As we've seen, much popular discourse imagines millennials to be armed with ways to collectively avoid corporate control, but they are also reported to be aware of and potentially accepting of the corporate claim on their identity. Recall Howe and Strauss's vision of millennials eager to spend and participate in the ever-growing commercial aspects of transmedia expansion. A white paper written by the Edelman Group, a consulting group for Levi Strauss, argues that millennials have "a strong sense of brand awareness and loyalty" and that they are likely to "define their personal brand" on social networking sites "by aligning with the brands they favor."[10] In their contradictory combination of commercial resistance and willing consumerism, millennials emerge as an elusive but valuable potential audience. Even as they slip past standard corporate methods of assessment and potentially threaten to bypass commercial/capitalist structures, millennials are still hailed as a promising market, as willing consumers ready to identify with and be loyal to brands across the landscapes of their lives.[11]

Millennial digital savvy is thus seen as bad when it threatens traditional modes of relating to media texts (think Ilsa's illegal downloading) but good when it can act as free labor to propel immersive brands seemingly co-created between millennials and corporations. Millennial consumer willingness makes them a heady prize for corporate interests, despite all the anxiety surrounding their coherence as an audience. I can't help but think of the refrain "how do you solve a problem like Maria?" referenced in the South by Southwest panel title mentioned above. To run with the *Sound of Music* parallel, in the musical/film, Maria's excesses are seen as a problem within the church, making the life of a nun unsuitable for her, but her perceived excesses — especially when performed by Julie Andrews — are her appeal to the Von Trapp family (not to mention the film's audience) and provide the story's romantic focus and ideological resolution.

While the CW may at times fall into the role of policing millennials' streaming habits, its televisual and transmedia texts more often seek instead to play up the illicit appeal of its millennial-oriented material. Again, *Gossip Girl* offers a case in which the series' perceived excesses became branding strategy. The series depicts the life of excessively wealthy teens who scrabble for power, fighting among themselves and wrangling with their usually impotent parents. *Gossip Girl* claims in its opening voice-over to depict "the lives of Manhattan's Upper East Side High School elite," and thus from the start it focuses on teens (and especially teen girls, as the title suggests) who wield excessive power in their class-entrenched hierarchy. The teens of *Gossip Girl* deal with the social problems of high school, but they also drink martinis in bars, have sex in New York City taxicabs, and even own their own burlesque clubs.

Adapted from a book series that had already received significant public scrutiny for its highly consumerist nature and its representation of teens engaging in inappropriate (that is, adult, illegal, and perverse) behavior, the TV version of *Gossip Girl* quickly received a maelstrom of critique regarding its depiction of teen characters. Watchdog group the Parents Television Council (PTC) accused *Gossip Girl* of corrupting young viewers and attacked the CW for housing such adult representations of teens: "The depictions of teenage behavior . . . were mind-blowingly inappropriate on any network at any time. This program exhibits Hollywood's concept of appropriate behavior for youth. The show further promotes the hedonistic irresponsible lifestyle that is captivating our country."[12] *Gossip Girl* became a visible representation of all that was supposedly wrong with millennial culture at the turn of the century—including most especially sexual knowingness and sexual activity—whether this was the fault of millennials themselves, the industries and media producers who sought to take advantage of them, or both.

Faced with this critique from the PTC, the CW chose to embrace and celebrate the taboo dimensions of teen experience, including teen sexuality and most especially female teen sexuality. A campaign in advance of *Gossip Girl*'s second season remixed images and dialogue from season 1 to make it seem even more salacious. Known as the OMFG campaign, the teasers depicted images of the characters in suggestive situations. The spots bleeped out words that weren't actual curse words to make them seem as if they were. One of the pieces opened with good girl turned manipulative "Queen B," Blair Waldorf, in a church confessional booth, confiding in an older priest that she has "succumbed to inebriation, and surrendered [her] virtue to a self-absorbed a . . ."

The rest of the word is bleeped out for a full second, allowing the viewer to fill in the even more taboo word "asshole," rather than "ass," the word actually spoken in the scene. This play with censorship on television presents a picture of *Gossip Girl* as pushing at the boundaries of television's long-accepted norms. The spot worked to make *Gossip Girl* seem more transgressive than it actually is, asking audiences to fill in the bleeps and imagine meanings not spelled out but still present in the series.

All of the short promo spots in the OMFG campaign did similar work to the one I described above. They did not significantly change the content of the original scene but rather reedited somewhat suggestive scenarios to make them appear more boundary pushing, inviting audiences to imagine more transgressive content. Each spot featured quick editing that also added a tone of hyped transgression. The letters OMG were intercut throughout, with the final image a black still with the large text OMFG hailing an in-the-know audience comfortable with sexual suggestiveness and armed with netspeak to elude authorities. By omitting and then including the F in OMFG, the spots avoided and simultaneously drew the audience's attention to the word "fucking," and in the same move hailed them as savvy decoders who didn't need to hear the word sounded out to know it was there.

If *Gossip Girl*'s episodes were already under fire from various cultural commentators, the OMFG campaign raised the critique to new heights. In response to the campaign, the PTC stated that it "deplores the CW's deliberate use of profanity and sexual imagery to exploit and further corrupt young viewers, and has warned its members about the show and the new ad campaign."[13] This critique was framed in generational terms, with the PTC arguing that "teenagers are a particularly vulnerable audience and are more apt to be influenced by the programming they watch than adults."[14]

The PTC's critiques depended on the assumption that the CW's prime audience was teens (and teen girls specifically) and that teen viewers need protection from representations of sexuality. However, because of the porousness of the millennial category, the CW could, when necessary, deny the teen component of their millennial audience in favor of an imagined older audience and thus avoid censoring its more transgressive material. CW representatives defended the series by arguing that while *Gossip Girl* may feature teen characters, it is a series that deals with adult issues and adult levels of sexuality, and thus has adult (and specifically female adult) appeal. In response to a later attack by the PTC for the series' hyping a supposed threesome, CW spokes-

REGISTER/LOG IN   THE RULES   ARCHIVE   FAN SIGNS

WHAT'S HOT: Britney Spears   Beyonce   Television   Film   Celeb Blogs & Twitter   Box Office

12:20 pm - 07/23/2008

All three (four, sorry!) Gossip Girl ads

__PAPILLON

Figure 5. Fans at the LiveJournal celebrity gossip site "Oh No They Didn't" shared, celebrated, and critiqued the CW campaign that appropriated the series' negative press.

man Paul McGuire described "the target audience" for *Gossip Girl* as "18- to 34-year-old women, with a median viewer age of 27 years old."[15] In *Gossip Girl*, the CW had created a show it could market simultaneously to teens and young adults, collapsing both into the target millennial audience; yet the CW could selectively emphasize or disavow either demographic as context required.

Rather than toning down the seemingly transgressive dimensions of the series, the CW embraced the critique and controversy. A billboard campaign launched in advance of the second season featured quotes of outrage from newspaper reviewers set against decontextualized, suggestive still imagery.[16]

This campaign sold *Gossip Girl* precisely as offering a taboo, sexualized (and sexually active) vision of millennials, a vision simultaneously alluring and policed—or perhaps alluring because it was or needed to be policed. The campaign included four different posters featuring medium close-ups of the individual main characters seemingly in the middle of various erotic acts. Each poster also included a selected negative quote from the popular press, including the PTC's "mind-blowingly inappropriate," the *San Diego Union Tribune*'s "very bad for you," the *New York Post*'s "a nasty piece of work," and the *Boston Herald*'s "every parent's nightmare."

Here the very censure expressed by the PTC became fuel for the CW's attempts to define itself as a boundary-pushing network that has its pulse on millennial change—as sexual, knowing, savvy, and nasty as it may be. In this way, the CW built its niche network branding around a core of millennial noir logic, collapsing teen and adult when convenient and celebrating the very threats that millennials seemed to pose.

Transforming Noir

Just as *Glee* reworks the genre of the movie musical to map out a vision of millennial hope, millennial texts like the TV series *Gossip Girl*, *Pretty Little Liars*, *Veronica Mars*, and *Revenge* draw on and rework elements of film noir to express the contradictions of millennial experience, contradictions about morality, religion, gender, sexuality, and individual versus collective worth. Not all darker narratives about millennials come in the trappings of film noir, but for many millennial texts, noir offers a language to capture and celebrate the alluring danger of millennials.

In *More Than Night*, James Naremore argues that our understanding of film noir cannot be limited to a specific period or media—not to America, the 1940s and 1950s, or even the medium of film. Naremore contends that far from disappearing or concluding in the end of the 1950s, noir continues to extend into all realms of our culture, including film, television, and even fashion.[17] With this expansive approach to noir in mind, we can find noir elements running throughout millennial media, either indirectly reworking noirish aesthetics and themes or more purposefully hailing back, with a nostalgic tinge, to film noir as a recognizable media tradition.[18] In both dimensions—indirect noir and purposefully nostalgic noir—noir elements do not remain static but transform into new cultural formulations.

Millennial noir transforms popular perceptions of classic noir through its reworking of gendered noir tropes, most especially the private eye and femme fatale, as well as through its address to a millennial female audience. In her study of American pulp modernism in the 1930s, Black and White and Noir, Paula Rabinowitz argues that the reach and significance of film noir goes far beyond the canon of noir films constructed by film scholars.[19] She finds noir not only in the classic films broadly recognized as noir, but, significantly, in the popular "detritus," pulp texts, and female-associated texts that preceded and accompanied the films now canonized as noir.[20] She argues that noir is more than a body of films or a delineated genre; rather, it constitutes the "context" through which we must "make sense" of America's "landscape and history."[21] With this perspective of a larger but more liminal history of noir in mind, and given millennial media's merging of niche and mainstream, it makes sense that contemporary noir discourse surfaces in millennial media. Millennial noir manifests especially in media texts marked as low quality, taboo, and, not incidentally, feminine, in texts like Gossip Girl that straddle the line between liminal and mainstream and that are often marked as not only millennial but—doubly taboo—millennial and feminine. These millennial noir texts arguably follow in the footsteps of noir's less celebrated histories—noir's B film and female-associated popular/detritus heritage. Millennial noir thus fits in with invisible noir traditions while simultaneously transforming the popular and dominant vision of noir.

Millennial Interiority, Noir Style

The noir tradition provides codes for representing ambiguities of all sorts—moral, sexual, gender—that emerge from the contradictions built into conceptions of the millennial generation. As we have seen, popular discourse imagines the millennial generation as a synthesis of idealist and corporate, pragmatic and utopian, innocent and sexual, and ethical and realist. Millennial noir media texts revel in these contradictions and ambiguities by deploying a new and/or revised language of noir. Noir becomes a route to depicting complex characters that embody millennial contradictions.

One of the most obvious noir elements permeating millennial noir narratives is the voice-over. The voice-over is especially crucial for millennial noir serial texts because it functions to provide access to shifting character interiority over time. In millennial noir television series like Veronica Mars, Gossip Girl, and Revenge, the voice-over seems to offer access to a character's authentic self, cutting past the ambiguity of social interactions and the falseness of everyday performances of self. The iconic noir voice-over emerges as a key trope providing entry into character interiority, and—given the female focus of many of these series—specifically female millennial interiority. In so doing, it renders accessible millennial ambiguity and excess, taking characters that might be seen as threatening villains (often femmes fatales) and turning them into the series' main points of identification.

The noir voice-over is a complicated trope about which much has been written; Karen Hollinger suggests that nonnoir 1940s genres deployed the voice-over to "increase audience identification with their narrators' stories," with voice-overs "associated with authority, heroism, and power."[22] In contrast, Hollinger argues, film noirs of the 1940s "contain weak, powerless narrators" whose voice-overs "tell a story of their past failures or of their inability to shape their lives to their own designs."[23] When appearing in combination with that other staple of film noir, the flashback, classic noir voice-overs actually often destabilize the perceived authority of the central male narrator. If the content of a flashback conflicts with voice-over narration (as is often the case in classic noir), then the narrating character's objectivity and moral compass can come into question. Discrepancy between voice-over narration and flashback can open up for the viewer the question of where (or whether) one can locate any kind of objective truth. In Robert Miklitsch's words, the discrepancy between voice-over narration and image can "trigger . . . a proliferation of competing perspectives."[24]

In classic noir, this struggle for narrative control is gendered in particular ways. The narrating voice attempting (but failing at) narrative coherence is usually a masculine investigating voice, probing and attempting to resolve the problem of the woman. What the classic noir voice-over often fails to contain is the (visual) power of the femme fatale. The femme fatale in classic film noir already pushes at and beyond the norms of representation of women in classic Hollywood films. As Hollinger notes, "Film noirs release the female image from . . . fixed female roles" as "weak, ineffectual figures," giving them instead "overwhelming visual power."[25] The narrative tension of film noir thus often plays out as the narrating male figure tells the story of his attempt and failure to contain the threat of the femme fatale: "The male voice-over in film noir, while it may attempt to control the female image, serves instead to pit the femme fatale's dominant visual presence against the male voice."[26] To oversimplify, in classic noir, voice narration represents a failing attempt at masculine control, while the visual image channels the unruly feminine.

Often the voice fails to fully control the image; the femme fatale may prove "fatal unto herself," but she takes the male "hero" with her, and, in the end, her (visual) power stays with us.[27]

Fast-forward to the millennial noir of the twenty-first century. First off, we have one very noticeable shift: the voice-over is more often than not no longer a male investigator but a female one. And the problem she is investigating is not (only) the problem of the femme fatale (which may or may not be the narrator herself) but the problem of the victimization of the femme fatale—the very problem of patriarchy—or rather, to be more specific, the problem of the femme fatale's younger counterpart, the fille fatale, and thus a compounded problem of gender and generation. Within this revised noir, the voice-over's subjectivity does not necessarily prompt us to question the control of the narrator, as Hollinger argues happens in classic noir. Rather, it forges a sense of connection between her marginal, subjective perspective and ours, as we are given access to her seemingly private inner thoughts. As viewers, we may be aware of the limited nature of her perspective, but we still feel its value and significance within the larger millennial collective.

Indeed, millennial noir series depict multiple young female characters (both across series and within a single series) who fight for and then wield power, often through their use of digital technologies. These young women narrate their power struggles—or perform their power—through voice-over, bringing the audience along for the ride. As we are drawn into the fille fatale's perspective, we are interpellated into the millennial collective and invited into a space of millennial/generational interiority, one marked simultaneously as public and intimate, individual and plural. The following chapter will look at four case studies of millennial noir serial television to consider the pictures they paint of female millennial individual and collective experience. These series take the perceived threat of the feminine digital millennial collective and render it as a powerful and significant cultural network. In so doing, they transform taboo visions of (female/feminized) fandom into a compelling new vision of audience transformative agency.

FIVE

The Attack of the Filles Fatales

In millennial noir media texts, millennial girls (or young women) negotiate an adult world full of corruption. They face dangers both digital and physical, including the dangers of sexual violence and patriarchal abuse of power. Digital technologies color a treacherous world that these girls must navigate. Yet at the same time, digital tools give millennial girls omniscience and mobility. Millennial noir media texts depict young women fighting digital terror with digital networks, claiming and deploying the technologies that seek to further entrap them within hierarchical, patriarchal systems of power. Cell phones and laptops become tools millennial girls use to uncover corruption across generations. Digital technologies also give voice to millennial female perspectives, as millennial women use technology to shape the plot, to connect with one another, and to guide viewer experience and understanding of the narrative.

This chapter explores these themes of digitally empowered female networks in four millennial noir television programs directed primarily at a female millennial audience: the CW's *Gossip Girl*, The UPN/CW's *Veronica Mars*, ABC Family's *Pretty Little Liars*, and ABC's *Revenge*.[1] These four series aired on different TV networks, but all offer visions of young women driven to using digital power to gain control and expose corruption. As I've already described, *Gossip Girl* features a group of teenagers living a decadent life in

New York City under the watchful eye of pseudonymous blogger for whom the series is named. *Veronica Mars* depicts a teen private eye investigating her best friend's murder. *Pretty Little Liars* tells the story of four friends researching the murder of their best friend while being digitally terrorized by an unknown figure pretending to be the same (dead) friend. Finally, *Revenge* depicts the vengeful Emily Thorne digitally orchestrating the destruction of the corrupt socialites who were responsible for her father's wrongful incarceration and death. These four millennial noir TV series offer an evolving picture of threatened yet empowered millennial feminine networks, and by extension of gender and community in millennial culture.

Across the four series considered here, I trace transformations in classic noir components including the voice-over, the private eye, the femme fatale, and moral ambiguity. These series merge teen and noir to different degrees, some more obviously or purposefully than others. They feature characters driven by individual circumstance to form networks to fight larger societal systems, thus insisting on the feminist recognition of the political in the personal and vice versa. In these series, young women use digital technology to attain omniscience and wrest power within a society that has rendered them powerless. With their newly seized power, they build a new millennial landscape, one modeled on the decentered network rather than on traditional hegemonic hierarchies. Together, these series offer a darker, more ambivalent picture of millennial experience than we saw in our examination of *Glee* and *Kyle XY*, specifically one colored by gender, class, and generational inequity. At the same time, these series also offer a vision of millennials creating a new social order in their own image.

"A girl, a teenager, a detective. I'm a triple threat."
Noir Transformations in *Veronica Mars*

Cult favorite *Veronica Mars* aired for its first two seasons (2004–2006) on the UPN network and continued for one more season on the newly created CW network (a merger of two networks with differing claims on the youth market, UPN and the WB). The series depicts a particular vision of millennial identity: savvy yet hopeful, intent on uncovering truths and righting moral inequities in an immoral, sexist, and ageist world. *Veronica Mars* features an unmistakably noir framing, deploying noiresque elements within the series itself and in the series' marketing and hype to distinguish the show from other teen programming.[2]

However, *Veronica Mars* also transforms the tropes of film noir to offer a vision of female millennial subjectivity that does not shy away from cultural and social critique. The series acknowledges that the issues that teen private eye Veronica faces individually (her own rape, her best friend's murder) are systemic issues that millennials must come together as a network to combat. In this way, *Veronica Mars* uses and adapts noir to offer a realist and feminist vision of millennial experience. Yet this vision is also a hopeful one, arguably quite in tune with the more hopeful (and commercially viable) millennial discourse, as the series depicts the possibility of a realist millennial collective— led by a proactive teen girl and empowered by digital technology—dedicated to shaping a better world through the pursuit of truth and justice.

Veronica's father, Keith Mars, is a private eye cut to the classic noir mold: he works out of a small office, is visited by femme fatales, and is consulted by members of Southern California's underbelly and elite alike. This allows the familiar textual noir background of Southern California (albeit San Diego rather than LA), a dimly lit private eye's office, unethical police, and wealthy but troubled families that hide their immorality behind closed doors. This noiresque frame provides a familiar generic tone and context for the series.

But despite being the nominal private eye, Keith Mars is not the series' lead or narrator. For *Veronica Mars* deviates from traditional noir expectations in crucial ways. The position of narrator is taken by teen Veronica, a high school student who moonlights as an assistant on her father's cases and who soon begins to work her own cases as well. Veronica's cases take her into the corruption within her high school, but also into the systemic corruption of the larger city and society. In keeping with film noir expectations, a voice-over frames the narrative, but it is Veronica's voice and words guiding us through the series' mysteries. Veronica's narrating voice-overs serve as direct route to her millennial perspective. They are one of the defining aspects of the series and one of the key elements that mark it from the start as recognizably noir.

Veronica Mars charts Veronica's dogged interrogation of the inequities around her as she investigates her best friend's murder and her own rape, and then, in a third season, a series of rapes on her college campus. Her voice-over guides us through her investigations, aligning us with her marginality as those around her (especially the adults) continually fail to take her seriously as an investigator despite her skill at uncovering the corruption that surrounds her.

Two versions of the pilot for *Veronica Mars* exist, the aired version and the director's cut, the latter available on DVD.[3] Both versions open with Veronica's noiresque voice-overs. The director's cut most explicitly announces itself as noir from the start; it opens with Veronica (played by Kristen Bell) narrating while on a stakeout, with all the accompanying noir visuals one might expect: Veronica uses a telephoto lens to survey a seedy motel, dark street, neon lights, and the shadows of an illicit tryst in the motel window. But this is not simply neonoir redux or nostalgic mimicry. Veronica's opening voice-over in the director's cut proclaims her intended status outside of heterogendered norms and adult life patterns: "I'm never getting married. You want an absolute? Well, there it is. Veronica Mars, spinster." The director's cut presents itself clearly as revised noir, attacking noir assumptions about gender and sexuality that dictate that men are the ones to narrate and investigate, and women are to be silent images subject to the investigating gaze. Instead, here the narrating voice and investigating gaze belong to a young woman, one who is declaring her choice to opt out of the normative institution of marriage.

Even the version of the opening that aired on the UPN—which is decidedly less noiry in visual terms, since it is set outside Veronica's high school rather than a neon lit-motel—uses the noir voice-over as a tool for Veronica to offer her class critique of her high school world, entrenched as it is in larger structures of adult corruption: "This is my school. If you go here, your parents are either millionaires, or your parents work for millionaires. Neptune, California, a town without a middle class." The voice-over here situates Veronica as an outsider female adolescent voice with a strong critical subjectivity, aligning us with her social critique and her interior emotional state. This opening brings noir's focus on systemic corruption to the everyday school space of millennials, a social terrain usually depicted as comparatively innocent, personal, and local.[4]

Veronica's voice-over opens and closes both versions of the series' pilot and resurfaces throughout the series, providing access to Veronica's perspective as she pursues the mysteries of her best friend's murder and her own rape. These voice-overs mimic the hard-boiled noir protagonist's subjective narration of (usually) his descent into a corrupt underbelly. *Veronica Mars*'s situating of the girl as the investigative force is clearly significant, as it flies in the face of the codes of classic noir and of long-standing gender tropes about girls and girlhood. Veronica is not a girl who must be seen and not heard; rather, she is the one who does the speaking (through voice-over) and the listening as she seeks out the truth of her world's corruption.[5] She performs femininity as means to an end, using it to entrap the unsuspecting objects of her investigation. Veronica chooses when her presence should be hidden in pursuit of her goals and when she should be seen and heard.

In the previous chapter, we considered Karen Hollinger's argument that classic noir flashbacks combined with voice-over call into question the noir narrator's total objectivity and control.[6] For Hollinger, this is critical in that it marks noir's destabilization of masculinity, when at first glance masculine control seems so embedded in the genre. Such destabilization might, we could imagine, play out less progressively if it undermined a young woman's already no doubt suspect (if not taboo) narrating voice. And to some extent, the combination of voice-over and flashback in Veronica Mars does call into question Veronica's seeming control over her environment. Editing, cinematography, and narrative structure emphasize the fact that Veronica's perspective is limited; the first episode shows us soft-focus flashbacks, including an ellipsis meant to represent a period of missing memory where Veronica believes she was raped but does not know by whom. The use of nostalgic soft focus in the flashbacks insistently reminds us that everything we see in flashback is from Veronica's perspective, and from her perspective before her loss of innocence, before the awakening trauma of her best friend Lilly Kane's death. The soft-focus filter visualizes Veronica's subjective interiority at the beginning of her journey. In contrast, the sharper imagery of the narrative's present conveys the clarity of Veronica's vision as a more mature, even jaded, young woman. Rather than distancing us from Veronica, the flashbacks thus draw us more closely into her point of view. We come to understand her perspective more deeply and to appreciate her growth over time.

In its insistence on Veronica's emotional subjectivity via voice-over and flashback, Veronica Mars performs a significant synthesis: it merges the subjective noir voice-over, usually meant to signify beleaguered masculinity in the face of corrupt modernity, with another media tradition: the teen girl narrating her personal experience as if through a diary entry. This diarylike narrative trope features in formative teen TV programs from the 1990s such as My So-Called Life (ABC, 1994–1995) and Roswell (WB and UPN, 1999–2002). Like these earlier teen TV series, Veronica's voice-overs personalize the narrative, bringing us inside the perspective of the young female lead.[7] In Veronica's case, her voice-overs function to personalize the series' noiresque politicized narratives of sexual violence and adult corruption. Our alignment with Veronica's emotional, subjective perspective gives weight to the series' exploration of immorality and sexual violence. We feel with Veronica as she struggles with the complexities of a millennial world in which she is a teen girl with adult problems.

Veronica's voice-over makes us aware of the limited and subjective nature of her narration, but this does not necessarily undermine our belief in the morality of her perspective. The series does not demand that we question the truth of Veronica's struggle. Rather, Veronica's emotions validate our sense of the rightness of her mission. We do not doubt that gender, class, and race inequity shape her community and life experience, as she attests. Veronica's voice-overs serve as a tool to connect us with the personal significance of her pursuit of corruption.

In addition to being personal, human, and intimate, Veronica's investigations are also digital and networked.[8] We cheer on her navigation of digital tools to aid in her truth seeking. Veronica orchestrates her investigations via her omnipresent PDA (personal digital assistant), the T-Mobile Sidekick, which at the time was a cell phone with a keyboard and web-accessing power popular among teenagers.[9] As in the other millennial noir texts we will examine in this chapter, Veronica does not wield her digital power in an isolated fashion; rather, she uses technology to connect with others and to build digital networks. In addition to her T-Mobile Sidekick, Veronica depends on two human sidekicks, her (millennial-aged) friends Wallace and Mac, to orchestrate her investigations of societal corruption. Mac is worth special mention here as another millennial girl who uses technology to break through masculine and institutional barriers: a teen girl with extensive technological skills, Mac hacks into corporations or tracks down the origin of e-mails at Veronica's request. Veronica wields digital tools and social networks as joint weapons, while her narrating voice-over aligns us with her emotional perspective and sense of purpose. *Veronica Mars's* millennial noir world is one in which young adults, and especially young women, must unite via digital technology to face the depth of adult corruption and to build new millennial networks and ways of being. The noir elements align us with this cultural critique and at the same time frame it within—and perhaps take away some of its sting via—a comforting nostalgia.

Narrating Digital Power: XOXO *Gossip Girl*

Based on a successful young adult novel series by Cecily von Ziegesar, the CW's *Gossip Girl* depicts an immoral world in which millennials must struggle to make their way despite adult (and millennial) abuses of power. Like *Veronica*

Mars, Gossip Girl uses the voice-over to create a sense of social discomfort while simultaneously connecting viewers with character experience. Each episode of the series begins with the voice-over of Gossip Girl, the unknown and omnipresent blogger, presumably female and millennial but not necessarily so. These voice-overs narrate diegetic blog posts supposedly read by all of the characters on the series; we see the visual of the blog post at the same time that we hear Gossip Girl's voice-over narration catching us up on the drama and intrigue of the Upper East Side teenage socialite world.

Via its framing blog posts, Gossip Girl colors its narrative with the uncertainties of anonymous and pseudonymous digital communities, and it offers a look into this world from a (presumably) millennial female perspective.[10] Gossip Girl's voice-overs nod directly to Veronica Mars because extratextually, they share a narrator. Both series' voice-overs are voiced by actress Kristen Bell. Because Gossip Girl rose to prominence just as Veronica Mars was facing imminent cancellation, in the minds of many viewers the voice of Gossip Girl was Veronica Mars. In Gossip Girl, however, we do not see Bell's face to match her narration—at least, not until a metatextual joke in the final episode, when Bell appears in a cameo. In comparison to Veronica Mars, our access to teen girl interiority is channeled through (the representation of) digital technology, as Gossip Girl uses digital publication tools to voice her perspective to others.

Gossip Girl's vision of gender, generation, and power differs from Veronica Mars in significant ways, and these differences are visible in the series' play with gendered noir tropes. Where Veronica inhabits a position somewhere between femme fatale and private eye, Gossip Girl expands and digitizes the trope of the femme fatale as dangerous spider woman, making her spiderweb the World Wide Web. From her position of digital power, she serves as the narrator in place of a policing private eye. Enabled by social networking and digital technology, Gossip Girl's voice-overs convey her omniscience: Gossip Girl seems to know everything at all times, however impossible it may seem. Further, Gossip Girl—an unnamed teen millennial—appears to set the agenda and plot of the series. It is almost as if she wields narrating power from beyond the story world.

Gossip Girl's narrations are significant in their merger of omniscience and millennial perspective. Their lack of realism (how could one individual know all this information and be so perfectly in tune with the needs of the series' multiple, interweaving story lines?) fuels our sense of Gossip Girl's power as digital, millennial fille fatale. On the surface, Gossip Girl represents the manipulative and terrorizing power of the digital fille fatale who is everywhere and nowhere, and who wields power over her millennial victims. She threatens and punishes all of the characters in regular intervals by sharing information about (and with) them on her blog.

However, on closer look, Gossip Girl is not an isolated but powerful fille fatale, nemesis to her millennial victims. Rather, she represents the power of the networked web, run by and for millennials. The millennial characters living under Gossip Girl's reign are not necessarily disempowered by her omniscience, because they all could potentially be her. Indeed, they regularly deploy her by sending her e-mails with information or images that often become the content of her next blog posts. Thus, Gossip Girl's power as digitally omniscient fille fatale extends to potentially everyone else in the series. The series repeatedly makes it a point to drive home that any of its millennial characters could in fact be our narrating fille fatale.

This sense of digital multiplicity is a crucial part of Gossip Girl's reworking of the femme fatale. Gossip Girl as symbol rather than individual links together all of the millennials in the series (as well as arguably the series' viewers), uniting the millennial collective in a narrating voice.[11] This sense of Gossip Girl as everyone is made explicit in a season 2 episode, "The Goodbye Gossip Girl," in which Gossip Girl plays a trick on everyone by getting them to congregate in a bar, each thinking that the other is Gossip Girl. In an e-mail blast, Gossip Girl tells them that they are all Gossip Girl because she would not exist if they didn't use her. She is herself just a digital tool.

In later seasons, Gossip Girl is temporarily locked out of her account, and particular characters take over her role, unbeknownst to their friends. With various possibilities playfully envisioned by the series (or guessed by characters), it becomes clear that Gossip Girl is more a role waiting to be filled, a role anyone could fill, than a particular individual subjectivity. Any sense that the voice-over gives us access to an individual emotional interiority is a MacGuffin, masking Gossip Girl's real function as nonindividualized networked power. Even the reveal of Gossip Girl's true identity in the series' final episode is quickly despecified, as a new Gossip Girl narrates the closing voice-over (yet still in Bell's voice), while a long shot pans over the milling high school students of the Upper East Side, any or all of whom could be Gossip Girl. On some level, then, the series hails all its characters and viewers to fill the role of the power-wielding, digitally enabled Gossip Girl. Gossip Girl, like Glee, ultimately emphasizes a collective interiority, but in this case with an individual woman's narrating voice standing in for the internal negotiations of an evolving generation.

By emphasizing multiple interiorities, *Gossip Girl* destabilizes familiar moral schemata, creating a noiresque landscape of millennial moral ambiguity. *Gossip Girl* offers up multiple ambiguous millennial antiheroes, both male and female, for our identification. Characters who seem at first to fit into more traditional gendered archetypes—hero or ingenue—transform into the various *filles* and *hommes fatales* that characterize the millennial noir collective. In a key moment of character transformation in *Gossip Girl*'s first season, "Queen B" Blair Waldorf performs in a burlesque club, moving from prudish audience member to exhibitionistic seductress. She strips off her iconic headband and slips out of her prim dress to reveal a risqué, vintage-style nightgown. Blair's performance allows her to speak back to the restrictive constructions of traditional femininity and to try on a new, more overt expression of female sexuality and desire. Blair's transformation through performance also elicits a transformation in her eventual love interest, Chuck Bass. Both characters evolve from this moment into morally ambiguous figures that perform excessive and transgressive sexuality in their everyday actions and dress. In this millennial noir reworking of familiar noir character tropes, Blair transforms from prudish ingenue into the *fille fatale*, and Chuck transforms from simplistic heavy into the *homme fatale*. In the multiplicitous millennial noir world of *Gossip Girl*, such a doubling represents an ideal romantic focus, a center of ambiguity and excess.[12] These two are at the core of the series' larger collective of *filles* and *hommes fatales*, a collective that eventually comes to envelop all of the series' characters.

"Justice, like beauty, is in the eye of the beholder": Inverting Moral and Gendered Assumptions in *Revenge*

The ABC series *Revenge* returns us to the single millennial female narrator more in the mold of *Veronica Mars*, except this time she is a full-fledged femme fatale. Unlike the other three series examined in this chapter, *Revenge* airs on a Big Three broadcast network, ABC, rather than a niche millennial-focused network like the CW or ABC Family. Likewise, its characters' ages skew older and it has received broader critical recognition than the other series discussed here. The series features older millennial characters negotiating the path from childhood to adulthood, and it uses noirish elements to explore their experiences of liminality and crisis.

Veronica Mars's narration was driven by her personal circumstances and located in her interpersonal relationships, thus merging teen and noir for a feminist insistence that the personal is political and the political is personal. Likewise, subjective emotion and moral indignation drive *Revenge*'s narrator, Emily Thorne, to speak, and her speaking makes up the episode's framing voice-over. The narrative is set into motion by Emily's desire for revenge (hence the series' title) against the wealthy socialites who framed her father as a terrorist and facilitated his murder. Each of the first episodes depict her enacting revenge on one person who was in some way complicit in her father's murder.

As in *Gossip Girl*, each episode opens with a voice-over, so that Emily becomes our guide for the series. However, Emily's voice-overs do not fill in plot details; nor do they function as "and here's what you missed on *Revenge*." They also—crucially—do not provide a direct line into Emily's thought processes. Instead, Emily narrates ethical and philosophical truisms, charting her determination for revenge and justifying her questionable moral choices with the force of her general ethical insight. Indeed, her voice-overs seem to work against any viewer desire to catch up on plot intricacies. Instead, they ask the viewer to focus on the series' larger thematic preoccupations through Emily's emotional philosophizing.

Although Emily's narration is highly subjective, her voice-overs also provide a sense of omniscience. Emily's subjective voice becomes a tool for articulating the series' core themes; we are asked to share her moral (or amoral) perspective through voice-overs that also seem to carry the weight of the series, making explicit its core concerns. We connect with Emily not because she tells us the plot from her perspective but because she announces the themes of her narrative as she sees them, most often in the form of lofty musings on morality and moral ambiguity.

Emily's truisms simultaneously share her personal insights, convey her omniscience, and indicate her access to (and control over) the series' larger narrative concerns. At any given moment, Emily seems to know more than the viewers or any of the other characters. Despite our supposed access to Emily's inner voice, she interferes in plots in ways we as viewers don't see coming. If we are ever privy to a plot development that she is not, she quickly realizes what's happening, then masters the events in ways that seem impossible and catch us by surprise. Although the voice-overs function to tie us to the force of Emily's subjective perspective, she still maintains narrative power over us and over the other characters in the series. She thus merges Veronica Mars's subjective insight (the insight of one on the margins) with Gossip Girl's empowering omniscience.

Emily uses digital technologies to enable her omniscience and her exacting of revenge. *Revenge* envisions digital technology as a tool with which a millennial woman can gain knowledge and thus wrest power from a system that has rendered her powerless, unseating old hierarchies in favor of a new decentered (or, in Emily's case, ravaged) millennial landscape. In this way, even more than *Gossip Girl*, *Revenge* erects the figure of the digitally empowered young woman and invites us to identify with her perspective while maintaining her mystery. We are teased through voice-overs with the promise of access to her interior perspective, but her omniscience makes her more unknown and unknowable, and more of a significant (if fantastic) threat to the power structures she seeks to unseat.

Like the femme fatale of classic film noir, Emily deceives the various men and women in her life as she ruthlessly follows her own agenda. However, Emily is not completely alone. As the series unfolds, she develops working relationships that amount to a small core collective, yet her relationships with these character often appear to be ones of manipulation. She uses her supporters when she needs to and doles out information to them as she sees fit. She uses her millennial network to infiltrate the Hamptons' upper echelon in order to enact digital revenge, but she only lets her friends in on her plans for revenge when she needs their help.

At first, Emily appears to be a clear invocation of the femme fatale. An iconic season 1 poster pictures her looming tall in the image, emerging from a vast black gown of thorns—a visual pun on her femme fatale–appropriate name, Emily Thorne. However, a closer examination of *Revenge*'s serial narrative suggests that Emily represents a significant shift in the femme fatale trope. The femme fatale's importance in classic noir is most crucially in her relation to the private eye and what she represents to him: temptation, moral ambiguity, and descent into immorality. But we do not judge Emily through the eyes and moral compass of a male private investigator, as was common in classic noir. Instead, we accompany Emily on her journey for revenge, and we sympathize with her goals, no matter how illegal. Even more so than Veronica Mars, Emily is an investigating femme fatale, a complete synthesis of two previously distinct generic categories. Emily as femme fatale is moral narrator and moral compass, taking up the private eye's narrating and assessing voice.

However, as a femme fatale, the ethics that Emily articulates in voice-over are far from clear-cut. If she conveys to us any clarity about morality, it's the notion that morality is itself a lie. Take, for example, one of Emily's voice-overs from the opening episode: "When I was a little girl, my understanding of revenge was as simple as the Sunday School proverbs it hid behind, little morality slogans like 'do unto others,' and 'two wrongs don't make a right.' But two wrongs can never make a right, because two wrongs can never equal each other." Undermining our expectations on multiple levels, Emily speaks in truisms, but those truisms break down commonly held ethical assumptions. She speaks with moral authority, yet uses that authority to destabilize moral dichotomies. As a femme fatale on a mission, Emily is a powerfully doubled figure—emotional yet calculating, digitally networked yet individually powerful. She does not simply inhabit or overturn traditional, masculine forms of power. Rather, she replaces them with millennial ambiguity.

Emily's voice-overs often frame flashbacks in which we see Emily as she was in the past, an innocent girl powerless to stop her family from being destroyed. The flashbacks encourage us to root for Emily, to feel for her, and to connect with her emotional state, past and present. However, these flashbacks do not threaten our sense of Emily's power in the narrative's present. Flashbacks in classic noir may have served to destabilize the sense of the narrator's authority, but in *Revenge*, the flashbacks do the opposite: they allow us to sympathize with Emily's femme fatale plotting and to believe in the rightness of her moral authority in the series' present, no matter how seemingly unethical her course of action. Rather than featuring a female character who is either wholly an innocent ingenue or wholly a manipulative femme fatale, *Revenge* gives us the two in one, and moreover suggests that they are fundamentally connected, thus challenging traditional gendered tropes, noir and otherwise. Put another way, *Revenge* insists on the presence of the personal and individual (Emily's tragic childhood) in the social and political (Emily's revenge-driven adulthood), and in so doing, *Revenge* creates a prototypically ambiguous millennial noir antiheroine.

"I'm still here, bitches, and I know everything": Omniscience, Multiplicity, and the Hitchcockian in *Pretty Little Liars*

ABC Family's *Pretty Little Liars* fully embraces the uncontrollable, omniscient, digitally empowered millennial fille fatale in the character of A, who is supposedly the digital embodiment of the four main characters' dead best friend. Crucially, A is denied the interiority that comes out of a voice-over directly addressing the viewer. We're given no access to her interiority through voice-over—and more than that, no hint as to her identity. Or rather, we're barraged with hints that never materialize into knowledge, raising the question of whether A even has a coherent identity to be known. Like Gossip Girl, A could be anyone, but where in Gossip Girl this anonymity seems somewhat inclusive, in Pretty Little Liars, it comes across as primarily threatening.

The texts A sends to the series' characters refuse to make A humanly visible or audible. We do not get to hear A's voice as she threatens the various characters; instead, we see only the texts as characters receive them. Each episode concludes by aligning us visually with A's perspective, but these sequences equally alienate us from A and tie us to her. These episode-closing moments enforce a a subjective point of view, executed in such a way that although we see through A's eyes, we can't completely see what she is doing, know what she looks like, or know her motivations. We see leather-gloved hands creating a symbolic tableau, perhaps cutting flowers for a funerary wreath, or playing a sinister game of spin the bottle with the main characters' pictures plastered on each bottle. With extreme melodrama, each episode closing's vision of A playfully introduces new tension and mystery, furthering the ongoing sense of a dangerous world that the millennial protagonists must navigate.

As in Gossip Girl, A is an anonymous potential collective; he or she could be any of the characters or even, as the series strongly suggests, a network of characters. Every time a plot revelation indicates that a particular character is A, it's like peeling another layer of an onion; there are more As lurking in the background, waiting to come forward as digital terrorizers. Here the expansive millennial collective is simultaneously power and threat, especially to themselves. In A, the digital millennial collective takes on a more ominous facade than in the other series we've examined, mostly devoid of a sense of illicit celebration. Yet this sinister tone makes the millennial collective seem more powerful, more significant: A's digitally networked power comes across as limitless, entirely beyond the grasp of societal rules and systems of order. Pretty Little Liars thus depicts a more radical and dangerous (and far less hopeful) embodiment of the digital millennial collective.

Although A is invisible in that he, she, or they are everywhere but nowhere, A does have a visualized and heard counterpart, the (assumed to be) dead Alison. Although Alison is already assumed dead when the series begins, in the opening season, we see her in subjective flashbacks from the point of view of the four main characters. The flashbacks are dispersed at particular moments to advance the narrative, usually simultaneously revealing a clue and opening up a new dimension to the mystery. We also see Alison in digital videos that the girls discover as clues. Much like Veronica Mars's murdered best friend, Lilly, we sew Alison together piecemeal through subjective flashbacks and partial, interrupted videos whose status as evidentiary, captured truth we constantly question with the discovery of new footage or contextual information.[13]

This subjective and subject-to-change mosaic of Alison depicts her as cruel, as someone who was full of disdainful glee as she bullied her friends. Indeed, the past picture we get of Alison looks very much like the present presence of her virtual "ghost" poser, A. Alison combines with A to create a vision of a powerful, multiplicitous, millennial fille fatale figure who controls those around her digitally and in embodied form. As the seasons progress, we learn that Alison herself was fighting for survival against A, and indeed may have been murdered by A. Alison offers a version of the powerful, networked fille fatale who is threatening and disruptive, yet still potentially a figure for identification.

A/Alison's version of the elusive and invisible fille fatale has antecedents in film noir history. In *The Women Who Knew Too Much*, Tania Modleski writes of another everywhere-but-nowhere, multiplictious female threat, the titular character in Hitchcock's *Rebecca*.[14] We might see *Rebecca* as the matriarchal heritage of *Gossip Girl* and *Pretty Little Liars*. Not only is *Rebecca* also cinematic gothic noir, but *Rebecca* and *Pretty Little Liars* (and for that matter *Gossip Girl*) are based on popular literary works directed primarily at female audiences, works that met with more than their fair share of cultural scorn as well as popularity. Both *Gossip Girl* and *Pretty Little Liars* are properties of Alloy Entertainment, originally a book-packaging division of a marketing company directed at millennial young women; in 2012, Alloy was purchased by Warner Bros. Television (the production arm of the CW, which produced *Gossip Girl*).[15] Both *Gossip Girl* and *Pretty Little Liars* are thus marked as part of the millennial female–oriented, marketing-suffused, franchise-first domain, often reviled as being overly consumerist oriented and lacking in high art value. Daphne Du Maurier's original novel, *Rebecca*, was likewise enormously popular among female readers, and Hitchcock's film was conceived by producer David O. Selznick with this already mobilized mass female audience in mind.[16] However, Hitchcock was resistant to *Rebecca*'s association with a ready-made mass female audience and market. *Rebecca*, *Gossip Girl*, and *Pretty Little Liars* thus all hold culturally suspect positions as transmedia franchises designed to appeal to young female audiences.[17] And as part of this questionable appeal, they all feature powerful yet invisible female leads who connect the multiple women within the diegesis and likewise connect the real-life networks of female audience members, readers, and fans.[18]

In *Rebecca*, Du Maurier offers a blueprint for the elusive, absent femme fatale and for the fraught female collective. The character of Rebecca functions as a figure of terror and desire for the narrating character, the nameless second Mrs. De Winter, who seeks to take the late Rebecca's place. Like A, Rebecca represents a dangerous multiplicity that threatens (or promises) to encompass other female characters as well. Rebecca comes to embody female desire that exceeds the constraints of patriarchal structures.

Like Lilly in *Veronica Mars* and Alison in *Pretty Little Liars*, Rebecca is already dead at the beginning of narration. Neither the film nor the book version of *Rebecca* deploys flashbacks to convey the power and allure of its dead but central character. In Hitchcock's adaptation specifically, Rebecca remains outside the visual language of the film that bears her name; she exists only in the objects she has left behind, in characters' spoken recollections of her, and in their actions based on those recollections. Rebecca exerts power by slipping past the visible, by being everywhere and nowhere, and thus she is not flattened or captured by the structures of the male gaze. In addition, Rebecca is not only powerful in her absence but in her presence in the multiple objects that stand in to represent her and in the multiple characters who think of her, including the housekeeper who mourns her and the narrator who seeks to take her place. As Tania Modleski puts it, "Rebecca takes malicious pleasure in her own plurality. . . . [She] is an intolerable figure precisely because she revels in her own multiplicity."[19] Modleski sees Hitchcock's representation of Rebecca as a reworking of the noir expectation of the femme fatale: "The eponymous and invisible villainess, then, is far from being the typical femme fatale of Hollywood cinema brought at last into the possession of men in order to secure for them a strong sense of their identity. Occupant of patriarchy's 'blind space,' Rebecca is, rather, she who appears to subvert the very notion of identity—and of the visual economy which supports it."[20] While at first glance *Rebecca* seems to tell a tale of female submission and punishment of female desire/power, the film has feminist subcurrents, and its powerful representation of multiplicitous yet invisible female subjectivity arguably accounts for its popularity among female audiences.

Like *Rebecca*, *Gossip Girl* and *Pretty Little Liars* offer visions of female power as a decentered multiplicity that functions beyond a visual/image economy. Like *Rebecca*, *Gossip Girl* is titled after a central character who is powerful—seemingly omniscient—yet never seen, but who represents the many who respond to her, react to her, and feed her significance. And though we do see *Pretty Little Liar*'s Alison in flashback, the meaning of her image is never fixed and is constantly changing. The figure of A emanates from Alison as a digital extension that is simultaneously everywhere and nowhere.

The title of *Pretty Little Liars* encompasses the plurality of the female network. It seems to refer to the four main characters, who keep secret the fact that they are being terrorized by their dead friend. The "liars" part of the title seems almost disingenuous given the series' premise, conjuring a sense that the show is about multiple immoral characters who use their beauty and youth as masks for falsity—a collection of Alison/Rebeccas—when in fact the series' core four (living) characters lie only out of necessity, and they usually lie only by omission. The narrative depicts the four main characters engaging in immoral behavior (lying) for moral reasons: to protect their family and friends or to avenge their friend's death.

The series' distinctive title sequence is worth examining at length because it paints a darker vision of the millennial noir girls' collective than even the series itself and includes Alison and us/the viewers in that collective. It suggests that the trappings of femininity are yet another tool—or technology—that millennial young women master to solidify their networks of power. The title sequence shows the four girls around Alison's coffin. Set to The Pierce's "Got a Secret," the opening credits offer a montage of close-up details of what seems at first glance to be a girl getting ready to go out, constructing a masquerade of femininity: we see someone applying mascara and lip gloss, buckling a high-heeled sandal, curling hair, and painting nails. As we see this series of images, we hear a girlish voice sing about promising to keep a secret, implying that the secret in question is bound up in this masquerade—or perhaps is this masquerade of femininity.

The images then shift, adding a sinister tone to this construction of femininity. We see a different hand (indicated by a different color of nail polish) closing the eyes featured in the earlier shot, and we realize, retroactively, that we have been watching the dressing up of a corpse. A slightly wider shot reveals the midsection of the corpse lying in a coffin as someone else folds her hands into a display of peaceful rest. The credits thus take a darker turn precisely with the introduction of the millennial female collective. The image momentarily fades to darkness—a fade we soon realize is diegetically caused by the advancing shadow of a descending coffin lid. Threatening lyrics insist on our secrecy as we, for a brief moment, contemplate the finality of the coffin that fills the image. A flickering cut then leads to a medium shot (the widest yet in this fairly claustrophobic sequence) that reveals the four main (living) characters, Aria, Spencer, Hannah, and Emily, standing above the coffin. Here we have the series' archetypal image of the millennial fille fatale foursome (or fivesome) linked together through death, terror, and the masquerade of femininity.

The larger project of this credit sequence is not simply to depict the fille fatale collective but to enlist us, the viewers, in said collective. A series of quick cuts returns us to a close-up of Aria, who breaks the fourth wall by raising her eyes to look directly at us/the camera. She puts her finger to her lips to shush us, and we realize that we're the ones whose lives are being threatened by the credit sequence. The combination of image and audio effectively renders Aria our terrorizer. We have been conscripted into the secret-holding collective and threatened with death if we tell.

Through Aria's secretive shushing, we are interpellated into the pretty little lying millennial collective and bound into this network through terror. The secret that ties us to the collective appears to be the knowledge that millennial femininity is a necessarily strategic construction, a masquerade hiding the realities of terror, violence, and corruption that the young women of the series must face on a daily basis. Possessing this dangerous knowledge enlists us into the collective, just as it does the girls within the series. Like them, we are hailed as innocent and knowing, terrorized and terrorizers—a multiplicity shown to be key to millennial (noir) identity more generally and to millennial female experience specifically.

A 2013 article in *Entertainment Weekly* article suggests yet another layer to *Pretty Little Liars* noiresque brand of the millennial collective. The headline reads "How This Twisty, Over the Top Teen Mystery is Changing TV," suggesting that the millennial noir feminine franchise has influence beyond its supposed niche, liminal, gendered origins.[21] This article focuses, however, not on the series' multiplicitous narrative structure but on its deployment of social media as an extension of that narrative structure. The article dwells on *Pretty Little Liar's* use of social media as a franchising strategy, built in part on the self-branding labor of its young actresses, who reach out to their audience

Figure 6. A fan artist interprets *Pretty Little Liars'* archetypal visual of the four main characters linked by a coffin. Yenni-Vu, http://yennivu.deviantart.com/art/Pretty-Little-Liars-389741054. Reprinted with permission.

Figure 7. In the opening credits of *Pretty Little Liars*, Aria binds
the viewer into the noir millennial collective.

on social networks. The article describes the actors' use of Twitter and Instagram to forge a sense of aspirational intimacy with their audience: "*Pretty
Little Liars* isn't just a teen soap on TV—it's a teen soap off screen as well. . . .
The show's quartet of stars consistently share the minutiae of their lives on
social media as if it's their job. . . . The cast's real gift is for unleashing details
of a more personal (and often cleverly aspirational) nature on their fans."[22]
From this perspective, *Pretty Little Liars* not only offers a narrative mystery that
thematizes millennial women's negotiation of digital culture but also has
launched a digital network that links young female actors as laborers with
their millennial-aged audience, building a larger collective through their production of aspirational consumerist narratives of self.

Here we have envisioned a further expansion of the millennial noir collective. *Pretty Little Liars*' narrative depicts a powerful and potentially dangerous female collective, bound by shared knowledge of the constructions of
femininity and the realities of sexualized violence. In turn, the series' transmedia extensions purposefully blur fiction and reality, character and actress,
and producer and audience. Transmedia extensions such as actors' Twitter

Figure 8. Actor Lucy Hale's Twitter presence (https://twitter.com/lucyhale) merges self-representation and commercial marketing.

accounts thus further enlist the audience members in the *Pretty Little Liars* collective, asking them to merge the personal and the social/political, the fictional/fantastic and lived reality. *Pretty Little Liars'* deployment of transmedia highlights a digital landscape in which fiction and fantasy blur in self-authored narratives of self and desire, a climate in which young women have the potential for visibility via digital self-publishing, including those whose voices might otherwise be silenced or dampened by cultural and industrial hierarchies. In the following chapter, we will examine how millennial noir extends and transforms within this realm of producer–audience interaction and audience authorship, envisioning a millennial noir collective with an even broader and perhaps more destabilizing impact.

An Invitation to Transgress

Millennial noir enrolls fan transgression and desire into a commercial framework, integrating what has been perceived as fan excess into the consumerist branded landscape of millennial noir culture. Millennial noir has the potential to transform the threat of fan's unruliness, excess, and obsession to allure, and thus to something industrially palatable, albeit within limits and without shedding the veneer of taboo and guilty pleasure. However, at the same time, millennial fan engagement with noir goes further than commercial millennial media texts do themselves. Audiences turned authors use the elements of noir to offer political critiques or to launch cultural attacks on the seeming bastions of millennial hope discourse. In this chapter, we will look at how millennial noir media texts invite viewers to transgress and transform media culture within commercial frameworks, and how fans respond to and at times exceed those invitations through transformative production and cultural critique. We will begin with the figure of the millennial fille fatale and the way she redefines dominant cultural assumptions about girls' use of technology and girlhood more broadly. We will consider how these new visions of tech-savvy girls invite viewers to interact with a program's transmedia extensions and even encourage viewers to act on a sense of ownership and control over the medium of television. Finally, we will turn to millennial fan authorship to see how fans turned media producers take up and deploy millennial noir tropes, merging nostalgia with political and cultural critique, often spinning even darker and more transgressive narratives than those offered by the commercial media industry.

The Fille Fatale as Feminist Fan

All four millennial noir texts examined in the last chapter—*Veronica Mars*, *Gossip Girl*, *Revenge*, and *Pretty Little Liars*—depict millennial female protagonists using digital technologies to network and investigate, and then to speak back, act, or take revenge. This vision of digitally adept girls is significant: by using digital tools to expose and overturn cultural hierarchies, the fictional digital filles fatales in millennial noir offer models for troubling traditional gendered and generational roles. In *Girls Make Media*, Mary Celeste Kearney writes that girls making media represents a shift in assumptions about girlhood.[1] Teen girls' use of digital technology troubles traditional notions of gendered media engagement that dictate that boys and men are the ones with technological skill, digital know-how, and the desire to build things. Media production also offers teen girls a route to express their resistance to the prescribed gendered roles they face in their everyday lives. According to Kearney, many girls make media that specifically demonstrate "their resistance to, if not refusal of, the traditional ideologies of gender and generation."[2] In turn, the media texts authored by young millennial women launch new narratives and models for girls' cultural engagement and sense of self.

Millennial noir representations depict teen girls as powerful wielders of media tools, yet render that power potentially uncanny, frightening, and beyond human. Kearney celebrates "young female media producers" as "the newest generation of cyborgs" who invade the "domains of adult male power and privilege using not just pens and paper, but computers, video cameras, and musical instruments."[3] Kearney celebrates this development, as do I, but in millennial noir, the vision of filles fatales as invading cyborgs comes across more ambivalently. Millennial noir texts depict digitally empowered young women as filles fatales who are to some degree beyond "natural" femininity. In the programs we considered in the previous chapter, millennial young women use digital tools not only as means for connectivity but also as weapons, and even as tools of terror. *Pretty Little Liars'* four young female leads deploy digital technology to battle the terrorizing A, but at the same time A uses technology to terrorize them. In *Gossip Girl*, the eponymous blogger uses her blog to terrorize all of the main characters, and all of the characters use her blog to terrorize each other. Figures like *Revenge*'s Emily Thorne are simultaneously heroines and uncanny figures that threaten to collapse societal understandings of femininity. We root for Emily Thorne's distribution of damage, but at the same time, she is an unknowable, othered, monstrous figure. Even sympathetic, seemingly harmless everygirls like *Pretty Little Liar*'s Aria sometimes become uncanny, either because of their use of digital power or because of their inclusion and participation in the digital network, as, for example, Aria does in her extradiegetic role as enforcer of secrets in the *Pretty Little Liars* opening credit sequence.

Thus, the empowered digital girl producer is both allure and threat— indeed, an alluring threat—in her resistance to the hegemonic, heteronormative, and even generational status quo. This duality fits squarely within the millennial noir project, which seeks not to erase but to sell the millennial's potential excesses and mystery as attractive. If, as Kearney argues, girls producing media marks a significant shift in traditional gendered conceptions of young girls from passive consumers to active meaning makers, then within the new millennial frame, girls making media become alluring and marketable precisely because of their perceived transgression. Even girl media producers' supposed unruliness as producers becomes a potential selling point.

What does this mean for long-standing conceptions of the female, feminine, or feminized media fan? The digitally empowered, (supposedly) excessively obsessed fangirl, traditionally a taboo figure of excess whose unruliness can be seen as a threat to media corporations, starts to look uncannily (pun intended) like the heroines in these series—or perhaps it is that the series' heroines start to look like the unruly fangirl. Where in the past media fans recognized their likeness on screen primarily in marginal or parodic characters, now we can recognize the figure of the fangirl as the core characters of these series. It is the fille fatale's desire, drive, and purpose that defines these texts' overarching narratives. And this celebration of unruly excess and empowered digital authorship informs the way these series court their audience. Millennial noir texts invite us to imagine ourselves as part of the digital fille fatale collective, a collective defined by fighting back and speaking back with digital tools. The celebration of transgressive digital empowerment extends to the way these series address fans via televisual text and transmedia extensions. Millennial noir series invite fans to intervene, and in some cases transgress, remix, and recreate, in the image of their own imaginings.

Gossip Girl and the Invitation to Intervene

All four series examined in the previous chapter reach out to their fans in a range of ways, but I will to return to *Gossip Girl* to show how the series uses multiple avenues to create a sense of the viewer as a noirlike, creative transgressor and thus a member of the series' celebrated illicit culture. *Gossip Girl* invites viewer participation and intervention through transmedia extensions and also through the aesthetic codes of the televisual text itself.

Transmedia extensions offer an obvious space to hail fans and to invite viewer participation in a narrative's fantasy world. *Gossip Girl* has had its fair share of transmedia extensions and world-building games that invite viewers to enter the *Gossip Girl* universe online. The first large-scale transmedia extension took the form of a digital version of the New York City lifestyle featured in the series, represented through the interface of Second Life.[4] *Gossip Girl*'s Second Life extension allowed viewers to explore a virtual Upper East Side, where they could create an avatar who could shop in digital representations of high-end department stores, attend online parties at the invitation of the series' characters, and interact with other viewers' avatars.[5] In 2008, the CW teamed with online fashion retailer Bluefly to translate the digital shopping imagined in *Gossip Girl*'s Second Life into actual online shopping.[6] Visitors to Bluefly.com could shop in the *Gossip Girl* store, where they could purchase clothing and brands that the characters on the show might wear, rather than the *Gossip Girl* T-shirts and merchandise that one might expect. The *Gossip Girl* store was divided into sections by character, so viewers turned online consumers could purchase clothes as part of their identification with or appreciation of the style of a particular character in the story world. In 2011, a year before its cancellation, *Gossip Girl* launched the Facebook game "Social Climbing," in which players earned "spotted points" by attending the various social events on their agenda and causing just the right amount and kind of scandal.[7] Though short lived, "Social Climbing" in particular shows what a transmedia campaign that celebrates the perceived transgressive excesses of millennials could look like. All of these transmedia extensions invited viewers to participate in the processes of excessive consumerism and collective monitoring featured in the *Gossip Girl* series.

These transmedia extensions are certainly worth dwelling on to consider what routes for participation they encourage and facilitate, as well as what limits they place on viewer entrance into the *Gossip Girl* world. *Gossip Girl* Second Life and the Bluefly *Gossip Girl* collaboration both encouraged viewers/

players to engage with the fantasies of excessive consumerism so central to the series. "Social Climbing" shifted emphasis to instead invite a celebration of bad behavior combined with social savvy.

While it is easy to recognize these transmedia extensions as tools intended to invite viewer participation, what is perhaps more remarkable is how *Gossip Girl* embeds into the television text itself invitations for viewers to digitally interact with the series. *Gossip Girl*'s transmedia dimensions extend participatory invitations already at work in the series' televisual text. In *Beyond the Box*, Sharon Ross describes how TV texts can invite viewer participation through a mix of direct and indirect address to viewer knowledge and viewer interactive practices.[8] *Gossip Girl*'s engagement with film history through intertextual reference indirectly reminds the viewer of the series' status as media representation. This self-reflexivity combines with the series' integration of do-it-yourself aesthetics to invite viewers to intervene on a visceral level with the text itself and to use remix to infuse the text with their own interpretations and emotional responses.

Each *Gossip Girl* episode title is modeled after the title of a well-known Hollywood film, and episodes often feature dreamlike sequences that cast main character Blair (herself a cinephile) in the role of a famous figure from classic cinema. For example, the episode "The Blair Bitch Project" (season 1, episode 14) opens with a dream sequence in which Blair approximates the role of Holly Golightly in *Breakfast at Tiffany's*, running through the rain in a trench coat to find her cat. Through these consistent media references, *Gossip Girl* asks its viewers to notice episode titles (more the type of knowledge an active fan would have than a casual viewer) and to recognize when the series is invoking a prolonged homage. The series also invites viewers to recognize or research each media reference in order to pull out the parallels and any ensuing insights. In this way, *Gossip Girl* demands that the viewer be consistently aware of the series' status as televisual text and representation. *Gossip Girl*'s consistent references to past media function as a broad-based invitation to participation by implying/assuming that both producers and viewers are working with the same toolbox of cultural referents. When *Gossip Girl* plays with media history by recreating a scene from *Breakfast at Tiffany's*, it positions producers and viewers as kindred cultural participants with a shared knowledge of media history.

This recognition of viewer cultural knowledge also manifests when *Gossip Girl* calls attention to the medium of television itself and to the series' status as stylized visual representation. At key moments, the series' visual language reminds the viewer of its artifice by interrupting or freezing the image, creating an aesthetic of the interrupted process of celluloid film projection. One of the most iconic—and fan beloved—of these moments occurs when two fan-favored characters, power-hungry teen Blair Waldorf and power-entrenched teen billionaire Chuck Bass, first become involved with each other. In the season 1 episode "Victor/Victrola," Blair and Chuck kiss for the first time in a cab racing through a New York City night. As the music crescendos and they lean in to kiss, the image flickers, becomes desaturated, and skips. The kiss is thus represented as if it were simultaneously an old projected silent film with accumulated dust and a skipping TV image. Finally, the image ruptures and burns away, like projected celluloid film on fire. This playful yet affective visual imagery layers various indicators of pastness in media, collapsing them into a collective aesthetic of nostalgia and emotion conveyed through form. The aesthetic play interrupts the series' realism (such as it is) with highly reflexive mediation; the moment draws attention to Gossip Girl's status as television by layering on the codes of previous media forms. Emotional melodrama overtakes realism and offers the viewer entrance via the form of the series itself. This moment invites the viewer to consider all of Gossip Girl's status as codified representation; pastness becomes a sign of mediation, indicating that it is possible and acceptable, even desired, for producer and viewer alike to intervene—to stop the text, to get inside it, to dwell on it, and to tear it apart or burn it up. Invasive editing becomes a route to represent emotion—one open to the viewer as well as to the official producer.

Gossip Girl's nostalgic play with past media is tied to a larger move within millennial culture to recreate an analog film aesthetic with digital tools. We can see this trend in iPhone apps like Hipstamatic, Instagram, and 8mm, all of which simulate the look of analog photography and filmmaking, approximating through digital means Polaroid-, Holga-, and eight-millimeter-style film imagery to communicate an emotional interpretation of a found moment. Gossip Girl draws on this nostalgic millennial vernacular to invite viewers to enter in and rework the digital text via remix editing, or at least to imagine doing so. In comparison with the series' transmedia extensions like "Social Climbing," Gossip Girl's aesthetic play invites a more open-ended form of viewer engagement, including a marked shift from audience to author. Where the "Social Climbing" player must navigate the game's restrictions to achieve specifically delineated goals and rewards, Gossip Girl's moments of nostal-

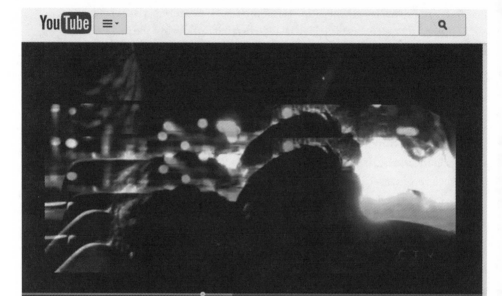

Blair and Chuck - Bittersweet Symphony

Figure 9. Kelsey Wilson's fanvid "Blair and Chuck—Bittersweet Symphony," available on YouTube, mediates the already highly mediated *Gossip Girl* episode imagery.

gic, do-it-yourself aesthetics invite viewers to imagine themselves as creators transforming the raw material of the series itself.

Indeed, these moments of digital cinematic fissure become favorites in fan reworkings through digital remix. Many fan-made remix videos (fan vids) build to the moment described above of Chuck and Blair kissing in the cab, with its skipping image and burning film strip, using this stylized imagery unaltered at the climax of a song or in its climactic refrain. For example, the vid "Blair and Chuck—Bittersweet Symphony" offers an interpretation of Blair and Chuck's character development by slowing down and repeating the already slowed-down imagery of the cab scene.[9] Where more commonly vidders move rapidly from image to image and scene to scene, "Bittersweet Symphony" (much like the song it uses as its soundtrack) builds slowly and dwells on *Gossip Girl* footage that already bears the marks of mediation.

In addition to focusing on this already mediated footage, many *Gossip Girl* fan vids use the tools of video editing, such as filters, to create a similar feel of pastness throughout. Vidders alter more realistic *Gossip Girl* footage with sepia filters, desaturate imagery to black and white, or interrupt footage with white flares that mimic an image burning up. For example, the vid "I'm Already Gone" layers partially transparent visual textures throughout, unevenly desaturating the image to heighten the vid's emotional tone.[10] *Gossip Girl* connects high melodrama with do-it-yourself stylization, inviting viewers to imagine reworking the televisual image themselves; in turn, viewers turned vidders use digital media tools to intervene, to transgress, to break apart, and then to recreate *Gossip Girl* along the fault lines of their own desires and fantasies.

Commercially produced millennial noir programming like *Gossip Girl* does not encourage transgression for its own sake; rather, it strives to co-opt fan transgression and desire and fold them into a commercial framework, so that millennial noir culture becomes a distinctly branded, consumerist landscape. *Gossip Girl*'s product advertising builds on the series' invitation to viewers to intervene with televisual form—for example, through the promotional campaign for the Nikon Coolpix digital camera. In spots that ran within commercial breaks, these ads directly reworked *Gossip Girl* scenes (not unlike the OMFG spots discussed in chapter 4). Serving double duty as promotional spots for the show and for Nikon, the advertisements rendered *Gossip Girl* footage in a campy yet nostalgic aesthetic. Like the scene from "Victor/Victrola" analyzed above, these spots refer to a range of past media styles, using an over-the-top male voice-over, filters that add flickering for an old home movie feel, and a laugh track for a classic sitcom flavor. All of these elements reshape carefully selected clips of salacious dialogue between *Gossip Girl*'s romantic pairings, making the series seem like a racy screwball comedy with 1940s pacing and twenty-first-century sexual innuendo. The camera advertised through this playful synthesis features internal editing abilities. With the campaign tagline, "create in any light," the Nikon Coolpix's advertising emphasizes its in-camera special effects tools (including what Nikon terms a "nostalgic sepia" option), framing, and other creative filters that could be used for exactly the type of modern/nostalgic remix intervention modeled by the advertisement itself. Thus, both the aesthetics of the advertisement and the digital tool being advertised encourage the viewer to take a position of playful and creative mediation with the televisual text—a position already posited within *Gossip Girl* itself. In this way, the CW network, *Gossip Girl*, and Nikon together interpellate a viewer who is simultaneously consumer and producer, and who will use digital tools to transgress, intervene, write over, and recreate.

In the last chapter, we considered how *Gossip Girl*'s millennial noir depicts digital technologies as tools for social policing and for collective empowerment through self-expression. The series' play with the aesthetics of mediation highlights the latter, encouraging the viewer to approach the series as representation—as raw digital material for creative intervention. *Gossip Girl*'s continued emphasis on playful aesthetic manipulation, echoing and in turn echoed in fan practice, suggests a shift away from the fear of digital dangers and toward an embrace of the powers and pleasures of digital play. *Gossip Girl* initially created a deeply ambivalent picture of digital culture, with its characters trapped within, dependent on, and only reluctantly embracing the digital power infusing their lives. *Gossip Girl*'s transmedia extensions echoed this sentiment, culminating with the "Social Climbing" game, situated as it was (albeit temporarily) within Facebook users' everyday online experience. However, *Gossip Girl*'s most significant legacy may be the way in which the series invited audience authorship and digital productivity in a celebration of viewer power. *Gossip Girl* invites viewer emotional investment in power-hungry characters like Blair Waldorf and Chuck Bass, then channels that investment into a sense of assumed viewer right to the power of re-representation and transformation.

Fans Take Over Millennial Noir

In the book's opening discussion of *Kyle XY*, we saw how transmedia extensions can be used as an attempt to control millennial fan participation and production. We focused in the introduction on the hopeful, positive vision of millennials that emerged from this construction. However, it would be spurious not to also acknowledge the millennial noir component of *Kyle XY*'s transmedia extensions.[11] The transmedia extensions for *Kyle XY* invited players to hack into various (fictional) corporate digital interfaces in order to (as it was finally revealed) come to the aid of a young female cyborg created by Madacorp. However, as we saw, this encouragement of hacking for a good cause did not extend to the series' embrace and encouragement of unguided fan play. ABC Family encouraged viewers to engage with a sense of transgression as play only in limited, distinctly guided ways and only as a fictional extension, not as an embrace of fannishness itself as transgression.[12] Indeed,

ABC Family canceled the alternate reality game halfway through, indicating a reluctance to more fully engage with millennial investment in transgressive digital coordination.

In this chapter so far, we have been examining instances of millennial fan address that take the next step, inviting viewers to partake in the pleasures of collective transgression, even in some cases inviting viewers to rip and re-mix à la Ilsa in the *Casablanca* antipiracy remix. To say that millennials respond to this invitation to transgress would be to miss the point. They do, but they were already transgressing before they were invited to do so, and their modes of intervention, creativity, and production often resist the lines or exceed the limits suggested by industry invitation. Let us look now at what fans do with these millennial noir texts in their own authorship, how they respond when they are directly invited to do so, and how they respond when they are not. Fans build on and revise the noir discourses at work in the various series we have examined here and in others as well, including those not already marked as noir. They deploy the noir frame to take further the darker vision of millennials on offer in millennial noir texts. Like the *Gossip Girl* vidders who make their vid footage even more clearly manipulated, fans make millennial noir more explicit, more nostalgic, or more politicized. Recall Mary Celeste Kearney's suggestion that girls making media often take the opportunity to make visible their resistance to the gendered and generational limitations that they face as teen girls.[13] The same is often true for millennial female fans and for millennial fans in general. Millennial fans, both male and female, face gendered and generational taboos and restrictions associated with both millennials and fans. Fan production and engagement with millennial noir provide tools to challenge or resist these taboos.

Millennial fan authors use stylistic elements of film noir to offer even greater moral ambiguity or a darker worldview than the source text; they out-noir millennial noir, so to speak. A significant number of millennial noir fan fiction stories use first-person hard-boiled narration to offer a different vision of a character's perspective or to create compelling, complex versions of characters who may not be as fleshed out in the original source text.[14] Like the voice-overs in the millennial noir TV texts I have analyzed, the hard-boiled-style first-person narration in millennial noir fan fiction functions to give us access to character interiority. In millennial noir fan fiction, first-person narration also often gives female characters a gender-bending quality, assigning to them voices and phrases more commonly associated with male tough-guy private eyes. For example, Isdonisgood's story "Switching Places" adapts *Veronica Mars'* opening and continuing narration but brings us into the mind and perspective of sexualized fille fatale Lilly Kane in a narrative that casts Lilly as the PI and Veronica as the murder victim:

> Neptune, California, a town without a middle class. . . . My afternoon job involves tailing philandering spouses or investigating false injury claims but I suppose that's what you get when you become the disgraced daughter of a billionaire. Don't get me wrong daddy dearest still helps out. Once a month I get a check, just enough to cover a tiny apartment and food, anything else I need I have to buy with the money I make because I burnt my platinum card bearing bridge almost a year ago.
>
> Who am I? I bet that's what you're saying and what could be so important that a spoilt rich kid would give up everything. I'm Lilly Kane, once beloved daughter of Jake and Celeste Kane, and I gave up everything to try to get justice for my best friend in the whole world, Veronica Mars.[15]

"Switching Places" closely mirrors *Veronica Mars'* millennial adaptation of noir, but it invites us directly into the perspective of the fille fatale who remains an enigmatic mystery in the TV series itself. In the television series, Lilly Kane speaks in sexualized, teasing riddles ("I've got a secret," she teases Veronica in a flashback set shortly before her murder). This fan fiction layers onto Lilly's spoiled and sexualized rich-girl/fille fatale persona the qualities of the disenchanted and jaded private eye. We are aligned with her—and given access to her secrets and interior monologue—via her first-person narration. Where, to a certain extent at least, *Veronica Mars* as a television series maintains the divide between fille fatale and private eye, with Lilly filling the former role and Veronica the latter, Isdonisgood's story truly merges the two in the narrating, investigating voice of Lilly.

Not all fan fiction uses noir elements like first-person narration to further revise noir for the millennial age. Some fan stories instead uses noir to demonstrate media literacy and authorial skill, reveling in a more traditional noir nostalgia. For example, Amber477's *Gossip Girl* fan fiction, "The Big Sleep" (title borrowed, of course, from the iconic noir film), restores the traditional male private eye and (with a brief framing device) places him solidly in the era of classic noir. This story takes the power of narration away from the power-wielding digital fille fatale and gives it instead to poor-boy aspiring author Dan Humphrey, who, struggling with writer's block, imagines himself to be a hard-boiled private detective.[16] This story's Dan (as diegetic author) uses a hard-boiled literary style to write himself into a highly nostalgic noir world of excess, intrigue, and murder.

New York City

1940

I can't believe it. Nothing's changed, not even my old office. I might have found the only vacant room in New York City.

I returned to the city like the sap returning to the girl he knows is just going to hurt him again. I tried to move on and forget her. But I had to go back.

The city still needs me.

And I still need her.[17]

With Dan filling the role of the private eye, "The Big Sleep" seems to take power, centrality, and subjective interiority away from Gossip Girl and the series' many female protagonists. While this story seems to retreat from much of what makes Gossip Girl a femalecentric noir revision, it does recreate Gossip Girl's sense of the multiplicitous fille fatale who is everywhere yet invisible, who is embedded in the spaces of the city itself, and who maintains power over the protagonist ("The city still needs me. And I still need her."). In this way, this nostalgia-laced fan fiction continues some of the millennial noir thematics and gender politics present in Gossip Girl, even if its more full-fledged return to classic noir seems to partially undo the gender revision present in the TV series by taking the narrating voice away from the digital fille fatale.

In contrast, some millennial noir-inspired fan works use noir to directly or indirectly critique the millennial noir source text. The vid "Martina" critiques Veronica Mars' exploitation of noir's more problematic gender tropes.[18] At first the vid seems to paint a millennial noir landscape not unlike the one we're introduced to in the series itself, where sexual violence lurks in dark corners and gender inequity colors all. The vid opens with a shot of Veronica's eyes, followed by a collage of images of objectified female bodies from the series' diegesis. We then see Veronica slapping us/the camera—an aggressive act that implicates us in the series' problematic recreation of the male gaze. As the vid continues, it highlights the way in which Veronica's own (televisual) image is bound up in these representational codes of female objectification and female powerlessness, including noir and horror genre codes that position Veronica as victim, as female body entering into male territory, and thus as target of sexualized violence. The spoken-word lyrics of the song emphasize the threat of sexual violence and color it with a noir aesthetic, invoking the sound of clicking heels on pavement and steamy alleyways, warning the listener: "Don't get raped / knock on wood." "Martina" echoes *Veronica Mars'* critique of gender inequity and gender violence, and it also critiques the program's gender representation, pointing to the ways in which the series itself trades on the representation of Veronica as potential victim through common visual codes—indeed, through the codes of noir.

Fans also draw on noir, in both its nostalgic and revisionist variations, when a source text does not already do so. Such instances may be the most striking use of noir by millennials because they resist preprescribed narratives that keep separate the hopeful and more negative visions of millennials. Fan works bring millennial noir to bear on millennial hope, aggressively merging these two divergent views of millennial identity. By layering millennial noir elements on nonnoir texts, these fan works demonstrate how fans can intervene in media in unintended and uninvited ways. These works call attention to how millennial fans use cultural and digital tools to reshape the raw materials of media culture.

Fan authors deploy nostalgic noir references to announce their knowledge and skill across multiple realms, sometimes bringing starkly different sources to bear on one another. Such is the case in mothergoddamn's *Glee* fan fiction story, "The Lost Nightingale," which is the first in the author's "Noir Series."[19] "The Lost Nightingale" announces its noir status through its literary style, with language that reminds the reader of the story's nostalgic historical setting by mimicking hard-boiled literature's expressive yet minimalist style: "I glanced back down at the photograph and felt a chill in my throat. The image was black and white but it filled my mind with colour. I pushed it away." "The Lost Nightingale" layers onto *Glee* this hard-boiled/noir ethos (specifically referencing cinematic noir via its mention of black-and-white imagery), not unlike the way the *Gossip Girl* vids we analyzed earlier deploy desaturating filters to announce an emotional shift. This story offers readers the double pleasure of recognizing noir and *Glee* elements mated together: the names of *Glee*'s various singing groups become nightclubs and cabarets (Vocal Adrenaline, New Directions), Blaine slots nicely into the role of the private investi-gator, and Kurt becomes a beautiful but mysterious nightclub singer whom Blaine must find some way to save. This story engages with themes of homo-phobia and sexual violence; it could perhaps be seen as a critique of Glee's han-dling of these issues; however, this story also revels in its nostalgic play and in the author's skill at finding unexpected but resonant commonalities between Glee and classic noir. Yet this celebration of authorial skill is in itself transgres-sive because it announces the fan author's (and reader's) media literacy and resulting power to intervene and to create within a larger cultural landscape, one beyond the limitations of the source text.

Some fan works unleash the dark themes of millennial noir onto the inno-cent landscape of millennial hope without recourse to the pleasures and safety of nostalgia. A chilling example, the multiauthored "Gleeful Little Liars" role-playing game (RPG) tells the story of the main characters of Glee, now grown into adulthood, and their teen children, all of whom find themselves terrorized by their own version of Pretty Little Liar's anonymous fille fatale, A.[20] "Gleeful Little Liars" brings the terror (digital and otherwise) facing the characters of Pretty Little Liars to the teens of Glee and their children in a bleak vision of the future. A multiplicity of anonymous digital powerhouse filles fatales preside over the narrative: in this multiauthored story world, A has competition in the shape of Gossip Girl, who pits herself against A, offering herself as the site for the collective combination of knowledge, where secrets will be revealed:

> hello lima. i'm your own personal gossip girl. don't worry, you'll come
> to love me soon enough. i'm here to surface all those little secrets you all
> seem so keen to keep hidden. they won't be secret for long, don't worry.
> but i can't do it on my own. well, i can, but that would be way too much
> effort. don't forget to drop your gossip off in the submit box. true, false,
> uncertain, whatever. i'll get to the bottom of it. and don't worry; i'll do a
> better job at uncovering the dirt then that A girl.[21]

As this description suggests, in this RPG, Glee's seemingly innocent, small-town setting of Lima, Ohio, is invaded by A and watched over by Gossip Girl; the two work separately to reveal the secrets and darkness hidden within the suburban millennial hope setting. By the conclusion of the long-running RPG, all of the characters and their children have died, either by A's hand or by suicide. The authors of individual characters were able to decide how their

Gleeful Little Liars

ASK   LINKS

Figure 10. An image of the *Pretty Little Liars* girls in their iconic silencing pose serves as the header for the "Gleeful Little Liars" role-playing game, where *Glee* meets *Pretty Little Liars* and hope meets noir on Tumblr.

characters would die, but it was collectively decided by the RPG participants all should die, directly or indirectly, because of A.

Glee's hopeful diverse collective may seem to perform a different set of ideological acrobatics than the millennial noir of *Gossip Girl* or *Pretty Little Liars*, but for participants in millennial culture, the members of New Directions, A, and Gossip Girl do not live in separate universes just because they happen to be characters in different series produced by different networks; rather, they all share the same cultural ground. The hopeful millennial collective and the threatening fille fatale network live in the same intertextual media universe. By merging hope and noir in an aggressive act of ideological synthesis, "Gleeful Little Liars" highlights how both together shape the millennial experience.

Fan-authored texts like "Gleeful Little Liars" offer participants the opportunity to revel in the contradictions of millennial discourse and to expose the hypocrisies of the conflicting narratives that circulate around millennials. Fans challenge and dismantle dominant millennial discourse in their own noir productions, using the very tools of noir offered by millennial noir programming. Commercial millennial noir texts walk a careful line between allure and threat, using noir's illicit appeal to invite viewers to transgress within industry-approved lines. But the noir genre offers potent tools to critique social norms in ways that exceed industry invitation. Just as the digital fille fatale resists discursive and narrative containment in her multiplicitous transgression, so too do millennial fans as they produce their own transformative noir texts.

Millennial Transformation

3

Transformativity is a key value in fan culture and in millennial culture more broadly. Fans and millennials both assume that it is their right to transform, and they expect others to rework media as well. The US Supreme Court defines a transformative work as one that uses already existing media but "adds something new, with a further purpose or different character, altering the [source] with new expression, meaning, or message."[1] The Supreme Court stipulates transformativity as a legally defensible position for creators of derivative work (that is, creative work that reworks or remixes already existing copyrighted media).[2] Fans frequently cite transformativity as a qualification for fair use in order to explain the value of fan fiction, art, and video. The fan-run not-for-profit Organization for Transformative Works (OTW) protects the cultural and legal legitimacy of fandom and fan creative work. The OTW strives to "defend . . . fan work from commercial exploitation and legal challenge" through emphasizing the centrality of transformation to fan culture.[3]

Millennial fan celebration of transformativity does not always translate into a clear embrace of the rights of the audience over the rights of the author, or of transformation for its own sake. Instead, millennial fans value transformation when it is driven by love and respect for the source text. Many participants in millennial fan culture believe that those who transform source texts should cite and respect the original author, especially when said source text is already deemed culturally and artistically valuable—a work of high art or literature, perhaps, or even a work of "quality" television. Such respect, however, does not foreclose the viewer/producer right to critique or the right to poke satiric fun at the source text being re-worked and remixed. Millennial fan works may transform via critique and vice versa, but even critical works (like the *Glee*-critical fan fiction we explored in chapter 3) emerge out of a respect for the potential of elements of the source text, if not its official execution.

Millennial fan culture contains diverse and at times even conflicting opinions about author versus audience rights. This amounts to a complex moral ecosystem that embraces the right to transform in tandem with the rights of the original author, even if these two perspectives may sometimes seem opposed. Millennial fans negotiate this contradictory set of values—this celebration of transformation as a right, but one that should be driven by cultural respect and appropriate affect—through comment-based discussions on Live-Journal, Tumblr, and YouTube. Such comments themselves act as transformative layers that imbue media texts with new meaning via critical commentary.

The Warner Bros. *Casablanca* antipiracy remix again serves as a good example. This remix video was meant to warn against illegal downloading, yet audience commentary has transformed the meaning further, reading and rewriting this remix as a signifier of corporate misunderstanding of transformative culture. The video has gone on to have an afterlife on YouTube, where commenters come together to critique the remix and its corporate author. YouTube commenters attack the video's poor editing, its misuse of *Casablanca*, and its problematic message, questioning—and often openly mocking—the video's effectiveness and moral logic.[4]

The title of the YouTube posting appropriates the famous *Casablanca* closing line, "We'll always have Paris," transforming it by pun into "We'll always have pirates." This transformation subversively deploys the nostalgic power of the *Casablanca* line to suggest that any attempts to stamp out piracy (including the remix itself) are doomed to failure. This reframing of *Casablanca*'s most memorable dialogue turns the meaning of WB's remix on its head by suggesting the video's inevitable failure. The description of the video on YouTube reads as follows: "Casablanca repurposed as an anti-piracy PSA. Copyright Warner Bros. I am posting this video as a public service because I think piracy is very, very wrong. I also wanted to offer my public support for Warner Bros. efforts to stamp out the repurposing of their intellectual property for nefarious purposes. Yarrrrrrrrrrrrrrr. . . ."[5] While the poster claims that "piracy is very, very wrong," when taken together, the video, description, and title suggest the opposite. First, in order to post the video on YouTube, it needed to be pirated—that is, someone needed to break its encryption, rip the video, and upload the resulting file for recirculation beyond the original DVD release. This, combined with the closing "Yarrrrrrrrrrrrrrr," suggests that the poster identifies as a pirate and that he or she considers WB's heavy-handed policing of piracy to be the problem at hand. Overall, the YouTube post comes across as satiric and as implicitly lobbying for viewer access to media and against corporate control.

The comments posted in response to the video further transform the meaning of the text—or rather, they expand the text to include their commentary and in so doing transform its meaning. They suggest that the video's greatest failing is that it is a bad remix, and moreover one that fundamentally misunderstands the values of millennial transformative culture. One comment reads: "Yes, let's treat one of the most beloved classic movies in existence like a cheap two-dollar whore in our attempt to stop piracy! I think this just proved that movie pirates have more respect for films than Warner Bros. Good job, WB."[6] This comment poses a moral schema in which Warner Bros. is the offender and the pirates are the heroes, defenders of the honor of a classic film that Warner Bros. has degraded. Another comment argues that as a result of its wrongheadedness, the so-called PSA has in fact inspired the commenter to pirate in protest of the remix's poor execution and troubling intent: "Because of how offensively bad this is, and because it retools one of the best movies of all time for a selfish and stupid purpose, I'm going to make a point to pirate even more."[7]

These comments position millennial pirates as the true guardians of media culture, both old and new. The comments support collective sharing and respectful transformation while condemning corporate policing and WB's mercenary attitude toward media culture. They accuse the WB's remix of failing to respect the source that it supposedly aims to protect, and moreover of failing to recognize the significance of working with past media to create new meanings. Such comments demonstrate the nuanced moral framework guiding transformative authors in millennial fan culture. Millennial fandom's moral schema demands nostalgic respect of shared media culture alongside freedom of access to media texts. In instances such as this, millennial authors not only add new meaning to particular texts but also collectively transform popular notions of authorship, from individual act of creativity to ongoing creative process of transformation. They also transform understandings of what constitutes an authored text—from an individual, static, coherent creative work to a multiplicitous, contradictory, and fluid multitext, the fan text writ large in millennial culture. These conceptual transformations, also collectively negotiated and authored in an ongoing process, are perhaps the most significant contributions of millennial fan culture.

The remaining section of the book examines the millennial fan culture of transformation. Rather than focus on media representation of millennial fans using digital media, the chapters in part 3 explore millennials' use of digital tools to create media and communities—in other words, millennial fan self-formation and self-representation. We will begin by looking at the way in which digital media is transforming audience cultures and audience–celebrity interactions. We will then examine the new forms of media texts and creative work emerging from this evolving digital landscape. Here we will most closely probe the relationship we have been dancing around throughout: the relationship between millennial culture and fandom. As we have done throughout, we will look at the amalgam of millennial/fandom—audience members participating in transformational processes that would previously have been conceived of as the domain of fandom. Not all participants would call themselves millennials; nor would all call themselves fans. Together, however, they make up a millennial fan culture of transformation with a breadth beyond the marginal, niche, and cult.

The first chapter of part 3 focuses on the change from notions of the author as privileged individual to decentered, creative collective engaged in a continual process of transformation. The following (and final) chapter considers how this creative collective merges performances of high emotion and skill, and in so doing transforms perceptions of fandom from marginal to mainstream and from liminal or taboo to shared, popular ethos. The celebration of decentered authorship in millennial fan discourse has overtones of the ideologies of millennial hope, yet the emphasis on collective transgression—including piracy—in much of this discourse imbues the now more visible millennial fan culture with the threatening allure of millennial noir. The heralding of high emotion and affect within a collective, popular, celebratory ethos further collapses the divide between millennial hope and noir that commercial representations of millennials seek to uphold, leaving in its wake a vibrant culture shaped in fandom's image but exceeding its perceived cultural and commercial limits.

Misha Collins and the Power of Decentered Authorship

If you were to search for information about a TV actor on the search engine of your choice (also known as Google), you would likely expect to come up with details about his or her past and current professional acting work. It thus might be somewhat surprising if your search instead turned up reports of a charity organization giving out flowers to strangers on subways, or of a scavenger hunt that included clues such as a piece of the Berlin Wall suspended in lime Jell-O.[1] However, along with the expected Internet Movie Database profile and Zap2It interviews, this is exactly the material that one unearths when searching for Misha Collins, an actor who has embraced digital media's crowd-sourcing possibilities. Collins has rallied his fans to take part in transmedia projects ranging from the sublime to the sublimely ridiculous. In this chapter, we will explore the case of Collins and his fandom to consider the rapidly transforming relationship between producer and fan in the millennial media context.

Through digital media, including Twitter, TwitPic, Kickstarter, and YouTube, Collins positions himself as one of the decentered millennial collective. At the same time, he uses satire to acknowledge the power differentials that inform audience–producer relationships. Collins and his fans model a new mode of millennial stardom and fandom, one in which professional producers position themselves within the very cultures that they are courting and in which fans welcome their participation.[2] In the process, fans and Collins together author Collins's distinctive star text.[3] Moreover, by poking fun at notions of stardom, fandom, and the star–fan relationship, Collins and his mostly female fandom together acknowledge and subvert gender hierarchies that run deep within notions of fandom and within popular culture at large.

Digital Democratization?

In chapter 6, we saw how some broadcast television mimics the aesthetics and values of fan authorship, inviting viewers to actively intervene in and transform the television text à la fandom. We looked at how the series *Gossip Girl* invokes aesthetic codes of fan culture such as nostalgic filtering, image repetition, and visible editing. Viewers read the inclusion of these aesthetic codes as producer recognition of fandom's creativity and as an invitation to transform the official media text. Such invitations to fan textual reworking undo popularly held distinctions between professional and audience productions, for if aesthetics can be traded in a cultural conversation between commercial producer and fan, than how can the two be so disparate that the former would be respectable and the latter taboo?

The realm of millennial digital production compounds this seeming democratization of digital authorship: professional author and fan creators use similar digital tools for authorship and distribution. Many fans use professional editing software such as Final Cut Pro or Adobe Premiere, or they use the more limited but still powerful tools Final Cut Express or iMovie—all editing tools capable of creating polished, professional-feeling pieces. Likewise, corporate producers and amateur fan culture both deploy the interfaces of YouTube and Twitter to self-author and to build social networks. In addition, professional and amateur authors alike invoke particular sets of cultural meanings to foster shared authorship and to acknowledge shared community. Fan codes are no longer limited to the hidden realm of fan conventions or to the depths of obscure comment boards; they are now visible in highly publicized, buzz-feeding online spaces such as Tumblr and YouTube. This sharing of platforms, tools, and cultural codes undermines the centrality of the official author.

Moreover, as the various examples of fan work in this book demonstrate, digital media offers us the opportunity to trace the labor of audience members who write fan fiction, make response videos, and create reception cul-

Figure 11. In this TwitPic post, actor Misha Collins commemorates his coordination of the world's largest international scavenger hunt.

tures. Without digital access, much of the ongoing labor of fan creativity would remain hidden. Thanks to digital self-publishing, we see fans post fiction chapter by chapter, tweet about writer's block, or ask their readers for inspiration. Thus, the digital landscape provides access to the processes of fan authorship—processes that might otherwise remain invisible. Likewise, digital media provides record of the labor and creative processes of official media producers in the form of tweets, blogs, and YouTube videos. Show runners, directors, writers, and actors post photos from the production set or from their personal lives; they tweet about the production process or hype upcoming episodes. This double visibility—that of the cultural labor of fans and official producers—unites both within shared and overlapping digital networks. As a result, a plurality of commercial and fan creativity populate the millennial transmedia landscape. Official and unofficial producers together author transmedia texts, including star texts.[4]

Those in traditionally empowered authorial positions may have reason to fear this shift to shared authorship, tied as it seems to be to a dissolution of the divide between professional and amateur. However, this shared ground offers less ensconced professional authors the opportunity to inhabit new modes of celebrity that embrace the commonalities between producer and audience. These authors take up a sort of liminal position—a form of minor celebrity that embraces its relative lack.[5]

Misha Collins has developed his star persona by aggressively performing this middle place of transmedia stardom. He first came to fans' attention for his (initially guest spot) performance of the angel Castiel in the fan-loved cult TV series *Supernatural*.[6] Collins opened conversation with *Supernatural* fans using Twitter, and in so doing mobilized a vocal fan base that helped him shape his star persona. More than simply developing his own fandom in the image of fan clubs of years past, Collins uses digital tools to coordinate goal-oriented communities. He has developed a transmedia charity organization, launched a transmedia production company, and created a somewhat anarchic international scavenger hunt. Through these various enterprises, Collins has joined *Supernatural* fans as an unofficial transmedia creator.

This decentralization of power is not total, to be sure. Commercial producers still wield power in millennial culture, but they must be cognizant of how they perform that power over and alongside fans. While professional and amateur creative work may commingle in digital contexts, differences between the two still exist. Official commercial producers have so-called verified Twitter accounts; they sponsor videos on YouTube for increased visibility; and they bring extra attention to fund-raising campaigns thanks to their star power.[7] When an officially affiliated author such as Collins positions himself as joint creator, participant, and inhabitant of fan culture, the results may seem to dissolve the power differentials between official and unofficial producer, but in fact the relationship depends on those very differentials. Collins and fandom call attention to this contradiction: both dwell on themes of shared collective good and the power of the digital collective while also self-reflexively highlighting power imbalances in the hierarchical structures of web culture and of celebrity–fan relationships. It is in large part Collins's recognition of both the collective, shared state of millennial authorship and the uneven realities of contemporary media authorship that make him such a resonant figure among millennial fans.

The Transmedia Star Text

Fans build on circulating star texts just as they do the characters those stars bring to life, often combining the two or muddying the supposed distinction between fictional and real. Fans make star-focused music videos, fan art, and fan fiction, creating star texts as flexible and multiplicitous as any other fan texts.[8] Industry, celebrity, and audience together shape the transmedia star image in an evolving, collective conversation.[9]

In Collins's case, his transmedia persona has evolved out of a combination of his own self-branding online, the work of industry processes, and the labor of fans. The resulting star text emphasizes Collins's subversive power play and alternative masculinity in a way that resonates with long-standing fan preoccupations. Collins's star image was initially defined in large part by his performance of the character Castiel, who offered fans an appealing synthesis of transgressive masculinity and religiosity. Collins first appeared as Castiel on *Supernatural* in the fall of 2008, in the first episode of the series' fourth season. The first three seasons of *Supernatural* focus on the story of two brothers, Sam and Dean, who drive across the United States in a vintage Chevy Impala, fighting the forces of evil as they go. The fourth season—with Collins's entrance into the series—introduces a long-arc story line featuring angels who look, talk, and act like film noir heavies and private eyes. Collins plays the first of these angels to appear on screen. In millennial noir style, Castiel makes his debut in a rumpled Bogartesque trench coat, confounding main characters' Sam and Dean's (and most likely most viewers') concepts of what angels should be. (As Dean puts it, "I thought angels were supposed to be guardians. Fluffy wings, halos—you know, Michael Landon. Not dicks," to which Castiel replies, "Read the Bible. Angels are warriors of God. I'm a soldier.") *Supernatural* revises our (gendered) notions of angels via Castiel; instead of a nurturing, feminine figure, Castiel looks and talks like a beleaguered noir private eye cum discontent soldier.[10]

Collins's characterization of Castiel, especially as reshaped by fans, dramatizes themes of power, desire, and marginality key to the fan experience.[11] His alienness renders him both powerful and disempowered. This duality in turn resonates with the contradictions of the millennial fan position: fans are powerful in the realm of fan-authored digital media but wield little control over the official text that is the object of their fandom. In blog posts, discussion boards, photo posts, art, memes, fan fiction, and fan vids, fans revel in Collins's performance of Castiel's simultaneous power and lack thereof. For example, one post (of many like examples) at Tumblr entitled "Why We Love Castiel" offers a series of erotically charged statements with screen captures of Castiel for visual illustration, with phrases including, "He's a billion year old virgin," "He's amused by his pretty body parts," "He'll watch over you while you sleep," "He only eats during famine so you don't need to feed him every day," and "He's the perfect manslave, just ask Dean."[12] Through its combination of text and image, this post depicts Castiel simultaneously as godlike figure and disempowered object of fan interest.

Collins's own marginality as a struggling actor and subversive cultural figure further contributes to the fan sympathy for him and fosters fan investment in his star text. Collins came on the scene in a role only intended to last for three episodes, in a series notorious for only maintaining two main characters. Collins's marginal position within the cast allowed him to interact on more of a perceived even par with the series' fans on Twitter. His use of the same interface as fans seemed like a genuine act of commonality, even as he used Twitter to perform satiric narratives of self-important stardom.

Once Collins was in the fannish field of vision, fans uncovered biographical elements that meshed well with his character's liminal persona.[13] Before his role on *Supernatural*, Collins's casting history already hinted at a nonnormative masculine star text: his best-known role was as the son of a mafioso villain on *24* (Fox, 2001–2010); he played a serial killer in the film *Karla* (2006); and he played a well-endowed yoga instructor who couldn't stop pleasuring himself in a guest role on *Nip/Tuck* (FX, 2003–2010). In addition, Collins offered other tidbits from his personal history: he came to acting only secondarily as a career, as a college student he interned at the White House, and he has published poetry in the *Columbia Poetry Review*. Collins shared these facts readily with fans; he even shared some of his poetry. He also shared images of his wedding-renewal ceremony, in which he and his wife dressed in drag for a ceremony held in a supermarket's floral department.[14] Fans sewed together these available elements of Collins's personal and creative history with their interpretation of Collins's *Supernatural* character into a star text sufficiently playful, transgressive, and liminal to channel the collective desire and power of fandom.

@mishacollins: Negotiating Power and Play on Twitter

Collins entered a transmedia playing field where audiences expect to be authors and where they aggressively demonstrate female and queer desire, often through fan authorship.[15] Rather than fight these elements, Collins embraced them, integrating them into his developing persona through the use of digital media, most especially the social networking interface of Twitter. On Twitter, he plays to and with fannish discourses of desire and power, and in so doing, he conveys a sense of commonality with fans. He has built a shared subversive culture through in-jokes, over-the-top stories, and an ethos of satiric and Dadaistic play. Collins draws on this sense of shared culture as he and fans move beyond Twitter to a web of digital interfaces, as well as in-person interactions, all of which further his continually unfolding star text.

Within a digital landscape, social media necessarily affects the way stardom functions.[16] Social-networking interfaces such as Twitter give fans the perception of access to stars and vice versa. In their study of the most-followed Twitter celebrities, danah boyd and Alice Marwick observe that celebrities use Twitter to create a sense of affiliation and intimacy with fans through tweets to other celebrities, friends, and, in some cases, fans.[17] The Twitterverse links media professionals with their audiences, rendering them all authors of their own Twitter feeds and branded selves. Twitter brings together media authors and audiences; artists such as Collins, who have greater (if still limited) access to broadcast tools like television, nonetheless share a digital platform with viewers for whom communicating via television is not an option. On Twitter, both share the same basic digital framework and limitations: celebrity and noncelebrity tweets appear side by side, and all are limited to 140 characters, no matter how famous the author. While some Twitter accounts may be labeled as verified and thus affirmed as authentic by Twitter management, posts from verified accounts join unverified ones in a reader's Twitter feed. On Twitter, Collins and his fans all work together with the same sets of tools and limitations. The interface seems to render all equal.

Collins's tweets build on this common ground, suggesting connection beyond shared interface. His first tweets, from May 2009, expressed skepticism toward Twitter—a skepticism shared at the time by many of his fans:

> mishacollins: i am doing a tutorial on Twitter[18]

> mishacollins: I am trying to figure out what the f*** Twitter is for[19]

> mishacollins: okay. So, now i've officially signed up for a high-tech time-wasting device. Let the tweeting begin. . . . . . . Now what?[20]

In these early tweets, Collins presented himself as an ambivalent, amateur Twitter user. His skepticism reflected the perspective of many of his fans whose preferred interface at the time was not Twitter but rather the fan-favored LiveJournal. By expressing his wariness of Twitter, Collins aligned himself with the fans who would eventually follow him in significant numbers to Twitter.

Collins's next tweets (all posted within his first day of Twitter use) destabilized any sense of his being just another new Twitter user; instead, he interrogated the Twitter celebrity dynamic, in which celebrities rapidly accumulate many followers who vie for their attention:

> mishacollins: Hi everyone. This whole interweb thing is really something. 12 hrs and already 412 followers. Doesn't that word have a negative connotation?[21]

> mishacollins: Anyway, i'll think of you as friends not followers. But then again, maybe minions is a better term . . . I'll percolate.[22]

> mishacollins: I like that term: twelebrity. Let the ignoring begin. And, yes I did have Twitter email alerts set and it crashed my account. I'm learning.[23]

These tweets established a playful performance of power and fame. Collins satirically cast himself as a power figure in the social network of Twitter, ignoring his followers at will, promising them the intimacy of friendship while in the same 140 characters declaring them to be his minions—a label taken up as a self-nomer by Collins's fans, myself included.

Collins plays with and defies common expectations of celebrities using Twitter. Rather than tweet semi-intimate details of his life or use Twitter as an overt advertising tool, he uses Twitter to perform a satiric narrative of self in which he self-aggrandizes while also mocking his status as minor celebrity. For example, in an early narrative, Collins shared adventures of his capture and torture by the queen of England, who (as he told it) threatened his execution and forced him to drink tea with no biscuits. He also bragged about his fraught (and, one assumes, fully fictional) friendships with Mahmoud Ahmadinejad and Michelle Obama. These narratives satirically position Collins as captive and yet as connected to networks of power while implying the opposite—that Collins is a renegade and marginal free spirit who has no access to centralized power.

Like other celebrities, Collins uses Twitter to create a sense of intimacy with his fans. However, he uses satire to fuel this sense of closeness. He co-opts the star–fan relationship to expose, mock, and critique the power differentials embedded in media culture. Via Twitter, he calls attention to his role as desired figure at the center of a predominantly female fan base. Collins has demonstrated his comfort with fans' objectification of him by, for example, tweeting pictures of himself surrounded by underwear that fans have jokingly sent him and by retweeting a fan art picture of him hugging his nude body around the Chrysler building. He also frequently tweets pictures of himself in drag and/or with drag queens in ways that champion rather than ridicule various forms of cultural femininity. This feminist interpretation is buttressed by his genuine public critiques of the sexism of his own show.[24]

In tweets and images such as these, Collins draws on what Jonathan Gray, Jeffrey P. Jones, and Ethan Thompson have described as satire's potential for "defamiliarization, allowing us to see the social and scientific order anew."[25] Collins's satiric Twitter performances render his embodiment of dominant power strange and indicative of its opposite—not of a lack of power but rather of a nonnormative power, through which Collins allies with fans in feminist/queer communities of power. In mocking gender norms, celebrating fan work that objectifies him, and repeatedly allying himself with the cultural feminine, he aligns himself with his female minions and their self-aware, critical, and feminist perspectives.

Tons of u have posted this, but it's totally inaccurate! I'm much better built & I would never cheat on the Sears Tower

Figure 12. Here Misha Collins shares a piece of fan art, demonstrating his comfort with fan manipulation of—and objectification of—his star image.

Minions Unite: Millennial Fandom's Self-Depiction

At this point, it should be clear that Collins's fandom is much more than the online self-representation of a web-savvy star. It is a collective performance of queer and feminine/feminist-based satire with which Collins is complicit and supportive. Fans frame Collins as leader of a movement of affect, transgression, and excess, and they frame themselves as the steam behind that movement. They eagerly take up the mantle of minion, weaving it into their own self-representation, performance, and authorship.

The YouTube video "Minion Recruitment Advert" by @Manic_Minion presents a telling example of fan authorship that builds on and transforms Collins's star text to construct a powerful vision of millennial fandom.[26] This video plays with the language of propagandistic and instructional film to represent Collins and fans together as knowing performers of nationalistic fannish devotion. The video intercuts images from a wide array of sources, recontextualizing them as an instructional film in order to recreate the stories Collins has performed on Twitter. The video envisions the call to minionhood as the opportunity to participate in a communal, renegade military organization. The video renders Collins's and fans' shared narratives as playful collective myths, appropriating historical images of women engaged in military and industrial labor and using them satirically to illustrate minion training practices. Some of these practices, mined from Collins's tweets, lean toward the absurd ("advanced abacus skills to work out how many you are outnumbered by," "the fine art of emergency pony dissection"); others seem like more realistic threats of online collectivity, including becoming "an expert in crashing websites and cyberterrorism"—a skill that calls to mind the threatening collective of millennial noir.

In works such as this recruitment video, fans author Collins's star text, depicting him as a renegade artist who models an alternate mode of masculine authorship through satire. But perhaps more importantly, Collins's mostly female fans also perform and author their own fan personae, depicting themselves as transgressive, aggressive, and overtly sexual, yet at the same time intellectual, digitally skilled, and self-aware.[27] This fannish self-depiction invokes and then implodes stereotypes of excessively emotive, nonverbal female fandom. The call to minionhood emphasizes fandom as powerful collective rather than individual, internalized devotion.

Fans depict Collins as a talented artist creating despite (or at least in tension with) the official creative frame of *Supernatural* (what fans call "The Powers That Be"), and they depict themselves as a savvy if unruly collective, a force that The Powers That Be must reckon with. In this picture, Collins becomes representative of fans as transgressive authors, with Collins working to leave his imprint on *Supernatural* from within while he authors with more freedom via digital media. In the end, both fans and Collins perform roles that highlight their discursive construction and that gesture to their shared positions as nondominant authors working to transform the structures of media culture.

Transmedia Power Struggles

A series like *Supernatural* fosters its status as a cult TV show by cultivating an ongoing relationship with fans through conventions and fan-directed publicity campaigns. Because of the series' investment in its fans, developments in online fan communities cannot be ignored, and they sometimes find their way into the text of the series itself. *Supernatural* has directly acknowledged its online fandom via a plot contrivance in which, within the world of *Supernatural*, there is a fantasy book series called *Supernatural*. Over the years, the show has represented online fan forums; introduced the character of Becky, a slash fan fiction–writing fangirl; depicted a *Supernatural* fan convention; and staged a *Supernatural* musical written and performed by teen fangirls. These televisual representations of fandom offer a combination of mockery and love, sometimes depicting fans as obsessive, excessive, and delusional, but also showing them to be necessary, passionate, and creative. [28]

In a sixth season episode, *Supernatural* directed its double-edged fan service specifically at Collins and his fandom. The highly self-reflexive episode throws the heroes into an alternative universe in which *Supernatural* is a television series rather than their lived reality.[29] In the episode, Collins plays a fictionalized version of himself, tweeting to his fans from the show's set. Where previous episodes direct (arguably loving) barbs at the series' fans, now Collins as Twitter celebrity also comes on the receiving end of this ambivalent acknowledgment. However, *Supernatural* significantly alters the self-representation Collins has created on Twitter—and, for that matter, Collins's fans' representation of themselves. For one, the show replaces the word "minions," thus sidestepping Collins's and fans' satiric play with power and gender. Instead of tweeting to his minions, fictional Collins tweets to his "mishamigos," as follows

> mishacollins: IMHO j&j had a late one last night. Rotflmfao!

> mishacollins: Ola mishamigos! j2 got me good. Really starting to feel like one of the guys.

This shift from fan-favored term "minions" to fictional/imagined fannish term "mishamigos" removes the language of playful (erotic) domination so central to Collins's fandom, constructing instead a picture of Collins as naive narcissist. Indeed, one could argue that the term "mishamigos" depicts Collins as misguidedly representing himself as ethnically othered. In addition, fictional

Collins's tweets suggest his desire to be included in the inner circle of the series' two main actors, Jensen Ackles and Jared Padelecki, known to fans as J2. Where Collins has developed his Internet fame through satiric excess and self-reflexive performance of marginality, the *Supernatural* version of Collins tweets with eager earnestness, and he tweets precisely about wishing to lose his outsider status to become "one of the guys."

Yet the whole episode is satire—more so than usual for *Supernatural*. We could perhaps read the episode as co-opting Collins and fandom's satiric world building—a nonmasculinist, feminine form of satire—and removing it from the transmedia spaces where fans and Collins have authorial control. The episode uses satire to punish Collins and by extension his fans. It depicts him as a pampered actor who wears a sweater jacket and bursts into uncontrollable tears while pleading for his life. In the world of *Supernatural*, where machismo and the strategic release of male suffering (in the fan-favored form of "one perfect tear") are core values, fictional Collins's excessive emotion is taboo. In addition, fictional Collins's in-episode tweets suggest that he is too close in kind to fans; he uses fan terms like "J2" and mistakes for real intimacy an imaginary relationship with the series' stars. All of these representations seem to police and reprimand Collins's for stepping beyond the appropriate, marginal place of the guest star and/or the appropriate models of masculine authorship, as well as the appropriate relationship between actor and fan. Finally, as if these subtle reprimands are not enough, the episode firmly punishes Collins for his various transgressions by violently killing him within the alternative universe plot. And if fans identify with Collins's very marginality and transgression, then this mocking representation and violence against fictional Collins disciplines fans as well.

Supernatural's representation of Collins in this episode has contradictory purpose and effect. It overtly represents Collins's authorship, making his role as Twitter author visible on television, and by extension also gesturing to his Twitter-authoring fandom. (His Twitter follower count shot up remarkably during the night of the episode's airing.) However, it also denigrates Collins's alternative masculinity and violently punishes him for his transgressions, whether they be transgressions of broadcasting through means other than television or transgressions against masculine norms, though really those two representations are one and the same: *Supernatural*'s representation of Collins is marked by his omnipresent smartphone and sweater jacket, both which serve to indicate his lack of *Supernatural*-valorized masculinity.

Collins was among many actors and producers parodied in the episode, and he was not the only one to meet a spectacular demise. Among others, the episode did away with the series' past show runner, Eric Kripke, who left the show after the fifth season. The episode thus kills the absent father and the transgressive son, the original author who had abandoned his story and the actor turned renegade transmedia author. Derek Johnson writes that television producers hold "privileged means of answering challenges to their producerly . . . authority" and can "mobilize" television to critique or police "unruly" fans.[30] In the case of Collins, the *Supernatural* producers appear to have used their privilege to punish one of their own in the same move punishing unruly would-be fan authors who support him and what he represents.

The end of the sixth season surprised many fans by making Castiel temporarily more central to the narrative than his limited airtime during the season would have suggested. The season's closing episodes reveal that Castiel was working with the devil, and in the final moments of the season, he transforms from a renegade angel to a self-proclaimed god. Fans of Collins read the shift in Castiel's character as an integration of Collins's star text into the character of Castiel. While Collins's persona was built in part on Castiel's alienness, it has grown to encompass narratives of domination and extreme self-importance as well as Collins's penchant for over-the-top story lines and his elasticity as an actor. Fans recognized these elements of Collins's star text on screen for the first time in the season 6 finale; indeed, it was these aspects of his persona that the earlier self-reflexive episode had seemed to quite purposefully sidestep. However, the pleasure in recognition also came with fear that this representation could be a step toward the eventual removal of Collins from *Supernatural*—the final rejection of the new mode of authorship and decentered authorial community Collins represents. The question seemed to be, could this new god of decentered authorship and transgressive gender performance really be represented on television, or was Collins/Castiel being raised to godlike status only to be put to death for his hubris?[31]

Season 7 further flamed fears of more permanent punishment for Collins and fans. Castiel was killed in the opening episodes, and several months passed before then–show runner Sera Gamble revealed that Collins would eventually return to the show. This was followed by Collins's announcement on Twitter: "It's true. I'm going to be back on the reality show about the two brothers who drive around testing out seedy motels. Any questions?"[32] While it is tempting to read the temporary but lengthy removal of Collins from the series as a further disciplining of the mode of authorial and audience power that Collins and fandom represent, an equally viable reading would be to understand the series' reluctance to fully commit to Collins (at least in public press) as a move to rile up and court Collins's dedicated fan base, thus acknowledging the power of the new author–fan relationship Collins has managed to harness. In either case (or, most likely, both), Collins emerges like his character: a new self-proclaimed god potentially threatening the entrenched power structure from within its ranks.

Transforming Transmedia Authorship

While Collins's position on *Supernatural* remains somewhat marginal (although increasingly less so each season), his Twitter followers (currently numbering 1.78 million) celebrate his importance to their appreciation of the series. Fans celebrate Collins's accessibility and his willingness to interact with them on Twitter, and they have made clear their willingness to follow him from ideological stance to ideological stance, franchise to franchise, and media platform to media platform. For Collins's growing fandom, the interface of Twitter functions as the core of a much larger transmedia playing field. Collins initially fostered his relationship with his minions primarily on Twitter, but fans quickly embraced and propagated this label on a network comprising multiple online interfaces. Together, Collins and fans spread a narrative of celebrity/fan co-creation across multiple digital and physical platforms.

The Collins–fan interactions exemplify transformations in concepts of authorship in millennial culture as well as in the infrastructures that will shape media authorship and participation in the future. They deploy a concert of interfaces in tandem to mobilize a variety of projects. Together, they have created a nonprofit charity organization, Random Acts.[33] Random Acts organizes many projects, including recurring trips to Haiti to build housing for orphans and to address other community needs. Collins has now taken two trips with fans to Haiti as part of this initiative. Collins and fans do not leave behind their satiric power play as they move into the roles of coworkers in the nonprofit charity domain, as Collins's tweets illustrate:

> mishacollins: Ancestors, minions and trainees: Change your Twitter time zone and location to "Tehran." It'll make it look like we care about others.[34]

mishacollins: I went to Haiti with these bad-ass mofos. Each was a killer; green berets, MMA fighters, stay-at-home moms . . . http://lockerz.com/s /1151627080[35]

This utopian story of celebrity-endorsed charity work may retread a familiar narrative of star personae backing charity causes, but it is significant in the collective action involved and in the way that it asserts a shared ethics within transmedia millennial communities composed of audience and author.[36] Not only do Collins and fans coauthor a shared culture but they also transform that culture into online and off-line projects that they work on together and that are guided by their shared transmedia ethical ethos.

Collins drew directly on this sense of collective transmedia ethics in his work with the production company Maple Blood Productions on the web series *Divine*. Maple Blood Productions used the fund-raising interface Kickstarter to raise money for *Divine*. The Kickstarter website describes the fund-raising tool as "a new form of commerce and patronage."[37] Kickstarter crowdsources funding through small donations, much like the web-savvy funding strategies designed to reach millennials to support the Obama campaign in the 2008 election.[38] It represents itself as innovative not only because of its crowd-sourcing but also because of its efforts to restore and reshape of notions of authorship for millennial culture. The site uses language of creative owner-ship ("Project creators keep 100% ownership and control over their work"), yet it depicts creative authorship as something everyone can be involved in at all levels: "Each and every project is the independent creation of someone like you. Projects are big and small, serious and whimsical, traditional and ex-perimental. They're inspiring, entertaining and unbelievably diverse."[39] Kick-starter's business model thus relies on a (re)definition of authorship as simul-taneously individual and collective.

Kickstarter's reframing of authorship fed into the larger project of the *Divine* web series. At the Kickstarter site for *Divine*, Collins and the other mem-bers of Maple Blood Productions (including *Divine* show runner Ivan Hayden) described their intent to use *Divine* to transform traditional models of broad-cast television production:

We all know that the Internet will be the next evolution in storytelling, it's just that the guys in the old towers of power don't know how to make it work for them. [. . .] Since they're not trying to find solutions it's up to the rest of us to find that new business model so we can start producing the content we all want to enjoy.

And that's where you come in. [. . .] If our fundraising is a success, we can hold up the result and say the fans paid for one whole episode, or two, or all four, or even a whole season's worth. Then when we pitch our business model, the *"old money men"* will have to listen. No one could say we don't know how to reach the new generation of enthusiasts or that our business model isn't backed by proof. If we can do that, then maybe the door will finally be open for a new, easier way for creators to make ongoing, online entertainment. Wouldn't that be something amazing to be a part of?[40]

As part of their Kickstarter pitch, Collins and team depicted themselves as authors who could bridge the gap between the "new generation of enthusiasts" and the traditional, hierarchal structures of media production. Collins and Maple Blood Productions aligned themselves with fans in (generational) opposition to "old money men," a version of The Powers That Be that is striking in its overt gendered and generational tone. From this perspective, millennial fans become producers not by making fan vids or writing fan fiction but by funding the projects of creative producers not yet in control of the commercial broadcast avenues of production — creative producers who emerge from and will continue to be part of their shared digital authorship networks.

Despite the visionary goals framing the *Divine* project, support for the series did not spread independently in fandom, and fan investment dwindled upon the series' release. Although *Divine* invited fans to become producers, it imagined specific and somewhat restrictive structures for audience transmedia engagement. Maple Blood Productions created predetermined spaces for particular modes of fan engagement, with primary focus on producer-created fan discussion boards and calls for monetary support. *Divine* may have failed to garner an active fandom in part because it did not facilitate enough of a sense of collective ownership through authorship and through choice of the tools of authorship, core values manifest in the various millennial fan communities examined here.

In contrast, fans more enthusiastically claim allegiance to Collins's most recent transmedia enterprise, launched in 2011: an annual scavenger hunt known as Gishwhes, an acronym for the "greatest international scavenger hunt the world has ever seen." Although Gishwhes lacks the articulated strategy of a transmedia industrial shift seemingly present in *Divine*, it is a more fully coauthored transmedia experience. Gishwhes builds on the shared culture of Collins/minion fandom, combining satiric power play with a call for shared, decentered authorship. Collins and co-conspirator Jean-Louis Alexander (who may or may not be a real person) sporadically demand fan action on strict timetables within a rubric of extensive rules.[41] At the same time, Gishwhes functions with a relatively open framework that empowers participants to create as they see fit across a wide range of digital platforms. Participants in Gishwhes choose their own paths to group organization, forming networks on a range of digital interfaces including Twitter, YouTube, Facebook, Tumblr, and Google Docs to coordinate their entries into the competition. The various pieces of art created for Gishwhes populate Youtube and Flickr—for example, the many submissions to the 2011 Gishwhes item 193 of stop-motion films featuring Cabbage Patch dolls doing stripteases, or "a painting/drawing of Misha and the Queen of England as Tarzan and Jane posing in a red chair" (referencing Collins's Twitter origins).

Collins et al. describe the collective authorship of Gishwhes not as a strategic intervention but as a shared ethos of anarchic, transgressive creativity:

> The term *Gishwheshean* refers to any willing—and accepted—member of any GISHWHES movement that deplores artistic normalcy, social trivialities and small talk, is tired of the inherently flawed structure of our political and economic systems and chooses to initiate change through collective artistic (and un-artistic) creation and destruction. That being said, they create art for no sake or purpose whatsoever; otherwise, it would not be Gishwheshean art.
>
> Examples of a Gishwheshean's natural habitat include art galleries, seventeen-course picnic lunches, over-priced naturalist coffee shops, and dadaist poetry readings. Gishwhesheans are not above blatant hedonism as a recreational sport. They are typically the only patron in the Duchamp exhibit performing the Balducci Levitation whilst wearing the GISHWHES national flag as a cape.[42]

Gishwhes does not use the overt language of industrial reconfiguration; nor does it present itself as a "pitch" to convince the "old money men" of the power of the digital, millennial fan collective. However, through its shared satire and performative play, Gishwhes models the potential within millennial culture for a congregation of authors, both official and unofficial, to collectively create in the transmedia sphere.[43]

In this moment of uncertain transition in the media landscape, those involved in television and film production are eager to tame the threat represented by the agency of the millennial generation and by digital media. Producers seek to redefine their media production as something that incorporates the tastes and tendencies of the millennial generation while still maintaining television's cultural and aesthetic norms and hegemonic centrality.[44] Within this potentially reactionary context, commercial media productions may take the digital into account, but they do not necessarily reimagine the very form and definition of programming in itself, nor the relationship between producer and consumer. Collectively authored, decentralized projects like Gishwhes, with creators who fully immerse themselves in the surrounding digital cultures, show us the potential for future transmedia creative authorship in millennial culture. This transformed model of authorship does not disavow hierarchies of professional and amateur or of content owner and content transformer, but it nonetheless finds its engine in the collective coordination and agency of all involved.

EIGHT

Collective Authorship and the Culture of Feels

A post that has been making the rounds on the micro-blogging network Tumblr declares: "Reblog if you are a wizard or a witch." At first the post consisted of this missive only, but it has since come to include several images and additional text. The images begin with a screen capture of Ron Weasley (from the Harry Potter movies) holding a wand and looking sardonic, with text emblazoned on the image that reads "Obviously" (as in, obviously Ron and/or the person responding to the post is a wizard or a witch). The image and text, taken together, suggest that not only do many Tumblr users identify as wizards but that this identification is to be expected as a natural dimension of the Tumblr user base. Later images mark the growth in the amount of times the post has been reposted (in Tumblr-speak, reblogged) by other Tumblr users, starting with Harry and Hermione high-fiving to mark "1.4 million wizards on Tumblr" and eventually including a production out-take of Snape and Dumbledore dancing, in full wizard garb, to celebrate the approach of two million reblogs and thus the presence of two million wizards and witches on Tumblr. Yet later images—as the reblogging approaches seven million wizards—include moving image GIFs from the fan musical parody, *A Very Potter Musical*, of the Hogwarts kids dancing; and later still, at thirteen million reblogs, *A Very Potter Musical*'s Snape and Lucius dance in celebration, as

Reblog if you are a wizard or a witch

val3ntinus:

   i-am-whale:

      my-invisible-angel:

         nicalletteswigart:

      1.4 million wizards on Tumblr!

Figure 13. Tumblr's "Reblog if you're a wizard or a witch" exemplifies the collective authorship of an unfolding digital text within millennial fan culture.

text declares that wizards and witches encompass "just about every person on Tumblr." A cluster of the Tumblr post's organizational tags read, "This fandom, Tumblr, is ours."

This Fandom, Tumblr, Is Ours

The "Reblog if you're a wizard or witch" post hails the viewer/reader directly; it requests (or perhaps demands) individual collective affirmation through re-blogging, which involves simply hitting the reblog button or perhaps adding tags or additional commentary. This post embodies a key ethos of Tumblr, and arguably of millennial fan culture more broadly: a celebration of community that extends beyond a niche-in-hiding cultural identity to a vision of fandom as an expansive, even proselytizing, collective. As the tag "This fandom, Tumblr, is ours" suggests, the post equates fandom with Tumblr users as a whole and with the Tumblr interface. At the time of writing this chapter, the post has hit 14,754,373, or, as the post declares, "14 fucking million." The insertion of a curse word marks cause for celebration, pride, and perhaps some surprise—or at least an in-your-face "so there!"—imbuing the number with a sense of collectively felt emotion.

Of course, this count of fourteen (fucking) million includes individuals posting multiple times; Tumblr culture encourages users to periodically reblog the same post to reaffirm fannish devotion or to reify a strongly held point of view. The commonly seen phrase on Tumblr, "always reblog," indicates that there are certain sentiments so moving that Tumblr participants/fans will repost them any time they appear on their dashboard (the dashboard being the posting stream of the combined Tumblr blogs a given user has chosen to follow). Two of the embedded comments in the "reblog if you're a wizard or a witch" post read "instant reblog" and "I REBLOG THIS EVERY TIME IT'S ON MY DASH."

However, the precision of the number of reblogs as an assessment of Harry Potter fandom (or wizards on Tumblr) is not what's at stake here. Yes, fans do look to posts such as "reblog if you're a wizard or a witch" to gauge the size of a fandom or support for a particular character, pairing, or plot development.[1] However, what is more significant here is the way in which the accumulation of notes in such a post celebrates shared, collective passion. This reblogged and additively transformed post makes visible communally shared emotion, registered through asynchronous authorship. This is true whether a repost signifies an additional wizard/Tumblr user or a wizard who feels the need to post multiple times. Indeed, the slippage between these two possible reasons for the post's accumulation is crucial here; such posts revel in their amorphous, multiplicitous authorship and the immeasurable shared emotion it suggests. Millennial fans often tout emotional response—or what is known in millennial culture as "feels"—as a driving force behind their creative authorship communities. What I refer to here as feels culture thrives on the public celebration of emotion previously considered the realm of the private. In feels culture, emotions remain intimate but are no longer necessarily private; rather, they build a sense of an intimate collective, one that is bound together precisely by the processes of shared emotional authorship. In this equation, emotion fuels fan transformative creativity, and performances of shared emotion define fan authorship communities.

We can think of emotionally driven collective authorship as a quality of the blog and of digital culture more broadly. Paul Booth argues in *Digital Fandom* that a blog post is not only authored by the person who originally wrote or constructed the post, but also by all the others who come along and add comments and conversation. As a post grows, its authorship moves from individual to collective. Any blog post is always already a potentially collective text, waiting to be elaborated upon.[2] In Booth's words: "The blog is not just a post, but rather the combination of the post plus comments. . . . The 'writer' of a blog is ultimately a group, not an individual."[3]

Kristina Busse and Karen Hellekson's notion of the fantext similarly approaches fan production as an ever-shifting text created by multiple authors, which as a result encompasses and embraces contradiction: "This *fantext*, the entirety of stories and critical commentary written in a fandom (or even in a pairing or genre), offers an ever-growing, ever-expanding version of the characters. . . . The community of fans creates a communal (albeit contentious and contradictory) interpretation in which a large number of potential meanings, directions, and outcomes co-reside."[4] Booth's and Busse and Hellekson's formulations of fandom highlight collective authorship, describing a collectivity that emerges over time and that unites multiple authors through a sense of shared source text, shared fantext, and shared processes of authorship. For Booth, this collectivity is driven by our emotional involvement in media, and it is this emotional involvement that gets at why fan studies matters. He argues that in a sense, we are all included in the larger collective of fannishness, if not in particular fandoms, through our emotional involvement in culture: "Fans offer us something we can all relate to. Whether cult television, sports, food, opera or books—we are all fans of something out there, and we all become emotionally involved over something. Studying fans, in effect, is . . . a way of studying ourselves."[5]

I've opened this final chapter with the Harry Potter "reblog if you're a wizard or witch" post because it speaks to this notion of an expansive fannish collective to which we all belong. More than that, it celebrates our collective belonging through images of embodied emotion. The post suggests that the identity of wizard (and, arguably, fan) encompasses not only Harry Potter fandom but potentially all of Tumblr, and perhaps even all of a generation. It depicts this magical collective as a mediated dance celebration, driven to collective motion by collective emotion. Moving-image GIFs layer embodied affect to represent the shared emotions of Harry Potter fans, Tumblr users, and anyone who feels himself or herself hailed by and included in this post.

As an interface, Tumblr lends itself particularly well to the visual enactment of collective emotion. When Tumblr first came on the scene in 2007, it offered a microblogging platform that, in contrast to Twitter, allowed for the inclusion of images and video as well as text. Visual images, and especially animated GIFs, have become a dominant mode of discourse on Tumblr, with images sometimes standing on their own or layered in various ways with text for multimodal impact. Although Twitter now allows image posting via additional interfaces like TwitPic and Instagram, Tumblr culture has continued to foreground the exchange of images, punctuated by text, as a primary form of expression. The exchange of (often animated) images in Tumblr posts—distributed across users' dashboards—renders visible fandom's collective energy.

Millennial feels culture combines an aesthetics of intimate emotion—the sense that we are accessing an author's immediate and personal emotional response to media culture—with an aesthetics of high performativity, calling attention to mediation and to the labor of the author. Users apply text and tags in Tumblr to punctuate images, thus personalizing them or emphasizing a user's emotional and/or intellectual engagement with a particular image. Although tags are intended to help with categorizing, archiving, and retrieval, Tumblr users often include tags to capture their momentary response to an image, to theorize or extrapolate, or to inscribe the imagined audience into the post. Emotion-oriented tags often intertwine with tags that function as analysis or interpretation to swamp organizational schemas. Tags even become the site of fan fiction authorship in what is known as tagfic, with fiction comprised only of tags. In the case of tagfic (and also with tagmeta, or fan theorizing via tags), tags function as an opportunity for fan transformative authorship, often at the expense of tags as organizational structure.[6]

Feels culture is perhaps on most vibrant display on Tumblr, in GIF sets, tagfic, and the like, but it is by no means exclusive to the interface and communities of Tumblr. Tumblresque multimodal (that is, visual and textual elements combined) representations of personal emotion play out in a larger field that includes the visual landscape of everyday life on Instagram, the world of vlogging and response videos on YouTube, and the semiprivate social networks of Facebook. Feels culture's presence exceeds the bounds of Tumblr and the limits, such as they are, of fandom.

Millennial Fans in Defense of Professionalism

The "reblog if you're a witch or wizard" post celebrates a collective vision of millennial fandom so expansive that it blurs the lines between Harry Potter fandom, Tumblr fandom, and a larger generational ethos. Such an expansive culture necessarily includes a multiplicity of positions, values, practices, and aesthetics. Although the celebratory discourse surrounding feels culture may be highly visible and seem all-encompassing, millennial fan culture does not simply celebrate the democratic collective at the expense of all else. Discourses of collective celebration go hand in hand with an emphasis on professional skill and professional aesthetics.[7] Despite the overall taboo against making money off fan work, professionalized aesthetics and success in the commercial world still breed respect (or, depending on the instance, notoriety) in fandom.[8] Not all fan producers embrace an affectively driven do-it-yourself aesthetic. Many millennial fan creators prefer fan texts that adhere to professionalized aesthetic rules, and some offer resources to help aspiring fan creators attain a professional tone to their work. Indeed, the celebration of the millennial fan collective has brought about what might be termed a backlash: a call to protect the rights and values of the individual author, and a call to value professionalized skill.

In "Avoiding Mistakes in Fanfiction Writing: A Beginner's Guide," the author begins with the assumption that "we're all here to improve, right?" and then instructs aspiring fan authors: "Not knowing the difference between its and it's, tenses, grammar, and all of the other mechanics of writing will bring your work down a notch in the eyes of those that care."[9] This advice encourages self-policing of fan authorship, invoking an (imagined) adjudicating readership invested in the rules of proper grammar. Another fan author offers a set of "Tips for Writing Better Fan Fiction" that includes the following guidelines: "Angst does not always equal good drama. . . . Keeping the scale and intensity of your stories closer to reality than Opera means that the genuine emotion you provoke in the reader will be all the more powerful for being attained through subtlety and skill rather than cheap theatrics."[10] This advice illustrates how the pursuit of writing "good" fan fiction can mean subscribing not only to the rules of grammar but to value sets that rein in excessive emotion and performativity in favor of a more measured professionalism.[11] These discourses of professionalism in millennial fandom urge fan creators to downplay excess emotion, collective or otherwise, in favor of individual literary and artistic restraint.[12]

This investment in professional aesthetics extends into questions of ethics. Not all fans celebrate the ethos of collective sharing in a public commons; some fans emphasize the rights of professional authors to own and control their characters and story worlds. While many fans support the fannish right to transform and share, others emphasize professional authors' rights to own their original ideas and to thus limit transformation and distribution. Many fans will speak out in support of specific professional authors who do not want their works transformed. A discussion entitled "Professional Authors on Fan Fiction" includes a range of opinions on this question.[13] Quite a few posters argue that fans should respect professional authors' wishes, as in the following:

> I found it sad . . . how some fanfiction writers (and fans) are bashing professional authors for their views on fanfiction. We claim we are writers ourselves. We, of all people, should understand their sentiments. . . . So when they say they get mad when they see their characters in someone else's story or read works base on their works, let's respect their stance. End of story.

This commenter argues that because fan writers are authors too, they should understand the motivations of professional authors who wish to control their creative work.

This defense of professional authors extends to include fan authors and artists who do not want their noncommercial fan work circulated without their permission or at all, or who do not want their transformational work further transformed.[14] Just as professionalism as an aesthetic may move through commercial and fan work, so too may the ethics of professionalism extend into fan communities and to the creative works of fans. These ethics can come directly in conflict with even such a seemingly core fannish value as the fan right to transform. Rather than being uniformly held millennial fan values, affective collectivity and fan transformation exist in tension with discourses of individual professionalism and idea ownership, all of which fans hold as valuable in an expansively diverse millennial culture.

The Lizzie Bennet Diaries and Millennial Feels

One of the most visible transmedia series of 2013, Emmy-award-winning *The Lizzie Bennet Diaries*, draws on the values and aesthetic of millennial fan and feels culture to update Jane Austen's *Pride and Prejudice*. *The Lizzie Bennet Diaries* is an independently produced transmedia series that situates itself within millennial fandom and feels culture, and it tells its story through the vehicles of that culture. The series transforms the iconic character of Lizzie Bennet into an outspoken vlogger. The story is told through multiple digital platforms, including YouTube, Tumblr, and Twitter. The primary channel of narrative is Lizzie Bennet's vlog, in which she documents the exploits of her family and charts the journey of her relationship with one William Darcy from intense dislike to love.[15] Additional character vlogs supplement Lizzie's narrative.

The Lizzie Bennet Diaries gives us a compelling picture of what (trans)media storytelling and engagement may look like within a decentered millennial landscape in which fans and professional media producers alike celebrate millennial feels and the millennial right to transform. The series deploys the codes of YouTube's "broadcast yourself" aesthetic—specifically the seemingly amateur, single-camera, confessional-style video blog, or vlog—to adapt Pride and Prejudice to feels culture.[16] It situates its fictional characters within what Jean Burgess and Joshua Green call the "affective economy" of YouTube, in which success is determined by participation, interaction, and the sharing of seemingly "authentic" emotion.[17] The various vlogs that make up the narrative offer slightly different representations of the forms of vlogging culture, including Lizzie's sardonic media studies grad student and her sister Lydia's exuberant performance of millennial netspeak. Thus situated within the digital–social YouTube context, The Lizzie Bennet Diaries works within and plays with the language and logic of YouTube vlogging culture and millennial fandom.

As a transmedia series, The Lizzie Bennet Diaries extends beyond YouTube; all of the characters have web footprints as if they were real people, with Twitter accounts, Pinterest accounts, and the like. The story unwinds through micronarratives that play out on these various platforms. As such, the series offers a commentary not only on the YouTube community's cultural practices but also on the range of modes of creativity and self-expression within millennial culture. In its playfully realist transmedia form, the series looks like some of the decentered fan creative works we examined at the end of chapter 6, where we explored multiauthored fannish role-playing games like "Gleeful Little Liars." Fan-authored fictional profiles populate social networks including YouTube, Tumblr, and Twitter. The Lizzie Bennet Diaries joins a landscape already fertile with fan fictional self-representations.[18]

Indeed, in some ways, The Lizzie Bennet Diaries may be recognized as a mode of transmedia fan fiction: the series presents itself as a digital refueling of a beloved story, with its creators driven by respect for the source text and its fans to retell *Pride and Prejudice* in a new, transformed form.[19] As such, *The Lizzie Bennet Diaries* seems to be made both by and for fans and the culture of fan authorship and millennial feels. Before the first video was even posted, the series was situated squarely within contemporary millennial fandom and fannish traditions. Like the BBC's reboot of Sherlock Holmes, *Sherlock* (BBC, 2010–present), *The Lizzie Bennet Diaries* came into being with more than one already existing fandom ready to launch.[20] *Pride and Prejudice* author Jane Austen's fandom is one of the oldest fandoms and remains vibrant.[21] *The Lizzie Bennet Diaries* was able to draw on the enthusiastic Jane Austen fan base, with its organized networks of appreciation and community. In addition, one of the two series' creators came with a millennial fandom of sorts already invested in his work. Series producer Hank Green is a visible figure in millennial fandom; before *The Lizzie Bennet Diaries*, Green was well known as half of the YouTube-based "Vlogbrothers" and leader of the Nerdfighteria movement, a collective online and in-person subculture that organizes social action projects and offers itself as a haven for nerds, outsiders, and anyone who wishes to affiliate.[22] Between the Nerdfighters and Jane Austen fandom, *The Lizzie Bennet Diaries* was positioned from the start within established traditions of fandom and active networks of millennial culture, networks that were ready to engage with the transmedia series.

The series also emulated fan-favored representations of technologically savvy millennial females like *Veronica Mars*, *Gossip Girl*, and *Pretty Little Liars*. Like these three series, *The Lizzie Bennet Diaries* offers the perspectives of multiple digitally savvy female characters. The young women of *The Lizzie Bennet Diaries* use digital technology to tell their own stories and train their young female friends and family members to do the same. Lizzie and her best friend, Charlotte, work together to produce Lizzie's vlog; while they vlog about Lizzie's personal life, Lizzie offers the perspective of a PhD student in communication studies, and Charlotte runs the technological side of things as an aspiring media professional. Lizzie's two sisters are also digitally savvy producers: Jane Bennet works in the fashion industry and runs a fashion blog, and Lydia starts her own vlog and Tumblr, "The Lydia Bennet," in which she shares her perspective on the developments in her own life as well as in her sisters' lives.[23]

Lydia is the one Bennet sister whose digital engagement is more personal than professional, and as we shall see, it is Lydia who most fully seems to embody the millennial culture of feels. Through Lydia, *The Lizzie Bennet Diaries* offers a commentary on the place of emotion in millennial culture. Where *Pride and Prejudice* presents Lydia as a negative figure whose weak-mindedness highlights Lizzie's strength of personality, *The Lizzie Bennet Diaries* depicts Lydia's effusive personality and openness as positive qualities that Lizzie could stand to learn from. It is Lizzie who seems to have failed Lydia by not recognizing that her sister's exuberance comes from an honest human place: a desire for connection and acceptance in the world. When an online sex scandal threatens Lydia, Lizzie more than Lydia must learn from the experience. Lydia does not need to be punished for her millennial excesses; rather, Lizzie needs to embrace the millennial culture of feels. One of the series' two major climaxes involves Lizzie apologizing to Lydia and thus reuniting the family. This shift to a sympathetic focus on Lydia represents a significant transformation from literary source text to transmedia adaptation.

The character of Lydia became a major site of fan appreciation and identification over the course of *The Lizzie Bennet Diaries'* yearlong run. Viewers rallied around Lydia's character and spoke directly about what they thought she represented for the series' take on female identity and millennial culture. For her fans, Lydia recuperates taboo femininity, offering a relatable alternative to Lizzie's comparative emotional control. Where Lizzie's sardonic girl blogger calls up a trope familiar from *Veronica Mars* and *Gossip Girl*, Lydia embodies a celebration of the culture of feels. Unwilling to hide behind analysis and lack of affect, Lydia channels unabashed emotion and performance of emotional self.

In personal blogs and community sites, fans defend and celebrate Lydia's emotionally performative character. For example, the authors of the blog *Girls Love Giants: Thinking Big, Girls, Media, and Popular Culture* write:

> The Lydia of *The Lizzie Bennet Diaries* is a whole other kettle of exuberant, strong-willed fish. Sure, she's boy-crazy and a bit of a lush. She comes home from the mall weighed down with shopping bags despite her family's financial straits. She's prone to textspeak (she calls herself "the adorbs"), and she lives to be the center of attention. But the web series doesn't judge her for this, though Lizzie does. As audience members, we understand that her bright pink lipstick and tendency to try to high five everyone in sight is just part of what makes her Lydia. And thanks to the spin-off video diary series that runs concomitantly with episodes of

TLBD, *The Lydia Bennet*, we also understand beneath her bravado, Lydia's vulnerable, loyal, and much more perceptive than she seems.[24]

Likewise, a fan defends Lydia on Tumblr:

> The Lizzie Bennet Diaries' focus was not about Lizzie and Darcy getting together. Sure, that was a major plot point. But The LBD was about relationships. Family, friends, partners, and everything in between. Lydia was Lizzie's family, and a major part of The LBD was Lydia and Lizzie's relationship changing . . . don't you DARE try and tell me that Lydia is not as significant as Lizzie or Darcy. Because I will defend the crap out of that wonderful, beautiful girl.

Both of these fan-authored posts demonstrate the strong conviction felt throughout the fandom about Lydia's centrality to the series.

The actress who plays Lydia, Mary Kate Wiles, describes how surprised she was by the love for Lydia within fandom, given the character's usual status as a reviled or trivialized figure. Wiles attributes the power of the character to Lydia's embodiment of self-discomfort:

> The thing that I'm going to take away and remember years from now is that I have grown to care so deeply about Lydia Bennet. . . . Never in my life would I have imagined that I would be proud to play this famed silly flirt of girl. . . . Lydia is not like characters I normally play. I didn't feel at home in her skin. I felt strange and uncomfortable. . . . And maybe that's what made me grow so close to her. I began to realize that how I felt playing her was how she felt being herself. But before long it became clear that her story and her struggle, while our personalities may differ, were deeply, deeply personal to me. . . . And never would I have guessed that Lydia Bennet was the vessel through which I'd get to tell a story like this, a story that affected me deeply, and I hope did you too.[25]

Building off Wiles's analysis, if Lydia serves as an identificatory figure representing aspects of femininity that millennial young women have been taught to repress, then it is more powerful still that *The Lizzie Bennet Diaries* recuperates Lydia from her prior role as *Pride and Prejudice*'s bad object, transforming her into a key figure whose importance to *The Lizzie Bennet Diaries* must be recognized. As a performer of feels, Lydia facilitates engagement with (and maybe even the integration of) the darker experiences and senses of self that millennials face. Lydia's emotional displays encompass more than giddy exuberance. As a character, she performs a complex, seemingly uncensored mix of emotions, including self-doubt and fear. The result rises above many of the more limited representations and performances of millennial self in contemporary media, thus resonating for audience and actor alike. Lydia's feels are millennial noir and millennial hope integrated into something more multidimensional, something that cannot fit into a simple, preprescribed narrative.

This is not to say that The Lizzie Bennet Diaries is an unchecked celebration of feels via Lydia. It is not The Lydia Bennet Diaries, after all. Lydia is still a side character to Lizzie's more controlled center. Lydia may have had her own vlog, but it was positioned as a small transmedia offshoot, not fully necessary to follow the larger series' narrative. As The Lizzie Bennet Diaries' narrative reaches its conclusion, Lydia stops vlogging in the face of the threatening online sex scandal and appears much less frequently on screen, whether on Lizzie's vlog or her own. Furthermore, while Lydia may have been key to the synchronous, unfolding experience of The Lizzie Bennet Diaries as it was released in installments on YouTube, in the series' continued afterlife, Lydia may take a less central role.[26] Supporters of the series' Kickstarter campaign received a Lizzie Bennet Diaries–themed reprint of Pride and Prejudice with a cover that features Darcy and Lizzie in a romantic pose, with black-and-white images of the other characters relegated to the background periphery.[27] The DVD box set cover likewise features only a photographed image of Lizzie and Darcy, although the various cast members, including Lydia, are depicted on the covers of the individual discs within the set.

Of course, Lizzie and Darcy's romance itself feeds into the culture of feels. Fans celebrated their long-awaited kiss (in episode 98) by remixing it into many different variations of moving-image GIF on Tumblr. Feels culture still has a presence in The Lizzie Bennet Diaries post facto distribution and reception, but it is a diluted presence that suggests a censoring of the excess emotion of feels or a stepping away from the more ambivalent or transgressive elements of millennial experience that Lydia represents. Perhaps the added complexity and darker narratives of millennial noir and exuberant emotions of millennial feels that Lydia channels have not yet shed their taboo to the extent that they can characterize what will be canonized about The Lizzie Bennet Diaries.

Building an Intimate Collective

The logic of collective feels plays a more definitive role in other transmedia projects emerging in the wake of *The Lizzie Bennet Diaries*. For example, Wiles has nurtured a crossover fandom for her other web series, *Squaresville*, in which she plays the alienated but passionate Zelda, one of the series' two main characters. With the tagline, "A new web series about growing up and burning brightly," *Squaresville* tells the story of Zelda and Esther, two teenage girls longing for adventure but trapped in suburbia. The series depicts its young characters as participants in media culture and fandom, and it includes a focus on their emotional connection with media.

Through its engagement with the larger media and fannish landscape, *Squaresville* builds an emotionally intimate collective that includes characters, actors, writers, and viewers. Take, for example, Zelda's contributions to *Squaresville*'s supplemental "monolo7ues." These offer brief moments (in vlog form) in which various characters speak intimately and directly to the camera and viewer. In these monologues, the characters step outside of the progressing story line to muse about a topic that is on their minds. The monologue form is in itself one that forges a connection with viewers—a form that many young, aspiring actors perform and practice to gain acting skill. The monologue also has much in common with the YouTube vlog aesthetic, as both are often intimate, personal, yet one-to-many addresses. In Wiles's/Zelda's first monologue, Zelda speaks directly to us in a way that recalls Wiles's intimate vlog performances as Lydia.[28]

Zelda's monologue, entitled "Fell in Love with a Song," is itself about the intimate and emotional relationship we have with media. Zelda lies on the floor, listening to her favorite song, and tells us about how the song makes her feel. She contemplates the song's temporary but intense emotional power and her communion with it:

> This song just makes me feel like . . . You know how sometimes when you're really focused, like I am when I'm listening to this song, you forget that you're a person? You forget that anything exists at all? It's you and the song and nothing else is there because how could it be? . . . Eventually that magic will fade away, and the song won't work anymore. . . . And maybe a year or two later we'll be able to be friends, but for the time being this love affair is over, and it's not you it's me, and there's nothing neither of us can do about it.

In this monologue, Zelda invites the audience into her personal experience of her favorite song. Through its combination of first- and second-person address, the monologue playfully suggests that, like Zelda, we all have an intimate relationship with media, one that mirrors the give-and-take of human relationships. Wiles's quietly emotive performance conjures an image of millennial fandom that is simultaneously intimate and collective, and that is bound together by shared emotional investment in media.

The viewer response on YouTube to Zelda's monologue exemplifies this sense of expansive, mediated emotional intimacy. Commenters assert their connection with the fictional Zelda and with Wiles as actor, star text, and fellow millennial. Commenter after commenter share their favorite song of the moment, one that makes them feel the way Zelda describes. Some of them comment on the video clip as a representation; others don't. Some address Zelda playfully as if she were real; others address Wiles as an actress. Either way, virtually every comment offers the commenter's personal favorite song as a way of connecting with Zelda, Wiles, and the (imagined) audience of the monologue.

There's an ease to this collective list compiling that is especially worth noting within the interface of YouTube, infamous as it is for its flame wars. This ease emerges from *Squaresville*'s transmedia approach; the *Squaresville* producers have worked strategically to establish a sense of shared culture on YouTube and Tumblr and thus to build a rapport with their viewers. Zelda's monologue reaches out to viewers as an accessible and mimicable form, and fans in turn respond by creating their own versions of the monologue. In addition, in the closing moments of each episode, the actors (as themselves) pose questions for viewers to answer in the comments or in their own vlogs, then entreat viewers to "stay square" and "fight the robots." These two phrases have become hashtag rallying cries on Tumblr, connecting *Squaresville* fans and linking posts that feature *Squaresville* fan art and commentary.

On *Squaresville*'s main informational site (itself a Tumblr), producers encourage viewers to share their Squaresville mash-ups, artwork, monologues, and response videos. The *Squaresville* producers also contribute to the flow of posts on Tumblr. For example, they have posted the transcripts of the monolo7ues (including "Fell in Love with a Song") on the series' main site. The actors also actively participate as themselves on Tumblr, posting and reblogging on their own personal Tumblrs. Thus, from a whole range of entry points, *Squaresville* makes extensive use of the Tumblr community and participates in Tumblr culture. The official *Squaresville* Tumblr account participates in the cross-fandom "Fan Art Fridays," reblogging (on Fridays) *Squaresville*-inspired fan art, thereby encouraging and highlighting fan participation and contribution. Fans work with the materials offered by *Squaresville* producers and share their work on Tumblr, within a space and culture in which the *Squaresville* creators are already participants, and active ones at that.

In a moment when digital media producers seek to recreate the web–audience relationship in the image of the broadcast TV industry, independent transmedia productions like *Squaresville* differentiate themselves by positioning themselves within the intimate public space of a collective, transformative creative culture.[29] And perhaps as a result, at least in the cases of *Squaresville* and *The Lizzie Bennet Diaries*, we find representations of fannish media investment that move beyond stereotypical representations of incoherent fangirl squee. These series offer representations of millennial fans that are intimately emotional and buoyantly emotive, depicting millennial fans at the heart of contemporary digital culture.

Perhaps unsurprisingly, Wiles herself has begun to vlog. In her vlog, she negotiates questions of emotional performance and digital professionalism. She performs earnestness and enthusiasm, rather like Lydia and Zelda, but she also tones down her exuberance to emphasize the professionalism and intent behind her performances as an actor, highlighting the craft and construction of the characters she plays:

> Okay, so. I made a video, and I said some things about acting. . . . I only expected two people to see that video, and now I have a lot of subscribers. Not an inordinate amount but a lot for someone who doesn't even do anything. . . . It's a little bizarre. Don't get me wrong. I'm very excited that you guys think I'm interesting. So like, what do I do now? I realize that I'm being very Lydia in this video already, and I just started, and I don't know how I feel about that.
>
> Here are my thoughts on vlogging. I don't really know how to do it. I feel like I shouldn't be vlogging because (a) I don't really have anything to say (b) I'm not very good at sharing because who cares? (Did I do abc or did I do 123?) And (e) I am an actor. That's all I am. If I were anything else, then I would be something else. . . . But here I am. I've bitten the bullet, and I am talking to you good people of the Internet.[30]

Wiles, in this vlog entry and in others, performs a synthesis of amateur and professional, connecting with her characters and fans while also stressing her

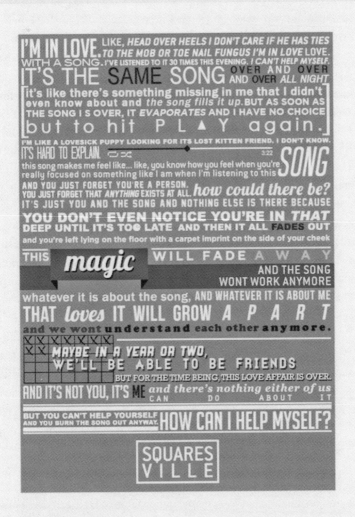

"Mom says dinner's ready."

"Okay, I'll be there in 3 minutes, 22 seconds." [x]

Fan art Friday - MonoLo7ue edition!

Figure 14. Shared as part of *Squaresville's* #fanartfriday, Mary Morales's "Mom Says Dinner's Ready" features the text of the monologue "Fell in Love with a Song."

separation from both. In the segment above, her phrasing and tone emphasize her amateur status as a vlogger while highlighting her professional status as an actor. She also simultaneously aligns herself with and distances herself from Lydia's feels-infused vlog performances. Her vlog balances a spontaneous, intimate, do-it-yourself-style with a discourse of professionalism. Her phrasing suggests that collective intimacy has won out ("Here I am, talking with you good people of the Internet"), yet it must be tempered with expressions of professional distinction. Wiles's self-representation suggests an ambivalence toward millennial feels culture on the part of millennials—one that arguably extends beyond her into the culture as a whole.

Wiles's balancing act reminds us that the reign of feels is not total in millennial culture. As millennials and millennial fans traverse cultural forums that confound assumed divides between public and intimate, they must negotiate the expression of emotion as simultaneous threat and asset. Discourses of millennial hope (of the sort discussed in part 1 of this book) encourage millennials to use their digital networks to built social communities in specific and guided ways, but discourses of millennial noir (as explored in part 2) simultaneously encourage the uncensored sharing of previously taboo cultural engagement, including fan emotion. The presence and power of emotion expressed online in millennial culture is undeniable; strong opinions, intense emotions, and playful performance of heightened self—all bring visibility and inflect whole communities. The digital world suffuses millennials' everyday lives, personal and professional, intimate and public (and intimate public). The contradictory messages about millennial excess and millennial noir create a challenging landscape for millennials to traverse. Some millennial fans seek to channel feels culture into professional or publicly visible social activist endeavors such as the Harry Potter Alliance and Nerdfighters, or Gishwhes and the Klaine box scene/Project Angel Food campaign; some millennial fans strive to protect feels culture and fan culture more specifically as semiprivate subcultures. Some seek to publicize the more aesthetically professionalized, skill-oriented dimensions of transformative millennial fan culture. In the end, most millennial fans—and any of us who engage with this culture—find ourselves constantly negotiating between these choices. In almost every moment of our personal and professional lives, online and perhaps even off, we must juggle the pros and cons as well as the pleasures and censures of engaging with millennial culture and millennial fandom.

Calling All Fandoms

Calling all fandoms, we have a chance to join and to rise.
Loki lies, you know it's true, if we stick together we'll see it through.
I can't wait to celebrate with you,
in that little town of Oregon,
we raise our glass, just get your ass
to LeakyCon!
—Opening Ceremonies, LeakyCon 2013,
by Tessa Nettings, Melissa Anelli, Melissa Lawson,
and Jordan Edwards (reprinted with permission)

I attended the 2013 fan convention LeakyCon in the midst of writing this book. First held in 2009, LeakyCon has evolved into multifannish yearly gathering.[1] LeakyCon features a web of interconnected fan texts, including Harry Potter, the StarKids musical theater troupe (most famous for their Harry Potter satires such as *A Very Potter Musical*), *Glee*, all things Disney, *Doctor Who*, *Sherlock*, *Supernatural*, thevlogbrothers, Nerdfighteria, web series such as *The Lizzie Bennet Diaries*, and young adult literature. In 2013, sessions also included broader discussions of the role of religion in millennial culture and the experiences of parents of fans over thirty.

In its diverse fannish energy, LeakyCon encapsulates millennial fan cultures and values in all their complexity and contradiction. LeakyCon's multifanishness (including not only multiple texts but also multiple media, from books to television to film to web series) models the fluidity of millennial fan culture. In particular, the StarKid musical theater troupe and fandom—very much a core part of

LeakyCon—have a particular energy that seems to me to embody where millennial fandom is headed.[2] The StarKids and their fans are passionate, playfully irreverent, and a little wacky. StarKid culture is somewhat utopian in that it embraces the idea that anyone can be a star, but in a millennial culture of microcelebrity and self-authorship, acknowledging the dispersion and construction of the star is perhaps more realist than not. Actors and fans are all part of one welcoming community known as Team StarKid, which works to foster cultural support and media literacy through performance, satire, and song, spread in person and online. This sense of fandom as a playful, cultural support network bridging author and audience extends beyond StarKid to characterize LeakyCon as a whole.

LeakyCon showcases the vibrancy of millennial-produced fan cultures, in which fans transform commercially produced media but also produce their own work, thus challenging assumed divides between transformative and original. LeakyCon also highlights the shift in fandom and fan identity from niche subculture to mainstream ethos. Congoers alternate between describing the con as a haven from a less fannish world and as a beloved, in-person, embodied version of their everyday lives, digital and otherwise. LeakyCon declares itself to be a hub for an intersection of largely female, queer-friendly youth cultures who use the media around them for their own (not necessarily normative) ends and who move freely from media text to media text, fandom to fandom, broadcast media to digital media, digital interface to digital interface, and most especially from the role of audience, reader, and viewer to (transmedia) producer.

In its celebratory multifannishness (and, in the broadest sense, queerness), LeakyCon gives the impression of being both unifying and extremely varied.[3] At the 2013 LeakyCon, held in Portland, Oregon, all attendees were given green LeakyCon bags. Within these bags were tags marking the wearer as belonging to a specific Harry Potter house: Gryffindor, Slytherin, Ravenclaw, or Hufflepuff. People energetically traded with each other until they had the house they wanted. (I had to do a bit of trading myself to get my proper Slytherin badge.) In the following days, folks at panels, meet-ups, and convention hall booths handed out additional tags that had been created by fans in advance of the con to represent particular fandoms, subfandoms, and online communities. By the con's end, individuals had long colorful banners of multiple identifiers, including "Everybody Deserves Tea" (a *Lizzie Bennet Diaries* reference), "9 Is My Doctor" (*Doctor Who*), "Nerdfighter," and many others.

Walking from the official con hotel in Portland to take the light rail to the convention center, you could tell fellow LeakyCon-goers by their green bags—or the fact that they were in full Hogwarts robes in the unusual Portland heat wave. Once there, you could get a sense of the multiplicity of their cultural engagement from the diverse ribbons hanging from their name tags.

Channeling millennial hope, the LeakyCon experience emphasizes a diverse multiplicity brought together in a celebratory collective. However, where *Glee* used its moments of collectivity to rein in the transgressive potential of its diversity, millennial-created fan culture celebrates precisely its shared transgression and its unbounded multiplicity. As we saw in part 1 of this book, millennial hope is an industrial construction driven by marketing and branding imperatives. When enacted and transformed by millennials themselves, however, millennial hope's diverse collective becomes a celebration of fannish multiplicity and fluid identities.

The 2013 LeakyCon closed with a playful reworking of *Rent*'s famous anthem, "La Vie Bohème," with *Rent* star Anthony Rapp reprising his role as Mark Cohen. However, the fannish remake replaces the "bohemian" life that Mark and friends celebrate with the multifannish life, as embodied in LeakyCon. *Rent*'s celebration of New York City's 1980s queer urban subculture here gets a fannish update, but not at a far remove; the very fact that Anthony Rapp plays his former character suggests how smooth the adaptation is from *Rent*'s depiction of a multifaceted, subcultural queer collective to LeakyCon's depiction of a multifannish community connecting online and off, cosplayers and fan writers, and web series actors and creators. The musical number celebrates multifannishness as queer in its multiplicity.

Millennial fandom merges hope and noir, then revels in the resulting combination. Millennial fans infuse their hopeful celebration with an insistent undermining of traditional moral, gender, and sexual hierarchies, and with the display of subcultural literacy. While not always deploying the aesthetics of film noir, fans celebrate millennial savvy as a shared cultural knowledge that surpasses single fandoms. The "To LeakyCon" number exemplifies the value fans place on this multifannish savvy. Performed by LeakyCon's many special guests (including the Team StarKid troupe and the cast of *The Lizzie Bennet Diaries*), the lyrics of the number are riddled with fannish codes, proclaiming LeakyCon a space for all fans to come together in person to rejoice in their shared fannishness.

Pleasure in the "To LeakyCon" number comes from the public, in-person

Make us some jifs or is it gifs?

▶ ◀)) 8:38 / 9:04   ⓘ ⏹CC ⚙ ▢ [ ]

LeakyCon Portland "La Vie Boheme" Fandom Parody -- Official Video

LeakyCon
▶ Subscribe   5,502

64,578

Figure 15. LeakyCon's many special guests perform the multifannish collective in the LeakyCon 2013 parody of "La Vie Bohème" in a performance that now has a digital afterlife on the official LeakyCon YouTube account.

performance, by various fan-beloved stars, of a diverse mix of fan codes, in lyrics like this:

> We're all weirdos, superheroes, *Homo sapiens*, Sherlockians, Jedis and
>   Wookies, Glee
> Edward Cullen
> Lily James, Gallifreyans, Hunger Games
> The Cumberbitches catching snitches, Snow White humming
> Cuz winter is coming
> To *allons-y*, 221B, I can't even, all the feels, OTP
> To those who cried, it's bigger on the inside

The references that make up these lyrics are recognizable across fandoms, yet still hold the charge of community secrets. (References to at least twelve fandoms are embedded in this one brief excerpt.) Millennial fan literacy means that fan culture can feel niche and mainstream, secret and collective, private and public, and even commercial and grassroots, all at once.

Millennial literacy encompasses sardonic and sometimes raunchy humor and evinces a comfort with sexual and gender play, which we saw in Misha Collins's fan minions and in Gishwhes fandom, and which is also certainly visible in the StarKid theater troupe's adaptations of Harry Potter. At a Leaky-Con panel for adult fans of Harry Potter and StarKid, members of the audience argued that contemporary fan culture (and LeakyCon specifically) offers a safe but multigenerational environment, where teens and twentysomethings have the opportunity to commingle and even become close friends. This multiage community may be read as a natural result of the marketing logics of millennial branding that invite teens and young adults into an expansive audience group. While this intergenerational mingling seems threatening to some parents because children and teens could be exposed to adult knowledge too soon, millennial fans argue that it offers an empowering route to knowledge within a supportive community. Thus, millennial knowingness—shared knowledge of multifannish culture—translates not only into media literacy but also into cultural literacy, community support, and even personal support. Millennial fandom in this context functions as a feminist, queer inclusive, intergenerational ethos—a way of life, a community, and a support system for young and old who identify as part of this expansive community.

LeakyCon's bringing together of younger and older fans is part of another key value at play in millennial fandom: the erasure of hierarchical structures and of the assumed divides between young and old, real life and online, producer and consumer, fan and star, high culture and low culture. The participants in LeakyCon, and in millennial fandom more broadly, see the culture as an inclusive, expansive, and fluid one, and as a powerful outlet that informs their lived experience beyond the con. In his conclusion to *Textual Poachers,* Henry Jenkins described fandom in 1992 as "subcultural" and as an "alternative social community."[4] However, LeakyCon is not an escape from fans' everyday lives; it isn't the fully separate domain of what Jenkins calls a "Weekend Only World."[5] Instead, LeakyCon is an in-person invocation of millennial fandom, a multimedia, multiage, multifannish community dedicated to embracing niche experiences but sewing them together in an interconnected web. LeakyCon offered a moment to revel as a visible, public community in the millennial fan culture that informs and even encompasses participants' everyday lives

In *Textual Poachers*, Jenkins writes that fans see fandom "as an alternative reality whose values may be more humane and democratic than those held by mundane society."[6] LeakyCon and millennial fandom carry on this tradition, but they direct it outward as they dissolve the divide between fan communities and a nonfannish, mundane world. Millennial fans envision fandom as an expansive community with subcultural energy that can transform the mainstream and that is already a growing part of popular culture. Even moments of purposefully oppositional millennial fan activism serve as building blocks for a larger culture built by millennials. By assuming the possibilities of transformative authorship as a broader cultural stance, millennial fans create a landscape in which commercial media is always already raw material for a culture of their design.

> To writing fiction . . . fanfiction
> A world without restriction . . .
> A prediction, my friend, we'll be geeky through and through.

Notes

NOTES TO INTRODUCTION

1. Neil Howe and William Strauss, *Millennials Rising: The Next Great Generation* (New York: Vintage Books, 2000).

2. Louisa Stein, "'This dratted thing': Fannish storytelling through new media," in *Fan Fiction and Fan Communities in the Age of the Internet*, ed. Karen Hellekson and Kristina Busse (Jefferson, NC: McFarland, 2006), 243–260; Mizuko Ito, "Machinima in a Fanvid Ecology," *Journal of Visual Culture* 10, no. 1 (April 2011): 51–54.

3. Melissa M. Brough and Sangita Shreshtova, "Fandom Meets Activism: Rethinking Civic and Political Participation," in "Transformative Works and Fan Activism," ed. Henry Jenkins and Sangita Shreshtova, special issue, *Transformative Works and Cultures*, no. 10 (2012), doi:10.3983/twc.2012.0303.

4. This position was suggested by Elizabeth Osder of Buzznet at the Futures of Entertainment conference in November 2007, when she distinguished between superfans and more mainstream consumers, with the latter offering sufficient ratings without the added complications of superfan investment. See Guy Brighton, "Report from the Futures of Entertainment 2 Conference: Labor," PSFK, November 20, 2007, http://www.psfk.com/. For a discussion of industry approach to different perceived stratums of fan engagement, see Suzanne Scott, "Dawn of the Undead Author: Fanboy Auteurism and Zack Snyder's 'Vision,'" in *Companion to Media Authorship*, ed. Jonathan Gray and Derek Johnson, 440–464 (Hoboken, NJ: Wiley Blackwell, 2013).

5. Jennifer Gillan, "Fashion Sleuths and Aerie Girls: *Veronica Mars*' Fan Forums and Network Strategies of Fan Address," in *Teen Television: Programming and Fandom*, ed. Sharon Ross and Louisa Stein (Jefferson, NC: McFarland, 2008), 185–206; Will Brooker, "Living on *Dawson's Creek*: Teen Viewers, Cultural Convergence and Television Overflow," *International Journal of Cultural Studies* 4, no. 4 (December 2001): 456–472; Derek Johnson, "Franchise Histories: Marvel, X-Men, and the Negotiated Process of Expansion," in *Convergence Media History*, ed. Janet Staiger and Sabine Hake London, 14–23 (New York: Routledge, 2009).

6. For other examples of studies that explore the interdependence of transmedia elements or of television and digital paratexts, see Will Brooker, *Batman Unmasked* (London: Continuum, 2001) and *Using the Force* (London: Continuum, 2002); Jennifer Gillan, *Television and New Media: Must-Click TV* (New York: Routledge, 2010); and Sharon Ross, *Beyond the Box: Television and the Internet* (Malden, MA: Wiley-Blackwell, 2008).

7. Although my analysis focuses on discursive fan texts rather than fans themselves, I am aware that there are people behind these texts. I have attempted to balance

respect for authors, acknowledgment, and rigorous citation with an awareness of the complex nature of fan spaces that merge private and public; indeed, this notion of an intimate public is a key topic of my later chapters. As a result, I follow in the citation practices recommended by the journal *Transformative Works and Cultures* and outlined by Karen Hellekson and Kristina Busse in "Identity, Ethics, and Fan Privacy," in *Fan Culture: Theory and Practice*, ed. Katherine Larsen and Lynn Zubernis (Newcastle: Cambridge Scholars, 2012), 38–56. When citing fan work, I do not give a full web address or URL; rather, I list the online site where the work is posted, such as LiveJournal or Tumblr. This prevents direct linking and excessive unwanted traffic to intimate yet public spaces while still offering citation. I enter into a gray area when citing work that lives somewhere in between fan and professional, like the StarKids' *A Very Potter Musical* and the video blogs and Tumblr posts of professional web series actors. In these cases, I have made citation judgments on the basis of the specifics of the situation. Also, when reproducing fan art for illustration, in specific cases, I provide a direct link at the request of the artist.

8. Jason Mittell examines the role of the community-editable wiki in the development of collaborative fan culture. Likewise, Julie Levin Russo examines how industrially instigated online fan engagement shapes fan digital production and fan cultures. Jason Mittell, "Sites of Participation: Wiki Fandom and the Case of Lostpedia," *Transformative Works and Cultures* no. 3 (2009), doi:10.3983/twc.2009.0118; Julie Levin Russo, "User-Penetrated Content: Fan Video in the Age of Convergence," *Cinema Journal* 48, no. 4 (2009): 125–130. See also my work with Kristina Busse on technological, cultural, and interface contexts for fan creativity: "Limit Play: Fan Authorship between Source Text, Intertext, and Context," *Popular Communication* 7, no. 4 (2009): 192–207.

9. Natalie Landau, "Are Millennials Too Dependent on Technology?" *Appeal Democrat*, September 1, 2011, http://www.appeal-democrat.com/; Charlie Warzel, "Study: Nobody Knows How All This Technology Will Shape 'The Millennials,'" *In the Capital*, February 29, 2012, http://inthecapital.streetwise.co/; Athima Chansanchai, "'Millennials' Lead the Wired Life' New Generation 'Digital Natives in a Land of Digital Immigrants,'" *NBC News*, September 5, 2006, http://www.nbcnews.com/.

10. Marc Prensky, "Digital Natives, Digital Immigrants," *On the Horizon* 9, no. 5 (October 2001): 1–6. danah boyd provides an invaluable overview of the persistent discourse of digital natives and its cultural ramifications. boyd argues that assumptions that today's teens are digital natives means that teens are often not taught important lessons necessary for media literacy. danah boyd, *It's Complicated: The Social Lives of Networked Teens* (New Haven, CT: Yale University Press, 2013), 176–198.

11. Julie Liesse, "Getting to Know the Millennials," *Advertising Age*, July 9, 2007, http://brandedcontent.adage.com/pdf/ABC_Family_Meet_The_Millennials.pdf.

12. Brett Hurt, "Millennials Are Socially Conscious Consumers," *Bazaar Voice*, October 25, 2006, http://blog.bazaarvoice.com/.

13. Obsession_inc, "Affirmational vs. Transformational Fandom," Dreamwidth, June 1, 2009

14. See Kristina Busse, "Geek Hierarchies, Boundary Policing, and the Gendering of the Good Fan," *Participations: Journal of Audience and Reception Studies* 10, no. 1 (May 2013), http://www.participations.org/. Academic discourse also plays a role in the disavowal of fannishness in millennial culture, with literature on young people's engagement with media often tactically emphasizing its socially productive dimension in ways that reify taboos against fan engagement. For example, as Melanie Kohnen argues in her review of S. Craig Watkins's *The Young and the Digital*, in order to emphasize the nondestructive dimension of young people's digital embeddedness, Watkins focuses on the ways in which young adults and teenagers use digital media to supplement and expand the relationships already present in their "real" lives; he does not include young adults connecting with others only online, a central part of media fandom. Melanie Kohnen, review of *The Young and the Digital: What Migration to Social-Networking Sites, Games, and Anytime, Anywhere Media Means for Our Future*, by S. Craig Watkins, *Transformative Works and Cultures*, no. 8: doi:10.3983/twc.2011.0357. S. Craig Watkins, *The Young and the Digital: What Migration to Social-Networking Sites, Games, and Anytime, Anywhere Media Means for Our Future* (Boston: Beacon Press, 2009).

15. Barbara Ehrenreich, Elizabeth Hess, and Gloria Jacobs, "Beatlemania: Girls Just Want to Have Fun," in *The Adoring Audience*, ed. Lisa A. Lewis (London: Routledge, 1992), 85. On discourses of failed masculinity in regard to Trekkies, see Henry Jenkins, *Textual Poachers* (1992; twentieth anniversary reprint, New York: Routledge, 2013), 9–12. Here and throughout, I use the term "queer" expansively, in the tradition of Alexander Doty, to mean nonnormative gender and sexual practices. Alexander Doty, *Flaming Classics* (New York: Routledge, 2000). On fandom as a queer female space, see Kristina Busse, Alexis Lothian, and Robin Ann Reid, "Yearning Void and Infinite Potential: Online Slash Fandom as Queer Female Space," *ELN* 45, no. 2 (Fall/Winter 2007): 103–111.

16. Henry Jenkins, *Convergence Culture* (New York: New York University Press, 2006).

17. Henry Jenkins, Sam Ford, and Joshua Green, *Spreadable Media: Creating Value and Meaning in a Networked Culture* (New York: New York University Press, 2013).

18. Paul Booth, *Digital Fandom: New Media Studies* (New York: Peter Lang, 2010).

19. Francesca Coppa, "A Brief History of Media Fandom," in Hellekson and Busse, *Fan Fiction and Fan Communities*, 41–59. Matt Hills similarly warns that we must resist any simple conflation between fandom and academia. Matt Hills, *Fan Cultures* (New York: Routledge, 2002), 15–17.

20. Jonathan Gray, Cornell Sandvoss, and C. Lee Harrington, eds., *Fandom: Identities and Communities in a Mediated World* (New York: New York University Press, 2007), 9.

21. Jenkins, *Textual Poachers*. For work on fandom as feminine and queer space published in *Transformative Works and Cultures* in particular, see Jennifer Stevens Aubrey, Elizabeth Behm-Morawitz, and Melissa A. Click, "The Romanticization of Abstinence: Fan Response to Sexual Restraint in the Twilight Series," *Transformative Works and Cultures*, no. 5, doi:10.3983/twc.2010.0216; and Francesca Coppa, "Women, *Star Trek*, and the Early Development of Fannish Vidding," *Transformative Works and Cultures*, no. 1 (2008), doi:10.3983/twc.2008.0044.

22. See, for example, Joanna Russ, "Pornography by Women, for Women, with Love," in *Magic Mommas, Trembling Sisters, Puritans and Perverts: Feminist Essays* (Trumansburg, NY: The Crossing Press, 1985), 79–99; Hui Min Annabeth Leow, "Subverting the Canon in Feminist Fan Fiction: 'Concession,'" *Transformative Works and Cultures*, no. 7 (2011), doi:10.3983/twc.2011.0286; Sarah Fiona Winters, "Vidding and the Perversity of Critical Pleasure: Sex, Violence, and Voyeurism in 'Closer' and 'On the Prowl,'" in "Fan/Remix Video," edited by Francesca Coppa and Julie Levin Russo, special issue, *Transformative Works and Cultures*, no. 9, doi:10.3983/twc.2012.0292.

23. Hills, *Fan Cultures*, 15–17.

24. Robert Seidman, "Join the Club: 'Gleek Week" Kicks Off Today on Fox,'" *Zap2It*, April 5, 2010, http://tvbythenumbers.zap2it.com/; Mary Beltran, "For the Love of Glee," *Antenna: Responses to Media and Culture*, April 15, 2010, http://blog.commarts.wisc.edu/.

25. ABC Family courted the millennial audience not only with *Kyle XY* but also with reruns of the *Gilmore Girls* (WB, 2000–2007) and with later series such as *Secret Life of the American Teenager* (ABC Family, 2008–2013), *Huge* (ABC Family, 2010), *Greek* (ABC Family, 2007–2011), and now *Pretty Little Liars* (2010–present) and *The Fosters* (2013–present), all of which fall under the banner of the rebranded network's "new kind of family."

26. Jeff Bercovici, "Disney Buying Fox Family Channel," *Media Life Magazine*, July 23, 2001, http://www.medialifemagazine.com.

27. Lynn Elbar, "ABC Family Banks on New Series," *ABC Local Go*, July 10, 2006, http://abclocal.go.com/; ABC Family Properties Inc., "Here's the XYZ," *Legal Force Trademarkia*, http://www.trademarkia.com/; ABC Family Worldwide Inc. History, *Funding Universe*, http://www.fundinguniverse.com/.

28. ABC Family is not the only network to set its sights on the millennials as an emerging demographic; the cable network Pivot has also entered the millennial television market. Emily Nussbaum, "On Television: Kids Today, Pivot, a new channel for Millennials," *New Yorker*, September 16, 2013, http://www.newyorker.com/. See also Sharon Ross on the niche audience address of The N network and Valerie Wee on teen (arguably protomillennial) marketing by the now-defunct WB network.

Sharon Ross, "Defining Teen Culture: The N Network," in Ross and Stein, *Teen Television*, 61–77; Valerie Wee, "Teen Television and the WB Television Network," in Ross and Stein, *Teen Television*, 43–60.

29. Liesse, "Getting to Know the Millennials."

30. Ibid.

31. Ibid.

32. After guiding the rebranding of ABC Family, Paul Lee became president of ABC Entertainment Group, a position he currently holds in 2014. Gina Keating, "Disney Tests 'Watch-Chat' Features on ABCFamily.com," *Reuters*, March 22, 2007, http:// www.reuters.com/.

33. Ibid.

34. "ABC Family Lets Viewers Share, Play, Go, and Celebrate," *Futon Critic*, April 12, 2006, http://www.thefutoncritic.com/.

35. Ibid.

36. Denise Martin, "ABC Family Hones Page," *Variety*, April 11, 2006, http://www .variety.com/.

37. Although the network made concerted efforts to develop a fan base for *Kyle XY* via official digital media extensions hosted on its website, this participation was not echoed in unofficial online spaces. The series' unofficial fannish response was limited compared to fan engagement with other similar shows such as *Roswell* and *Supernatural*. For example, at the time of writing, *Kyle XY* has 409 entries at FanFiction.net (http://www.fanfiction.net/tv/), where the similarly themed *Roswell* has 4.8 thousand and *Supernatural* has 85.7 thousand.

38. The website's revamped structure was outlined in a press release from ABC Family, accessible at *Futon Critic*, "ABC Family Lets Viewers Share."

39. Clue Tracker is now available in stand-alone format (no longer part of a larger alternate reality game) at the ABC Family site at http://a.media.abcfamily.go.com /abcfamily/Standalone/cluetracker/.

40. Mittell, "Sites of Participation." See also Denise Mann, "The Labor behind the Lost ARG: WGA's Tentative Foothold in the Digital Age," in *Wired TV: Laboring over an Interactive Future*, ed. Denise Mann (New Jersey: Rutgers University Press, 2014).

41. The ABC Family Insider Blog is no longer a component of the ABC Family website.

42. As is the case for most of ABC Family's ARG efforts with *Kyle XY* (beyond Clue Tracker), Coop's Scoop is no longer available online. The remnants of Cooper's Blog are available at http://www.781229.com/coopersblog/.

43. For analysis of a similar industrial strategy, see Avi Santos, "From Heroes to Zeroes: Producing Fan Vids without Fans," *In Media Res*, February 20, 2009, http:// mediacommons.futureofthebook.org/.

44. See Kristina Busse, "'I'm jealous of the fake me': Postmodern Subjectivity and Identity Construction in Boy Band Fan Fiction," in *Framing Celebrity: New Directions*

in *Celebrity Culture*, ed. Su Holmes and Sean Redmond (New York: Routledge, 2006), 256–267; Kristina Busse, "My Life Is a WIP on My LJ: Slashing the Slasher and the Reality of Celebrity and Internet Performances," in Hellekson and Busse, *Fan Fiction and Fan Communities*, 207–223; Stein, "This dratted thing."

45. Sian Lincoln posits that because of the presence of the Internet and other digital media, bedrooms in digital culture function as fluid spaces, simultaneously private and public. For Lincoln, this means that bedroom culture (for boys and girls) is no longer shaped strictly by the media and culture industry, as Angela McRobbie and Jenny Garber suggested in "Girls and Subcultures." Rather, bedrooms offer personal space where teens control and negotiate their cultural engagement. Sian Lincoln, "Teenage Girls Bedroom Culture: Codes versus Zones," in *After Subculture: Critical Studies in Contemporary Youth Culture*, ed. Andy Bennett and Keith Kahn-Harris (Basingstoke: Palgrave, 2004), 94–106; Angela McRobbie and Jenny Garber, "Girls and Subcultures," in *Resistance through Rituals: Youth Subcultures in Post-War Britain*, ed. Stuart Hall and Tony Jefferson (London: HarperCollins Academic, 1976), 209–222. See also Mary Celeste Kearney, *Girls Make Media* (New York: Routledge, 2006), 4.

46. Gillan, *Television and New Media*; Dan Harries, ed., *The New Media Book* (London: British Film Institute, 2002), 172, 178, 181.

47. Henry Jenkins, "The Cultural Logic of Media Convergence," *International Journal of Cultural Studies* 7 (2004): 33–43; Jenkins, *Convergence Culture*.

48. Ellen Seiter, Hans Borchers, Gabriel Kreutzner, and Eva-Maria Warth, eds., *Remote Control: Television, Audiences and Cultural Power* (London: Routledge, 1989); Jenkins, *Textual Poachers*, 151–184.

49. Henry Jenkins, "Transmedia Storytelling 101," *Confessions of an Acafan*, March 22, 2007, http://henryjenkins.org/.

50. Brooker, "Living on *Dawson's Creek*"; Will Brooker, "Overflow and Audience," in *The Audience Studies Reader*, ed. Will Brooker and Deborah Jermyn (London: Routledge, 2003), 322–335.

NOTES TO PART I

1. Kyle Sims, "Gleek Freak Out: Kurt & Blaine Kiss Reaction," YouTube, March 15, 2011.

2. SofisSwag and AllenSimansMusic, comments on "Gleek Freak Out: Kurt & Blaine Kiss Reaction," YouTube.

3. Other flamers may have posted negative and homophobic comments on this video, but YouTube allows users to request that inflammatory comments be removed. Thus, to some degree, fan communities can self-police and shape the tone of discourse on YouTube.

1. Howe and Strauss, *Millennials Rising*, 5

2. Howe and Strauss's previous work, including *Generations* and *The Fourth Turning*, established a vision of repeated and thus predictable generational cycles and archetypes. Their work posed the coming generation at a critical juncture—a fact Howe and Strauss claimed they could predict because of their knowledge of past generational archetypes and cycles. Neil Howe and William Strauss, *Generations: The History of America's Future, 1584 to 2069* (New York: William Morrow, 1991); Neil Howe and William Strauss, *The Fourth Turning: What the Cycles of History Tell Us about America's Next Rendezvous with Destiny* (New York: Broadway Books), 1997.

3. Howe and Strauss, *Millennials Rising*, 4. The popular and niche press provide ample stories of adolescents abandoning faith and traditional community formation in favor of technology and social networking. Ainsley Caffrey, "Religion and the Generation Y," *Miss Millennia Magazine*, March 9, 2013, http://www.missmillmag .com/; "Millennials Losing Faith in God," *Huffington Post*, June 5, 2012, http://www .huffingtonpost.com/; Brandee Sanders, "Are Millennials Losing Faith?" *Root*, July 26, 2010, http://www.theroot.com/.

4. For just a few examples of the myriad press that stresses young adults' destructive relationships to digital media, see Alexander Vassilliadis and John Mederich, "Digital Withdrawal: I'm a Teenage Addict!" *Huffington Post*, March 1, 2012, http:// www.huffingtonpost.com/; Rebecca Smith, "Facebook and MySpace Generation 'Cannot Form Relationships,'" *Telegraph*, July 3, 2008, http://www.telegraph.co.uk/; Pete Cashmore, "Trapped Girls Update Facebook Status Instead of Calling for Help," *Mashable*, September 7, 2009, http://mashable.com; Kashmir Hill, "What Employers Are Thinking When They Look at Your Facebook Page," *Forbes*, March 6, 2012, http://www.forbes.com/.

5. Howe and Strauss, *Millennials Rising*, 213–238.

6. Eric Hoover critiques *Millennials Rising* as based "on a hodgepodge of anecdotes, statistics, and pop-culture references, as well as on surveys of teachers and about 600 high-school seniors in Fairfax County, Va.," suggesting that these survey statistics are highly compromised because of Fairfax's economic stature. Eric Hoover, "The Millennial Muddle," *Chronicle of Higher Education*, October 11, 2009, http://chronicle.com/.

7. Ibid.

8. LifeCourse Associates, "Higher Education," http://www.lifecourse.com/.

9. Morley Winograd and Michael Hais, *Millennial Makeover: My Space, YouTube, and the Future of American Politics* (New Brunswick, NJ: Rutgers University Press, 2009), 3.

10. "Millennials: Confident. Connected. Open to Change," *Pew Social Trends*, February 24, 2010, http://www.pewsocialtrends.org/.

11. For example, *Harry Potter and the Millennials* examines the liberal values in the Harry

Potter series and considers their effect on the millennial generation. Anthony Gier-zynski and Kathryn Eddy, *Harry Potter and the Millennials: Research Methods and the Politics of the Muggle Generation* (Baltimore: John Hopkins University Press, 2013).

12. Henrik Temp, "With Apologies to Mitt Romney: 3 Reasons Millennials Vote Democrat," *AEI Ideas*, March 20, 2012, http://www.aei-ideas.org/.

13. Howe and Strauss, *Millennials Rising*, 234.

14. Ibid., 236.

15. Ibid., 265.

16. Ibid., 264.

17. Ibid., 266.

18. Lisa Bannon, "More Kids' Marketers Pitch Number of Single-Sex Products," *Wall Street Journal*, February 14, 2000, http://online.wsj.com/, cited in Howe and Strauss, *Millennials Rising*, 266. More recently, conversations around millennials and gender have begun to shift, as is evident in a recent NPR series on millennials, *New Boom*. See Lidia Jean Kott, "For These Millennials, Gender Norms Have Gone Out of Style," *National Public Radio*, November 30, 2014, http://www.npr.org.

19. Howe and Strauss, *Millennials Rising*, 266.

20. Ibid., 265.

21. Although Fox, Fox News, and their shared umbrella, Fox Entertainment Group, are not identical in terms of controlling forces or political positioning, we can trace ideological affiliations between them, as Jennifer Gillan demonstrates in her work on 24. Jennifer Gillan, *Television and New Media*, 76–134.

22. Contemporary academic literature on digital culture also emphasizes the positive social impact of online engagement. S. Craig Watkins argues that young people most often use digital technologies to enhance real-life relationships. S. Craig Watkins, *The Young and the Digital*, 47–74. danah boyd argues that young people are more savvy about the stakes of their online engagement than older generations give them credit for. See danah boyd and Alice E. Marwick, "Social Privacy in Networked Publics: Teen Attitudes, Practices, and Strategies," in *Proceedings of the OII Symposium on the Dynamics of the Internet and Society: A Decade in Internet Time*, University of Oxford, September 2011, 21–24, 1–29. The recent work of Henry Jenkins and others describes not only the media literacy built within fandom but also the collective social action and social impact increasingly mobilized within fan communities. See the March 2012 special issue of *Transformative Works and Cultures*, "Transformative Works and Fan Activism," http://journal.transformativeworks.org/.

23. Just as *Millennials Rising* has drawn criticism for its limited scope and seemingly self-fulfilling narratives, many scholars since Jenkins, including Sarah Gwenllian Jones, Alexis Lothian, Kristina Busse, and Julie Levin Russo, have pointed to blind spots created by *Textual Poachers'* celebratory emphasis on the value of community-instigated fan resistance. Sarah Gwenllian Jones, "The Sex Lives of Cult Television

Characters," *Screen* 43 (2002): 79–90; Alexis Lothian, "Living in a Den of Thieves: Fan Video and Digital Challenges to Ownership," *Cinema Journal* 48, no. 4 (Summer 2009), 130–136; Kristina Busse, "Podcasts and the Fan Experience of Disseminated Media Commentary," *Flow*, October 2006, http://www.kristinabusse.com/cv /research/flow06.html.

24. Jenkins, *Textual Poachers*, 277–287.

25. I don't mean to equate *Millennials Rising* and *Textual Poachers; Millennials Rising* may have some kernels of insight into millennials, or it may create self-fulfilling prophecies that extend at least as far as the television programs created in the book's mold. In contrast, *Textual Poachers* offers a nuanced, self-reflexive interrogation of specific fan communities in a specific moment.

26. "'Glee' Creator Ryan Murphy Talks Death Threats, Regrets, Controversy," *Huffington Post*, August 5, 2011, http://www.huffingtonpost.com/.

27. Adam Sherman, "Sing-a-Long-A Sex Education," *Independent*, November 10, 2011, http://www.independent.co.uk/.

28. "'Glee' Creator Ryan Murphy Talks Death Threats."

29. Ibid.

30. Where the popular press echoes the narrative of social progress put out by the series' producers, critical reception of the series—especially in the crossover sphere of academic popular criticism at sites such as *Flow* and *Antenna*—has questioned the show's progressiveness and positive social impact. For example, Mary Beltran takes *Glee* to task for offering only a veneer of diversity while upholding traditional hegemonic values. Mary Beltran, "Meaningful Diversity: Exploring Questions of Equitable Representation on Diverse Ensemble Cast Shows," *Flow TV*, August 27, 2010, http://flowtv.org/. Likewise, Alexander Doty criticizes *Glee*'s false sense of diversity, although he acknowledges that later seasons rectify some of the first season's wrong "by self-consciously addressing the series' own shortcomings" and by offering new focus on the series' previously marginalized characters. Alexander Doty, "*Modern Family, Glee*, and the Limits of Television Liberalism," *Flow TV*, September 24, 2010, http://flowtv.org/.

31. *Glee* played a contributing role in making Fox the network with the most gay characters on prime time TV in 2011–2012. According to a GLAAD report, "Fox leads the networks in gay representation, with eight regular characters out of a total of 117," with five of those eight being supporting and recurring characters on *Glee*. Associated Press, "Study: New Network TV Season Has Fewer Gay Characters," *Fox News*, September 28, 2011, http://www.foxnews.com/.

32. Sharon Ross argues that in contemporary millennial media, this multiplicity extends from multiple characters and story lines to multiple channels, platforms, and viewer entry points within the transmedia landscape. Ross, *Beyond the Box*, 20.

33. Jason Mittell, "Narrative Complexity in Contemporary American Television," *Vel-*

vet Light Trap 58 (Fall 2006): 29–40. See also Jason Mittell, *Complex TV: The Poetics of Contemporary Television Storytelling*, http://mediacommons.futureofthebook.org/mcpress/complextelevision/.

34. Mittell, *Complex TV*.

35. Sherman, "Sing-Along-A Sex Education."

36. In following chapters, we'll look at how the genre of film noir enters into this ideological dance in series such as *Veronica Mars* and *Pretty Little Liars*.

37. Richard Dyer, "Entertainment and Utopia," in *Only Entertainment*, 2nd ed. (New York: Routledge, 2002), 19.

38. Jane Feuer, "Hollywood Musicals: Mass Art as Folk Art," *Jump Cut* 23 (October 1980): 23–25.

39. Rick Altman, *The American Film Musical* (Bloomington: Indiana University Press, 1987), 28–50.

40. Ibid., 37.

41. In her study of theatrical performance in contemporary television, Abigail De Kosnik suggests that in a time of increased self-mediation through digital authorship, many TV programs feature theatrical performance in order to convey character transformation and authenticity of self. Abigail De Kosnik, "Drama Is the Cure for Gossip: Television's Turn to Theatricality in a Time of Media Transition," *Modern Drama* 53, no. 3 (2010): 377.

42. Mittell, *Complex TV*.

43. Ibid.

44. Jane Feuer, "The Self-Reflective Musical and the Myth of Entertainment," *Quarterly Review of Film Studies* 2, no. 3 (August 1977): 313–326. See also Feuer's "Hollywood Musicals."

45. That *Glee* is less likely to be discussed as "narratively complex" than, say, *The Wire* or *Breaking Bad* perhaps attests to the influence of industrial discourses of "quality" TV in our academic assessment of contemporary television. See Michael Z. Newman and Elana Levine, *Legitimating Television: Media Convergence and Cultural Status* (New York: Routledge, 2012).

46. Laura Mumford, *Love and Ideology in the Afternoon* (Bloomington: Indiana University Press, 1995), 92.

NOTES TO CHAPTER 2

1. Mumford, *Love and Ideology*, 72.

2. Feuer, "Self-Reflective Musical."

3. Allison McCracken, "*Glee*: The Countertenor and the Crooner," *Antenna: Responses to Media Culture*, May 3, 2011, http://blog.commarts.wisc.edu/.

4. Ibid.

5. Ibid. McCracken argues that *Glee* offers a significant departure for contemporary

American network television by showcasing young men singing pop songs to other young men without changing pronouns and without shying away from the potential queer meanings embodied in such performances.

6. Laura Mulvey, "Visual Pleasure and Narrative Cinema," *Screen* 16, no. 3 (1975): 6–18.

7. An article in *Bitch Magazine* outlined *Glee*'s double standard in regard to depicting bisexuality and sexual fluidity. Carrie Nelson, "Visi(bi)lity: *Glee*'s Problem with Bisexual Men," *Bitch Magazine*, March 20, 2012, http://bitchmagazine.org/.

8. Melanie Kohnen, *Queer Representation, Visibility, and Race in American Film and Television: Screening the Closet* (New York: Routledge, forthcoming).

9. This number is also significant in that it is a cover of a song cowritten and performed by k. d. lang, a singer/songwriter known for her gay rights activism, thus offering an additional dimension of queer voice and queer performance to the episode.

10. Lesley Goldberg, "Parents Television Council Blasts 'Glee's' 'First Time' Episode," *Hollywood Reporter*, November 8, 2011, http://www.hollywoodreporter.com/.

11. See Steve Cohan, "Feminizing the Song and Dance Man: Fred Astaire and the Spectacle of Masculinity in the Hollywood Musical," in *Hollywood Musicals: The Film Reader*, ed. Steve Cohan (New York: Routledge, 2002). See also Feuer, "Self-Reflexive Musical."

12. Edward Wyatt, "Not That High School Musical," *New York Times*, May 17, 2009, http://www.nytimes.com.

13. Kelli Marshall, "Show Musical Good, Paired Segments Better: *Glee*'s Unevenness Explained," *Flow TV*, July 16, 2010, http://flowtv.org/.

14. A nostalgic aesthetic characterizes much of millennial self-authored and official representation, a development that I will look at in later chapters on millennial noir and millennial transformation.

15. Kohnen, *Queer Representation*.

16. Cohan, "Feminizing the Song and Dance Man," 88.

17. Ibid.

18. See Allison McCracken's "Kurt and the Casting Couch" for a discussion of the series' and cultural authorities' discomfort with the feminized male as an erotic object for fans. Allison McCracken, "Kurt and the Casting Couch," *Antenna: Responses to Media Culture*, October 19, 2011, http://blog.commarts.wisc.edu/.

19. Cohan, "Feminizing the Song and Dance Man," 88.

NOTES TO CHAPTER 3

1. Michael Schneider, "Fox Greenlights 'Glee' Pilot," *Variety*, July 23, 2008, http://variety.com/.

2. Maria Elena Fernandez, "What 'Glee.' Choir kids rule." *LA Times*, April 26, 2009, http://articles.latimes.com/.

3. Lawrence Lessig, *Remix: Making Art and Commerce Thrive in the Hybrid Economy* (New York: Penguin, 2008).

4. Ibid., 28.

5. Ibid.

6. Cristina Kinon, "'Glee' Puts Edgy Spin on Top 40 Tunes," *Daily News*, May 16, 2009, http://www.nydailynews.com/.

7. *Glee* models a legal process for producing remixes and covers, as described in Todd and Jeff Brabec, "Glee: A Prime Example of How Music Branding Works; International Association of Entertainment Lawyers," *Midem Book*, April 16, 2012, http://www.musicandmoney.com/. However, *Glee* has also come under attack for taking advantage of artists and overlooking copyright. See Michelle Jaworski, "Serial Song Theft on *Glee*? 'Baby Got Back' Wasn't the First," *Daily Dot*, January 25, 2013, http://www.dailydot.com/.

8. Plot summary for *The Glee Project*, Internet Movie Database, http://www.imdb.com/.

9. Jane Feuer, *The Hollywood Musical*, 2nd ed. (Bloomington: Indiana University Press, 1993), 3.

10. Ibid.

11. Susan Wloszczyna and Ann Oldenburg, "Geek Chic," *USA Today*, October 22, 2003, http://usatoday.com. See also Busse, "Geek Hierarchies."

12. The Glee-related albums released in 2011 from Columbia Records include *Glee: The Music Presents the Warblers*; *Glee: The Music, Volume 7*; and *Glee: The Music—The Christmas Album, Volume 2*.

13. Jenkins, *Textual Poachers*; Lessig, *Remix*.

14. For another example of selection as transformation, see allforonexx, "When B Met K," January 1, 2012, YouTube. This video features all of the Kurt/Blaine scenes edited down to the key moments. The performances are included in brief shorthand as they motivate the plot; they are not presented as a spectacle in their own right.

15. Margaret Hartmann, "Glee Does Original Songs, We Only Care about Kurt & Blaine's Duet," *Jezebel*, March 16, 2011, http://jezebel.com/.

16. Totallypandacoffee, Tumblr note.

17. Shesaidclud, "Chris Colfer Doing Judy Garland. It's So Perfect," Tumblr.

18. Christie Keith, "Glee's Missing Klaine 'Box Scene' Revealed," *Backlot*, May 30, 2012, http://www.thebacklot.com/; "Give Your *Glee* Fan a Signed Script," *Charity Buzz*, April 26, 2012, https://www.charitybuzz.com/.

19. "The Box Scene Project: About Us," http://www.theboxsceneproject.org/.

20. Lulzychan, "The Klaine Box Scene Script Livestream, 5/29/12," May 29, 2012, YouTube.

21. Anna McCarthy, "Ellen: Making Queer Television History," *GLQ: A Journal of Lesbian and Gay Studies* 7, no. 4 (2001): 593–620.

22. Perhaps not incidentally, this scene also mentions Kurt's habit of purchasing clothes on the online site Rue La La, thus positioning him as a convergence consumer and digital participant akin to those who campaigned for the box scene script's release. Online viewers were finally rewarded for their convergence engagement when Ryan Murphy posted the actual video of the box scene on Tumblr and YouTube. Beth Douglass, "*Glee*'s Romantic Klaine 'Box' Scene: Ryan Murphy Will Release It—If You Do THIS," *Wet Paint*, July 31, 2012, http://www.wetpaint.com/.

23. Glee Equality Project, "Season 3 Kiss Compilation," YouTube, June 18, 2012.

24. Murphy also tweeted his support of the Glee Equality Project, now visible in a post reproduced on the Glee Equality Project's Tumblr as an indicator of the project's legitimacy: Glee Equality Project, "Thank You Mr. Murphy," August 9, 2012, Tumblr.

25. C. P. Coulter's "Dalton" is by far the most "favorited" piece of *Glee* fan fiction on FanFiction.net.

26. Mochacappucino, "Steal a Heart," *Archive of Our Own*, http://archiveofourown.org. This series was previously known as "Drive Myself Insane" and "Love Like Whoa."

27. SugarKane_01, "Come Here Boy," *Archive of Our Own*, http://archiveofourown.org.

28. Some *Glee* fan fiction works, both Klaine and otherwise, address issues of race, class, and disability in substantive ways that are often more rigorous than in the series: Herostratic, "Good (You Know What I Mean)," LiveJournal; AdiWriting, "HearingVerse: Integrating," Tumblr; and QuietlyGleeful, "A Singular Gentleman," Tumblr.

29. See, for example, the multiple Disney-focused sing-alongs and panels at the millennial fan convention par excellence, LeakyCon, in 2013 (http://leakyconportland2013.sched.org/).

30. Alex Juhasz, *Learning from YouTube* (Boston: MIT Press & Vector), http://vectors.usc.edu/projects/learningfromYouTube/texteo.php?composite=161&tag=23. A version of this essay was also published as "Learning the Five Lessons of YouTube," *Cinema Journal* 48, no. 2 (Winter 2009): 145–150.

31. Juhasz, *Learning from YouTube*.

32. Jean Burgess and Joshua Green, *YouTube: Online Video and Participatory Culture* (Cambridge: Polity Press, 2009), 98.

33. Izzyintan1992, comment on "Gleek Freak Out."

34. Lynn Spigel, *Make Room for TV: Television and the Family Ideal in Postwar America* (Chicago: University of Chicago Press, 1992).

35. Given the overarching flaming culture that thrives on YouTube, it is noteworthy that there is little to no truly negative response to the "Gleek Freak Out" video. However, as mentioned previously, viewers can request that highly negative, flaming comments be removed. There is evidence of this removal, in the form of miss-

ing comments and responses to missing comments, in the "Gleek Freak Out" video comment threads.

36. Elektrita9, comment on "Gleek Freak Out."

37. zeek4two, comment on "Gleek Freak Out."

38. doubleDdog09, comment on "Gleek Freak Out."

NOTES TO PART 2

1. E. Anne Kaplan, ed., *Women in Film Noir*, rev. ed. (London: British Film Institute, 2008).

2. Jessica Pressler and Chris Rovzar, "The Genius of *Gossip Girl*," *New York Magazine*, April 21, 2008, http://nymag.com/; Sonia Zjawinski, "*Gossip Girl*'s Online Success Is a Preview of TV 3.0," *Wired*, April 24, 2008, http://www.wired.com/.

NOTES TO CHAPTER 4

1. The threat of millennial collective empowerment and groupthink runs through discourses on young peoples' digital engagement. For example, an article in *Retail Wire* suggests that millennials make purchasing decisions only after consulting social networks and user-generated content: "Millennials are . . . the first generation to be 'always connected.' They are much more likely than the general population to consult user-generated content before making a purchasing decision, such as checking first with family, friends and peers via social media." "Getting Millennials: How Shopping Patterns are Shifting," *Retail Wire*, July 19, 2012, http://www.retailwire.com/.

2. Amelia Hill, "Internet Users Unaware of Illegal Downloading," *Guardian*, April 21, 2013, http://www.theguardian.com/; Rebecca Nelson, "Young Americans Won't Pay for TV. Will They Ever?" *Time*, May 9, 2013, http://business.time.com/.

3. "How Teens Watch: The Future (of Media) Is in Their Hands," *Nielsen*, June 16, 2010, http://www.nielsen.com/.

4. Such initiatives to educate workplaces and educators about how to work with millennials have become so ubiquitous as to be fodder for parody in OfficialComedy's "Millennials in the Workplace: A Helpful Guide," which urges bosses frustrated by millennials' work habits, "Don't fire them yet!" This parody pokes fun at millennials' supposed lack of a traditional work ethic, at bosses' negative labeling of millennial qualities, and at the disingenuous promises of consulting companies who claim to have solved the millennial problem. E. D. W. Lync, "Millennials in the Workplace: A Helpful Guide," *Laughing Squid*, June 5, 2013, http://laughingsquid.com/.

5. "How Do You Solve a Problem Like Millennials?" SXSW Panel Picker, http://panelpicker.sxsw.com/.

6. The predominance of traditional crafts like knitting and beading on sites like Etsy are heralded as the return of the crafting movement. See Jack Bratich and Heidi M. Brush, "Fabricating Activism: Craft-Work, Popular Culture, Gender," *Utopian Studies* 22, no. 2 (2011): 233–260.

7. Pressler and Rovzar, "Genius of Gossip Girl"; Zjawinski, "*Gossip Girl*'s Online Success."

8. Pressler and Rovzar, "Genius of Gossip Girl."

9. Leslie Bruce and Lacey Rose, " 'Gossip Girl' Cast and Producers Reflect on the CW Drama's Road to 100 Episodes," *Hollywood Reporter*, January 30, 2012, http://www .hollywoodreporter.com/.

10. Edelman/Strategy One, "The 8095 Exchange: Millennials, Their Actions Surrounding Brands, and the Dynamics of Reverberation," http://www.edelmanberland .com/documents/8095whitepaper.pdf.

11. For examples of public discourse emphasizing millennial consumerism, see Jennifer Frighetto, "Millennial Consumers Seek New Tastes, Willing to Pay a Premium for Alcoholic Beverages," *Nielsen*, November 26, 2007, http://www.nielsen .com/; Deirdre van Dyk, "The Global Millennial Generation: The Next Generation of Luxury Consumers," *Time*, February 21, 2008, http://content.time.com/; and Adrienne Selko, "How You Manufacture Matters to Millennials," *Industry Week*, October 17, 2012, http://www.industryweek.com/.

12. Parents' Television Council, "Worst TV Show of the Week: *Gossip Girl*," *Parents TV*, November 19, 2007, https://www.parentstv.org/.

13. Parents' Television Council, "PTC Study: Sexualized Teen Girls Are Tinseltown's New Target," *Parents TV*, December 15, 2010, http://www.parentstv.org/.

14. John Consoli, "PTC Takes Issue with 'Gossip Girl,' " *Ad Week*, April 23, 2008, http:// www.adweek.com/.

15. "Parental Advocacy Group Slams CW's 'Gossip Girl' for Intense Sexual Imagery," *Fox News*, November 5, 2009, http://www.foxnews.com/.

16. "OMG! Check Out the Sexy New *Gossip Girl* Ads," *People*, July 23, 2008, http://www .people.com/.

17. James Naremore, *More Than Night: Film Noir in Its Contexts* (1998), updated and expanded ed. (Berkeley: University of California Press, 2008).

18. Jason Mittell, *Genre and Television* (New York: Routledge, 2004).

19. Paula Rabinowitz, *Black and White and Noir: America's Pulp Modernism* (New York: Columbia University Press, 2002).

20. Ibid., 18.

21. Ibid.

22. Karen Hollinger, "Film Noir, Voice-over, and the Femme Fatale," in *Film Noir Reader*, ed. Alain Silver and James Ursini (New York: Limelight, 1996), 243.

23. Ibid.

24. Robert Miklitsch, *Siren City: Sound and Source Music in Classic American Noir* (New Brunswick, NJ: Rutgers University Press, 2011), 248.

25. Hollinger, "Film Noir," 246.

26. Ibid., 246–247.

27. Raymond Borde and Etienne Chaumeton, *A Panorama of American Film Noir*, trans. Paul Hammond (1941–1953; translation published 1955; reprint, San Francisco: City Lights, 2002), 9.

NOTES TO CHAPTER 5

1. We can trace millennial noir across niche and broadcast television networks as well as film and digital media. I choose here to focus on four femalecentric television texts because femalecentric serial television is a primary site for the negotiations of millennial ambivalence specifically in relation to notions of fandom and feminine excess. However, I would argue that we can also see millennial noir surfacing in more seemingly malecentric television series like *Supernatural* and *Teen Wolf* (MTV, 2011–present) and in filmic (and literary) texts like the Harry Potter and Twilight franchises.

2. Sarah Hughes, "Humphrey Bogart's Back—But This Time Round He's at High School," *Guardian*, March 26, 2006, http://www.theguardian.com/.

3. For an extended analysis and comparison of the two openings, see Jason Mittell, "These Questions Need Answers: An Essay on the *Veronica Mars* Pilot," *JustTV*, August 10, 2009, http://justtv.wordpress.com/.

4. On film noir's critique of systemic corruption, see Daniel Hodges, "The Politics of Crime and the Crime of Politics: Post-War Noir, the Liberal Consensus and the Hollywood Left," in *Film Noir Reader 4*, ed. Alain Silver and James Ursini (New Jersey: Limelight, 2004), 227–246. On the social spaces of school in teen film, see Timothy Shary, "Youth in School: Academics and Attitude," chap. 2 of *Generation Multiplex* (Austin: University of Texas Press, 2002), 26–79.

5. I will explore this shift from girls staying silent to speaking out through digital production in the next chapter. See Kearney's *Girls Make Media* for an invaluable look at this issue and the significance of girls speaking out through media production.

6. Hollinger, "Film Noir," 246–247.

7. For more on *Veronica Mars'* merging of hardboiled and teen media tropes, see Andrea Braithwaite's "That girl of yours—she's pretty hardboiled, huh?': Detecting Feminism in *Veronica Mars*," in Ross and Stein, *Teen Television*, 132–149.

8. Sharon Ross describes this type of representation of young characters using digital technology as a form of "organic invitation" in which characters offer relatable models of digital participation in media. Ross, *Beyond the Box*, 8. See also Gillan,

Television and New Media, 54, on characters' use of digital technology in TV programs in the early 2000s, including *Veronica Mars*'s omnipresent T-Mobile Sidekick.

9. "I Use My T-Mobile Sidekick to Get Online More Than My Computer!" *Black Digerati*, September 4, 2009, http://www.blackweb20.com/. T-Mobile (and the T-Mobile Sidekick specifically) sponsored both UPN and the CW, the two networks on which *Veronica Mars* aired.

10. The final episode of *Gossip Girl* reveals the infamous blogger to be poor-boy writer Dan Humphrey; however, this was not the supposition of viewers throughout the show's run. Moreover, the series final moments suggest yet again that Gossip Girl is a role to be filled rather than a particular person. The series concludes with a new, newly anonymous Gossip Girl narrating—with gender again undetermined.

11. *Gossip Girl*'s structure interpellates us, the viewers, as part of the Gossip Girl reading and e-mailing public. One of the series' many transmedia campaigns enabled viewers to receive Gossip Girl blasts on their phone, allowing the story world to spill over into viewers' daily digital interactions. "'Gossip Girl' Blast Reveals Scandalous Moments," *AceShowBiz*, March 25, 2009, http://www.aceshowbiz.com/.

12. This transformation from restrained viewer to transgressive millennial performer is one taken up by fans/viewers and even encouraged by the text itself, not only by interpellating us to identify with Chuck and Blair but also by invitations to transform the text itself. These invitations to fan transformation will be the subject of the next chapter.

13. Although season 5 reveals Alison to be alive, she still remains an enigmatic figure; we are constantly encouraged to guess whether she is in fact victim or terrorizer, powerful or powerless. Thus, even when Alison appears on screen alive, she remains an elusive, uncontrollable, powerful mystery.

14. Tania Modleski, *The Women Who Knew Too Much* (New York: Routledge, 2005).

15. See Amy Pattee, "Commodities in Literature, Literature as Commodity: A Close Look at the *Gossip Girl* Series," *Children's Literature Association Quarterly* 31, no. 2 (Summer 2006): 154–175.

16. Modleski, *Women Who Knew Too Much*.

17. Ibid., 44. Modleski suggests that this ambivalence toward female collective knowledge informed Hitchcock's ambivalence to *Rebecca*. Hitchcock objected to Daphne Du Maurier's intimate writing style in *Rebecca* and the female mass audience that came with it. However, Modleski argues that even so, Hitchcock found in *Rebecca* a key preoccupation: the strong, potentially oppressive/dangerous identification between women (seen most clearly in *Vertigo*), a theme we might read as being adapted into the millennial girl collective.

18. It is both ironic and appropriate, then, that *Pretty Little Liars* pays such frequent homage to Hitchcock, the most esteemed of film auteurs, whose films appear in

canon-constructing best-of lists. *Pretty Little Liars* frequently invokes Hitchcock in its plot, mise-en-scène, and character performance. Reviewers and fans alike take pleasure in noting and analyzing these various Hitchcock references. See Kayti Burt, "*Pretty Little Liars* Hitchcock Homages—From *Psycho* to *The Birds*," *Wet Paint*, April 25, 2013, http://www.wetpaint.com/.

19. Modleski, *Women Who Knew Too Much*, 54.
20. Ibid.
21. "How This Twisty, Over the Top Teen Mystery Is Changing TV," *Entertainment Weekly*, February 22, 2013, http://www.ew.com/.
22. Ibid.

NOTES TO CHAPTER 6

1. Kearney, *Girls Make Media*, xix.
2. Ibid., xxvi.
3. Ibid.
4. Popsugar Tech, "*Gossip Girl's* Second Life Secret," *Pop Sugar*, October 31, 2007, http://www.popsugar.com/.
5. Louisa Stein, "Playing Dress-up: Digital Fashion and Gamic Extensions of Televisual Experience in *Gossip Girl's* Second Life," *Cinema Journal* 48, no. 3 (Spring 2009): 116–122.
6. Deidre Woollard, "*Gossip Girl* Fashions on Bluefly," *Luxist*, October 26, 2008, https://web.archive.org/web/20100704095011/http://www.luxist.com/2008/10/26/gossip-girl-fashions-on-bluefly/.
7. "Live Like a Gossip Girl with New Social Game!" *Seventeen Magazine*, January 27, 2011, http://www.seventeen.com/.
8. Ross, *Beyond the Box*, 9.
9. Kelsey Wilson, "Blair and Chuck—Bittersweet Symphony," YouTube, November 19, 2007.
10. Florence Snow, "I'm Already Gone," YouTube, December 25, 2009.
11. Despite being the poster child for ABC Family's hopeful millennial discourse, *Kyle XY's* TV narrative also incorporates elements of millennial noir into its overall hopeful picture. Over the course of the series' run, Kyle and his female counterpart learn that they are in fact clones created by nefarious corporation Madacorp. They are corporate-created humans built by the very organization they are fighting. Many of the later episodes feature Kyle and friends breaking into the corporate fortress of Madacorp to discover further information about their origins. Although the narrative is overall one of millennial hope, the series often focuses on corporate transgression and moral ambiguity.
12. Ben, "Kyle XY Online: The Warehouse," *Scribble Ben*, May 19, 2009, http://scribbleben.com/.

13. Kearney, *Girls Make Media*, xxvi.

14. In most nonnoir fan fiction, fans self-police against overt self-insertion (known derogatorily as the Mary Sue), and they thus stay away from first-person narratives. However, hard-boiled style prose is one of the few exceptions to this rule. Ika Willis, "Keeping Promises to Queer Children: Making Space (for Mary Sue) at Hogwarts," in Hellekson and Busse, *Fan Fiction and Fan Communities*, 153–170.

15. Isdonisgood, "Switching Places," FanFiction.net, February 27, 2009.

16. This story was written before the TV series' conclusion. In retrospect, if we accept the series' ending, Gossip Girl and Dan Humphrey are one and the same. However, the TV series never has Dan narrating as himself; he always narrates as Gossip Girl, as voiced by Kristen Bell (aka Veronica Mars).

17. Amber477, "The Big Sleep," FanFiction.net, March 12, 2009.

18. Darlulu, "Martina," LiveJournal, August 15, 2007.

19. MotherGoddamn, "The Lost Nightingale," *Archive of Our Own*, June 7, 2012, http://archiveofourown.org.

20. "Gleeful Little Liars," community header image, Tumblr.

21. Role-playing games are temporary, transient texts. "Gleeful Little Liars" is no longer in active play, although many accounts remain. The "Gleeful Little Liars" gossip blog with the Gossip Girl component is no longer available on Tumblr.

NOTES TO PART 3

1. 510 U.S. 569 (1994). "Why Was This Terminology Chosen?" Organization for Transformative Works, http://transformativeworks.org/.

2. "Measuring Fair Use: The Four Factors," Copyright and Fair Use, Stanford University Libraries, http://fairuse.stanford.edu/.

3. "What We Believe," *Organization for Transformative Works*, http://transformativeworks.org/.

4. The video has been uploaded at least twice on YouTube: Nathan Jongewaard, "We'll Always Have Pirates," November 23, 2008; and "Pirating DVDs, Casablanca Style," July 10, 2008.

5. Jongewaard, "We'll Always Have Pirates."

6. Comment by Leechcode5 to Jongewaard, "We'll Always Have Pirates."

7. Comment by Gibberishtwist to Jongewaard, "We'll Always Have Pirates."

NOTES TO CHAPTER 7

1. "Prior Gishwhes Rhino Hunt Lists," Tumblr.

2. Other examples of television actors and celebrities positioning themselves within fandom include *Supernatural*'s Osric Chao and *Sleepy Hollow*'s Orlando Jones. In the following chapter, I look at performers in web series such as *The Lizzie Bennet Diaries* and *Squaresville* who push even further at some of these boundaries.

3. See Graeme Turner, *Understanding Celebrity* (Thousand Oaks, CA: Sage, 2004); and Richard Dyer, "A Star Is Born and the Construction of Authenticity," in *Stardom: Industry of Desire*, ed. Christine Gledhill, 132–140 (New York: Routledge, 1991).

4. I have used term "transmedia" flexibly to include any instances of storytelling or world building that takes place across interfaces, whether authored by official producers or by fans. Previous definitions of the word "transmedia" emphasize professional/commercial authorial control of a singular narrative across multiple platforms. However, if we do not prioritize transmedia storytelling as a narrative system controlled by a single author, we can recognize the multiplicitous expanse of audience or fan authorship as transmedia production. See Jenkins, "Transmedia Storytelling 101"; Henry Jenkins, "Transmedia Storytelling 202: Further Reflections," *Confessions of an Acafan*, August 1, 2011, http://henryjenkins.org/; and Andrea Phillips, *A Creator's Guide to Transmedia Storytelling: How to Captivate and Engage Audiences across Multiple Platforms* (New York: McGraw-Hill, 2012).

5. danah boyd and Alice Marwick call this form of small-scale celebrity fostered on Twitter "microcelebrity." danah boyd and Alice Marwick, "To See and Be Seen," *Convergence* 17, no. 2 (May 2011): 139–158.

6. *Supernatural* already had an active fandom with ready processes for recognizing and celebrating characters and actors. On *Supernatural* fandom, see Katherine Larsen and Lynne Zubernis, *Fangasm: Supernatural Fangirls* (Iowa City: University of Iowa Press, 2013). See also the special issue of the journal *Transformative Works and Cultures*, "Saving People, Hunting Things," guest edited by Catherine Tosenberger, http://journal.transformativeworks.org/.

7. Juhasz, *Learning from YouTube*.

8. Busse, "I'm jealous of the fake me."

9. Lindsay Hogan describes stars as "at once texts, commodities, and people, functioning both as the author and the authored." Lindsay Hogan, "The Mouse House of Cards: Disney Tween Stars and Questions of Institutional Authorship," in Gray and Johnson, *Companion to Media Authorship*, 296–313.

10. Frank Krutnik, *In a Lonely Street: Film Noir, Genre, Masculinity* (New York: Routledge, 1991).

11. Collins's performance of Castiel as a somewhat alien, subversive male figure activates media tropes that have long histories of fan resonance linking fangirl with alien male, with the two united in their shared alternative perspective. Castiel recalls the (female) fan-beloved alien figure of *Star Trek*'s Spock, whose character was originally written as a female love interest for Captain Kirk, and who thus evokes (in the words of Francesca Coppa) the "shadow of the missing woman" and "desiring female subjectivity." Coppa, "Women, *Star Trek*."

12. "Reasons Why We Love Castiel," Tumblr.

13. For an example of the paratextual biographic information circulating about Collins

emphasizing his nontraditional path to stardom, see "Misha Collins," *Buddy TV*, http://www.buddytv.com/.

14. "Vicki and Misha Renew Vows at Albertsons," *FanPop*, http://www.fanpop.com/.

15. For discussion of fandom as a queer female space, see Lothian, Busse, and Reid, "Yearning Void."

16. Elizabeth Ellcessor argues that the prevalence of social media and social networking must necessarily affect the way we understand the construction of stardom and star texts. Elizabeth Ellcessor, "Tweeting @feliciaday: Online Social Media, Convergence and the Subcultural Stardom of Felicia Day," *Cinema Journal* 51, no. 2 (2012): 46–66.

17. boyd and Marwick, "To See and Be Seen"; Alice Marwick and danah boyd, "I Tweet Honestly, I Tweet Passionately: Twitter Users, Context Collapse, and the Imagined Audience," *New Media and Society* 13, no. 1 (2011): 1–20.

18. Misha Collins, @mishacollins, *Twitter*, May 13, 2009, https://twitter.com/#!/misha collins/statuses/1781444376.

19. Ibid., May 13, 2009, http://twitter.com/#!/mishacollins/status/1781491998

20. Ibid., https://twitter.com/#!/mishacollins/status/1781776590.

21. Ibid., https://twitter.com/#!/mishacollins/status/1789654441.

22. Ibid., https://twitter.com/#!/mishacollins/status/1789720465.

23. Ibid., https://twitter.com/#!/mishacollins/status/1789920824.

24. "'Supernatural' Star Misha Collins Calls the Show 'Gratuitously Misogynistic,'" *Hypable*, May 14, 2013, http://www.hypable.com/.

25. Jonathan Gray, Jeffrey P. Jones, and Ethan Thompson, "The State of Satire, the Satire of State," in *Satire TV: Politics and Comedy in the Post-Network Era*, ed. Gray, Jones, and Thompson (New York: New York University Press, 2009), 4.

26. Magic_Minion, "Misha Collins: Minion Recruitment Advert," YouTube, August 7, 2009. This video was hosted on YouTube and circulated on LiveJournal and Twitter.

27. For a discussion of the gendered perceptions of fandom, see Busse, "Geek Hierarchies."

28. Over the years, these representations have led to deep ambivalence among fans about being represented on television. See Lisa Schmidt, "Monstrous Melodrama: Expanding the Scope of Melodramatic Identification to Interpret Negative Fan Responses to *Supernatural*," *Transformative Works and Cultures*, no. 4 (2010), doi:10.3983/twc.2010.0152.

29. The episode, entitled "The French Mistake," aired February 25, 2011, after Collins was already firmly established on Twitter, with over 300,000 followers. On *Supernatural*'s representation of its fandom, see Laura Felschow, "'Hey, check it out, there's actually fans': (Dis)empowerment and (Mis)representation of Cult Fandom in *Supernatural*," *Transformative Works and Cultures*, no. 4 (2010), doi:10.3983/twc.2010.0134.

30. Derek Johnson, "Fan-tagonism: Factions, Institutions, and Constitutive Hegemonies of Fandom," in Gray, Sandvoss, and Harrington, *Fandom*, 294–295.

31. See post and comments at Vlada Gelman, "*Supernatural* Exclusive: Misha Collins Won't Be a Series Regular for Season 7," *TV Line*, May 20, 2011, http://tvline.com/; Kevin Yeoman, "'Supernatural' Shake-up: Misha Collins Out, Jim Beaver In as Series Regular?" *Screen Rant*, June 9, 2011, http://screenrant.com/; Tierney Bricker, "*Supernatural*'s New God Misha Collins Spills on His Limited Season-Seven Role," *E Online*, August 4, 2011, http://m.eonline.com/.

32. Misha Collins, @mishacollins, *Twitter*, December 5, 2011, https://twitter.com/#!/mishacollins/statuses/143910127601328128.

33. Random Acts was originally hosted at Wordpress (http://www.therandomact.org/wordpress/) but now can be found at http://www.therandomact.org/.

34. Misha Collins, @mishacollins, *Twitter*, June 18, 2009, https://twitter.com/#!/mishacollins/status/2229238845.

35. Ibid., June 28, 2009, https://twitter.com/#!/mishacollins/statuses/85889823163949056.

36. Random Acts shares common ground with other fan activist movements, such as the Harry Potter Alliance, a fan-instigated nonprofit organization that channels Harry Potter fan investment into digital and real-world social action. See Henry Jenkins, "'Cultural Acupuncture': Fan Activism and the Harry Potter Alliance," in "Transformative Works and Fan Activism," ed. Henry Jenkins and Sangita Shresthova, special issue, *Transformative Works and Cultures*, no. 10 (2012), doi:10.3983/twc.2012.0305.

37. The quoted description is no longer available at the Kickstarter main site. The description was previously available at http://www.kickstarter.com/start, but now it can be found reposted on various online sites, such as Jason Wood, "Kickstarter: Patronage for the New Millennium, *I Fanboy*, October 20, 2010, http://ifanboy.com/. Kickstarter has since grown in visibility, in part thanks to the highly publicized *Veronica Mars* movie campaign.

38. See Watkins, "Conclusion: A Message from Barack," in *The Young and the Digital*.

39. "Kickstarter Basics: Kickstarter 101," *Kickstarter*, http://www.kickstarter.com/help/faq/kickstarter%20basics. This description is no longer available at the main site, but it remains in circulation online, quoted in blog posts like this one: "Technology Lessons," *Lessons for Old People*, http://lessonsforoldpeople.blogspot.com/2011/11/technology-lesson-kickstarter.html. It was originally available at "Defining Your Project: Kickstarter," http://www.kickstarter.com/help/school/defining_your_project.

40. Ivan, "Divine: The Series," *Kickstarter*, http://www.kickstarter.com/.

41. One rule declares: "Any whining, whimpering, yelling, screaming, crying, tantrum-throwing, challenging or contesting the judges or contest results will result in im-

mediate disqualification and revocation of your Gishwhes citizenship. Seduction, however, is allowed under certain circumstances." Although the items and rules (including this one) for the 2011 Gishwhes hunt are no longer posted at the official website, they have been reproduced in parts throughout Tumblr and LiveJournal.

42. This description is as originally found online at http://greatestinternational scavengerhunttheworldhaseverseen.com/faq/. It has since been reposted at "Frequently Asked Questions," *What Is Gishwhes*, http://whatisgishwhes.wordpress.com /frequently-asked-questions/.

43. I have different degrees of personal investment in all of the chapters in this book; however, this is a chapter to which I feel most especially tied. I have followed Misha Collins on Twitter since the start, and I have participated in his various enterprises. I supported *Divine*, and I signed on for the craziness that is Gishwhes, even dragging my husband into it. I've now participated in the hunt three times. In my third year of participation, my team won the hunt. In a few months' time from this writing, I will be headed to an island in Vancouver with my teammates (and my newborn son) to eat fish stew and hold a séance with Collins himself. Without a doubt, my own relationship to Gishwhes and my perception of it—and Collins—will be altered irrevocably after this real-life, in-person experience, which brings together fans from across the globe with the star who originally connected them. Although others may look in from the outside and see Collins's strategic manipulation of his fans, because of my ongoing participation in Collins's fandom, I find myself especially aware of how he has continually presented himself as an individual contributing to a creative network and how his fans—myself included—have responded and contributed in kind. As such, Collins's and fandom's authorship has been, to me at least, always already decentered and collective, thus offering a rich ground for collective transmedia authorship.

44. On the push toward televisual norms in a digital media landscape, see Melanie Kohnen, "Television's Queer Future? The Possibilities and Limitations of Web Series, Digital Distribution, and LGBT Representation in *Husbands*," in *Future Texts: Subversive Bodies and Feminist Performance*, ed. Vicki Callahan and Virginia Kuhn (Anderson, SC: Parlor Press, forthcoming).

NOTES TO CHAPTER 8

1. For similar posts gauging size of fandom or support of particular characters, see "Reblog if You're in the Welcome to Nightvale Fandom," Tumblr; "Reblog if You Want Gabriel Back on *Supernatural*," Tumblr; and "Reblog if StarKid Is the Blood in Your Veins," Tumblr.

2. On collective authorship and the blog post, see Kristina Busse, "The Return of the Author: Ethos and Identity Politics," in Gray and Johnson, *Companion to Media Authorship*, 48–68.

3. Booth, *Digital Fandom*, 43. See also Staci Stutsman, "Blogging and Blooks: Communal Authorship in a Contemporary Context," *Transformative Works and Cultures*, no. 11 (2012), doi:10.3983/twc.2012.0413.

4. Kristina Busse and Karen Hellekson, "Introduction: Work in Progress," in Hellekson and Busse, *Fan Fiction and Fan Communities*, 7.

5. Booth, *Digital Fandom*, 17.

6. Tagfic and tagmeta are usually ephemeral and are generally not archived or meant for reading beyond the flow of Tumblr. A search for the #tagfic hashtag on Tumblr may reveal recent instances of tagfic, but often tagfic and tagmeta are integrated into the daily flow of Tumblr posting without being labeled as fan fiction or analysis.

7. One significant counternarrative stems from fan—and fan scholar—desire to recognize the talent, skill, creativity, and innovation of fan authorship, and especially female fan authorship. Francesca Coppa argues that too much emphasis on collectivity in fan scholarship, especially in studies that document the mostly female communities of media fandom, may risk devaluing female authorship by labeling it as collective craft rather than innovative art or professional skill. Francesca Coppa, review of *Digital Fandom: New Media Studies* by Paul Booth, *Transformative Works and Cultures*, no. 11 (2006): doi:10.3983/twc.2012.0450.

8. The question of whether it is ever appropriate to make money from fan works has come to the fore as a result of the launch of Amazon's Kindle Worlds, which offers a route for fans to sell specific types of fan fiction for money. See Mel Stanfill, "Fandom, Public, Commons," *Transformative Works and Cultures*, no. 14 (2013), doi:10.3983/twc.2013.0530; Karen Hellekson, "A Fannish Field of Value: Online Fan Gift Culture," *Cinema Journal* 48, no. 4 (Summer 2009): 118; Nele Noppe, "Why We Should Talk about Commodifying Fan Work," *Transformative Works and Cultures*, no. 8 (2011): doi:10.3983/twc.2011.0369; and Rebecca Tushnet, "User-Generated Discontent: Transformation in Practice." *Columbia Journal of Law and the Arts* 31 (2008): 497–516. On the question of labor in fandom, see also the *Cinema Journal* In Focus section, edited by Kristina Busse, "Fandom and Feminism Revisited," *Cinema Journal* 54, no. 3 (2014).

9. Valis2, "Avoiding Mistakes in Fanfiction Writing: A Beginner's Guide," *Sycophant Hex.*

10. LJC, "Tips for Writing Better Fan Fiction," *My Geek, Let Me Show You It*, LiveJournal.

11. Likewise, in video form, Big Big Truck's "Cowboy Bebop: Failed Experiments in Video Editing" (uploaded by Alive1985 to YouTube, April 6, 2006) playfully critiques newbie vidder errors, yet—perhaps surprisingly—does so within a more DIY, almost grrrl zine–esque aesthetic.

12. Academic work on fandom (both in scholarship and teaching) can be complicit in this move to celebrating professionalized aesthetics and skill, even when this is

not intended, by drawing attention to and foregrounding creative work with a professional aesthetic to argue for the cultural value of fandom. See Kristina Busse, Flourish Kink, and Nancy Baym, "Acafandom and Beyond: Week Three, Part One (Kristina Busse, Flourish Klink, and Nancy Baym)" *Confessions of an AcaFan*, http://henryjenkins.org/. On debates within fandom regarding professionalization, see Will Brooker, "Going Pro: Gendered Responses to the Incorporation of Fan Labor as User-Generated Content," in Denise Mann, *Wired TV*, 72–97.

13. "Professional Authors on Fanfiction," forum discussion, FanFiction.net.

14. See Kristina Busse and Shannon Farley, "Remixing the Remix: Ownership and Appropriation within Fan Communities," *M/C Journal* 16, no 4 (August 2013), http://journal.media-culture.org.au/. See also Altocello, "Reccing vs. Reposting; Fandom Etiquette Musings," Dreamwidth, March 14, 2013; Cherrybina. "Plagiarism and Fandom Etiquette," Tumblr; and Bellumina, "Why I Have a Problem with Cassandra Clare and You Should Too," Wordpress, March 14, 2012.

15. "Lizzie Bennet—This Is My Diary," YouTube, https://www.YouTube.com/user/LizzieBennet.

16. *The Lizzie Bennet Diaries*, http://www.lizziebennet.com/.

17. Jean Burgess and Joshua Green, "The Entrepreneurial Vlogger: Participatory Culture beyond the Professional–Amateur Divide," in *The YouTube Reader*, ed. Pelle Snickars and Patrick Vonderau (Stockholm: National Library of Sweden, 2009), 95.

18. One of the more high profile of these fictional social networks is the *Mad Men* Twitter network (http://wearesterlingcooper.org/), which has received significant attention in part because many of its creators and authors work in the media industry. As an enterprise, the *Mad Men* Twitter network thus blurs the lines between amateur and professional. However, similar fan-authored profile-based role-playing games proliferate in fandom, with sites such as "Advertise My RPG" on Tumblr serving to connect role players with one another and to advertise media-based role-playing opportunities.

19. Aja Romano, "Behind the Scenes of the *Lizzie Bennet Diaries*," *Daily Dot*, August 27, 2012, http://www.dailydot.com/.

20. On *Sherlock*'s appeal to multiple fandoms, see Matt Hills, "*Sherlock*'s Epistemological Economy and the Value of 'Fan' Knowledge," in *Sherlock and Transmedia Fandom: Essays on the BBC Series*, ed. Louisa Ellen Stein and Kristina Busse, 27–40 (Jefferson, NC: McFarland, 2012).

21. Jane Austen fandom lives on in Austen-focused organizations such as the Jane Austen Society of North America (http://www.jasna.org/) and in digital multifandom spaces such as the Archive of Our Own (http://archiveofourown.org). See Deborah Yaffe, *Among the Janeites: A Journey through the World of Jane Austen Fandom* (New York: Houghton Mifflin Harcourt, 2013).

22. Brothers Hank and John Green first formed YouTube channel/project Brotherhood

2.0 (http://www.brotherhood2.com/index.php), which later transformed into the Vlogbrothers (https://www.YouTube.com/user/vlogbrothers), with its ever-growing fan community known as Nerdfighters or Nerdfighteria. On Hank Green and the Vlogbrothers, see Allison McCracken, "Redefining the Performance of Masculinity at LeakyCon Portland," *Antenna: Responses to Media and Culture*, October 11, 2013. The Nerdfighters have an established relationship with the Harry Potter Alliance (http://thehpalliance.org/), a branch of Harry Potter fandom concerned with organizing social action initiatives in relation to all things Harry Potter); see Jenkins, "Cultural Acupuncture."

23. "The Lydia Bennet," YouTube channel, https://www.YouTube.com/user/TheLydia Bennet.

24. "*The Lizzie Bennet Diaries* and the Reclamation of Lydia Bennet," *Girls Like Giants*, Wordpress, March 31, 2013.

25. Mary Kate Wiles, "What *The Lizzie Bennet Diaries* Has Meant to Me," Tumblr.

26. Myles McNutt has predicted that Lydia's presence will be downplayed in the series' long tail. Myles McNutt, "Lydia, Legacy, and the end of *The Lizzie Bennet Diaries*," *Cultural Learnings*, March 28, 2013, http://cultural-learnings.com/.

27. Jane Austen, *Pride and Prejudice*, reprint with an introduction by Hank Green (Pemberley Digital and DFTBA Records, 2013).

28. "*Squaresville* Monologue 1: Fell in Love with a Song," YouTube, February 8, 2013.

29. Melanie Kohnen argues that although web series may seem to push at the norms of television, both in terms of form and content, as often as not, they recreate industrial and ideological standards. Melanie Kohnen, " 'You Want Me to Be Anderson Cooper': Negotiating Queer Visibility on *Husbands*," *Antenna: Responses to Media and Culture*, October 23, 2012, http://blog.commarts.wisc.edu/.

30. Mary Kate Wiles, "On Vlogging and Answering Questions," YouTube, July 29, 2012.

NOTES TO CONCLUSION

1. The "leaky" in LeakyCon references the Harry Potter fan site, the Leaky Cauldron, which in turn references the Harry Potter pub of the same name. However, despite this seeming Harry Potter focus, LeakyCon has been from its inception inclusive of diverse fan texts and fandoms. The year 2013 actually debuted two LeakyCons in one year, one in London and the other in Portland. At the 2014 LeakyCon, the creators announced that the con would be renamed GeekyCon to represent its multifannish character. Jennifer, "LeakyCon Is Now GeekyCon," *Geeky News*, http://www.geekynews.com/.

2. Team StarKid originated as a musical theater production company at the University of Michigan. Darren Criss, the actor who plays *Glee*'s Blaine Anderson, is one of its founding members—thus the crossover into *Glee* fandom at LeakyCon. StarKid productions create musical theater satire playing with and poking fun at Harry

Potter and other popular cultural texts. Their productions are available on social media, including YouTube (https://www.YouTube.com/user/StarKidPotter). The actors interact with fans via a range of social media, including Twitter and Tumblr. Many StarKids travel to see the musicals in person, with LeakyCon being a key site for live StarKid performances.

3. As I have throughout the book, here I use the term "queer" in the tradition of Alexander Doty to refer to an assemblage of nonnormative positions that challenge assumed hierarchies of gender and sexuality.

4. Jenkins, *Textual Poachers*, 277, 280.

5. Ibid., 280.

6. Ibid.

Index

DeWinter, Rebecca, 108–109

Digital Fandom, 10, 157, 200n7

digital media: and bedroom culture, 182n45; fan/audience control, 74, 140; in Kyle XY, 15; markets, 22; and millennials, 84, 134, 153, 172; Misha Collins's use of, 135, 141, 145; practices, 7, 179n4; production, 168; research, 136, 138; as tool, 121. See also digital technology

digital natives, 7, 178n10

digital network: fan use of, 3; female collective as, 14, 93, 96, 109, 112; linking fans and producers, 138; millennials and, 14, 170; in millennial noir, 94; in Pretty Little Liars, 112; uncanny, 116; in Veronica Mars, 99

digital technology, 6, 7; addiction, 30; affordances and limitations, 6; generational comfort with, 7; girls' use of, 115; Gossip Girl and, 100, 103; interface, 6, 158; and the Lizzie Bennet Diaries, 162; and millennial noir, 14, 95–99; millennial use of, 5, 6; overdependence, 7, 8, 27; platform, 6; Pretty Little Liars and, 115; Revenge and, 104; representation of, 192–193n8; and television, 17; as tool, 4, 104, 122, 138; in Veronica Mars, 95–99; women using, 95. See also digital media

digital terror, 14, 78, 94–95, 101, 106, 109, 115–116, 127, 145

(dis)abilism, 35

disability, 13, 36, 72, 189n28

discrimination, 26. See also (dis)abilism; homophobia; racism

Disney: and ABC Family, 12, 16, 17, 22, 32; in fan fiction, 73; at LeakyCon, 171, 189n21

diversity: in fan culture, 10; in Glee, 35, 41, 46, 56, 60, 61, 70, 73, 173, 185n30; and millennials, 34, 56

Divine, 150–152

DIY. See aesthetics: do it yourself

Doty, Alexander, 179n15, 185n30, 203n3

Dreamwidth, 1

DuMaurier, Daphne, 107, 108, 193n17

Dyer, Richard, 38

emotion: aesthetics of, 158; celebration of, 15, 134; collective, 157–158; embodied, 157; of the fan, 118, 122, 153; in fan culture, 9, 14; in fan work, 70, 121, 126, 159; in feels culture, 156, 170; in Glee, 43, 45–47, 49; in The Lizzie Bennet Diaries, 163, 165; masculinity and, 147; in millennial noir, 7–8, 80, 97–99, 101, 103, 105; representations of, 119, 168; in Squaresville, 166, 167; on Tumblr, 158; on YouTube, 161. See also affect; feels

ethics: in fan studies research, 177–178n7; millennial, 33; of professionalism, 160; in Revenge, 104; shared by fans and official producers, 150

ethnicity, 26, 30, 146

Etsy, 191n6

excess: as allure, 78, 114, 116; digital, 8, 77–78; embrace of, 15, 87, 159, 163; of emotion, 15, 78–80, 147; fangirl, 9, 80, 116, 146; of fans, 4, 9, 15, 18, 33, 80, 81, 146; feminine, 87, 145, 159; in Gossip Girl, 87, 102, 118; and Lydia Bennet, 164, 165; in millennial noir, 77, 80, 92, 114, 118; millennials, 77, 78, 86, 117; and Misha Collins fandom, 144, 147; reining in, 159; sexuality, 80, 87, 102; of spectacle, 43–44 extensions, digital: ABC Family, 12, 17; Coop's Scoop, 20–21, 62; *Gossip Girl* Bluefly collaboration, 117; *Gossip Girl* Second Life, 117; *Kyle XY*, 12, 17, 18, 19; "Social Climbing," 117–118, 119, 120; transmedia, 12, 114, 116, 122. *See also* paratexts; transmedia

Fabray, Quinn, 35, 40–42
Facebook, 3, 117, 122, 152, 158
fair use, 131. *See also* transformativity
family values: ABC Family branding, 16, 17; millennial, 3, 33; in *Glee*, 27, 34; in fandom, 70, 75
fan affect. *See* affect: fan
fan activism: and *Glee*, 27, 70, 72, 184n23. *See also* Random Acts; Nerdfighteria
fan art, 11, 139, 143, 144, 167, 168, 169
fan art Fridays, 168
fan authorship, 6, 11, 17, 50, 66, 115, 136, 138, 141, 145, 156, 159, 162; communities of, 156; millennial noir, 123; as transmedia, 196n4. *See also* fan fiction; fan art; transformative authorship
fan codes, 62, 136, 174
fan communities, female, 11. *See also* fandom: female
Fan Cultures, 11
fan culture: aesthetic codes of, 136; celebrities within, 139, 195; collective authorship in, 155–157; corporately produced vs. grassroots, 15; feels culture and, 14, 159; professionalism in, 159–160; Leakycon as, 171–173, 175; and millennial culture, 5; negotiations of, 170; relationship with digital culture, 6, 10; research on, 33, 34; and social networks, 136;

transformativity in, 131–134. *See also* fandom
fan critique, 54, 114; as activism, 71; fan fiction as, 11, 72–73, 126–129, 132; fan videos as, 68–72, 125–126, 200n11; Glee Equality Project, 71–72; as media literacy, 66; on YouTube, 79, 137
fan dissatisfaction, 65, 66, 70
fan engagement: gendered, 25; taboo of, 33, 34, 179n14. *See also* fan investment
fan fiction, 11, 14, 27, 34, 72–73; making money from, 200n8; millennial noir in, 123–126, 131, 132, 136, 139, 146, 151; *Lizzie Bennet Diaries* as, 161–162; noir in, 14, 123, 124, 125; professional aesthetics in, 159–160; race in, 189n28; slash, 11, 34, 72–73; tagfic, 158; as transformative, 131. *See also* fan fiction stories
Fan Fiction and Fan Communities in the Digital Age, 10
fan fiction stories: "The Big Sleep," 124–125; "Come Here Boy," 72–73; "Dalton," 72–73, 189n25; "Gleeful Little Liars," 127–129, 161; "The Lost Nightingale," 126–127; "Steal a Heart," 72–73; "Switching Places," 124
fan investment, 15, 18, 122, 140, 151, 160, 167, 168, 177n4, 198n36, 199n43
fan portmanteaus, 62
fan remix video, 67, 68, 120–121, 125–126; videos: "Chuck and Blair—Bittersweet Symphony," 120; "Glee Equality Project—Season 3 Kiss Compilation," 71; "I'm Already Gone," 121; "Klaine Box Scene Script Livestream," 67–71; "Martina," 125–

126; "Minion Recruitment Advert," 145

fan studies, 9, 157; third wave, 10–12

fan vids. *See* fan remix video

fan work: citation of, 178n7

fanboy, 9; as construct, 22, 63

fandom: and academia, 11, 33, 179n19; affirmational, 9; and community activism, 27 (*see also* fan activism); as collective transgression, 18, 121, 134, 144, 173; as creative culture, 4, 168; as critical economy, 65–66; female, 78, 136, 145; gendered assumptions, 9, 81; as guilty pleasure, 114; industry appropriation of, 22, 57, 62, 121, 143, 147; international contexts, 6, 76; as intimate collective, 156, 166–170; Jane Austen, 162, 201n21; *Kyle XY*, 181n37; as millennial hope, 70; of Misha Collins, 144–146, 149–153; niche, 4, 172, 175; poaching, 65; and professionalism, 14, 15, 159–160; proselytizing, 155; as queer, 141, 143–144, 172–173, 175; as taboo, 9, 33, 34, 93, 114, 116, 134, 136, 170, 179n14; as threat, 9, 11; *Roswell*, 181n37; as selective economy, 63–64; *Sherlock*, 162, 171, 174; slash, 11, 34, 62, 146; as subcultural, 4, 13, 62, 173, 175, 176; as transformative economy, 65–72; on Twitter, 14, 135, 138–143, 146–149. *See also* cult fandom; Gleekdom; Klaine fandom; minions

fangirl, 9, 25, 63, 80, 116, 146, 168, 196n11

fans: transgressive, 4, 116, 127, 139, 141, 145, 173; unruly, 4, 15, 18, 116, 148. *See also* fan authorship; fandom

fantext, the, 74, 157

feels, 9, 14, 156, 161, 162, 165, 166, 170,

174; culture of, 156, 158–161, 163, 165, 170

female collective: digitally networked, 14; fandom as, 9; in *Pretty Little Liars*, 110, 112; in *Rebecca*, 108, 193n17

femininity: in millennial noir, 97, 102, 109, 110, 112, 115, 116; and Misha Collins's star text, 149; recuperated, 163, 164

feminism: and fan studies, 11; in millennial noir, 95, 96, 103, 108, 115–116; millennial fandom and, 175; Misha Collins's fandom and, 143, 144

femme fatale, 78, 91, 93, 95, 96, 101, 102, 105; digital, 14, 100; as feminist, 108; identification with, 92; as investigator, 14, 104; omniscient, 100; and private eye, 104; Rebecca DeWinter as, 108. *See also* fille fatale

Feuer, Jane, 38, 61

file-sharing, 58, 79, 84

fille fatale, 93, 100–102, 105, 110, 114–116; as cyborg, 115; and digital technology, 93, 101, 116, 125, 129; in fan fiction, 124, 125, 127, 129; and fandom, 80, 81; and gender trouble, 115; in *Gossip Girl*, 100; multiplicity, 78, 102, 107, 112, 127; in *Pretty Little Liars*, 105, 107. *See also* femme fatale

film noir, 53, 77, 78, 79, 83, 90–92, 96, 104, 107, 123, 139; in fandom, 173. *See also* millennial noir

filter, image, 52, 98, 119, 121, 126, 136

flashbacks: in millennial noir, 106, 107, 108, 109, 124; with voice-over, 92, 98, 105

flow: of narrative, 36, 38; queerness and, 50; transmedia, 23, 76; on Tumblr, 167, 200n6. *See also* overflow; transmedia: flow

112, 136, 138, 139, 145, 158; liberal
leaning, 31, 52; and masculinity, 44,
52–53, 81, 139, 147; and media fans,
9, 12, 15, 33, 134; morality of, 77, 78,
84, 90, 96, 99, 103–105; and Obama,
3, 31, 83, 150; as pirates, 133; and
religion, 31, 90, 171, 183n3; and sexuality, 11, 13, 27, 31, 35–37, 49, 65, 68,
70, 72, 80, 83, 87–90, 102, 187n7. *See
also* millennial generation
"Minion Recruitment Advert," 145
minions, of Misha Collins, 142–149, 175
mishacollins, tweets, 142, 146, 148, 149,
150
mise-en-scène, 19, 52, 194n18
Mittell, Jason, 36, 37, 41, 178n8
Modleski, Tania, 107, 108, 193n17
Monteith, Cory, 1–2, 83
Montgomery, Aria, 110, 112, 116
moral ambiguity, in millennial noir, 78,
95, 102, 103, 104, 123, 194n11
More Than Night, 90
Morrison, Matthew, 56
multiplicity: in millennial media, 36,
185n32; of fandom, 127, 159, 171,
173; in *Glee*, 48, 64, 67; of the fille
fatale, 101, 105, 108–110
Mulvey, Laura, 46
multifannishness: at LeakyCon, 171–
175, 202n1; as queer, 173
Mumford, Laura, 42, 43
Murphy, Ryan, 35, 37, 51, 56, 58, 59, 72,
189n22, 189n24
musical numbers: in *Glee*, 26, 27, 38, 39,
41, 42, 43, 51, 56, 59, 64, 65; in *The
Glee Project*, 59; reception of, 64, 65.
See also *Glee* musical numbers

Naremore, James, 90
narrative complexity, 36–37, 40, 54

narrative special effect, 40–42, 50, 51,
65
Nerdfighteria, 162, 170, 184n22; and
Harry Potter Alliance, 201–202n22; at
LeakyCon, 170, 171, 172
network branding. *See* ABC Family; CW
Network; Fox Network
New Directions (Glee Club), 41, 42, 45,
46, 47, 48, 51, 58; in fan work, 73,
127, 128
new media. *See* digital media
Nielsen ratings, 84, 85
noir, 29, 53, 83, 90, 91, 123, 173; *Casablanca*, 79; classic, 77; as cultural
critique, 99; in fan fiction, 125, 126;
femme fatale in, 92; gender in, 78;
indirect, 90; masculinity in, 98; nostalgic, 90, 99. *See also* film noir; millennial noir
nostalgia: in fandom, 115, 123–127, 132,
133, 136; in *Glee*, 51–53, 58, 66; in
millennial noir, 90, 97, 98, 99, 119,
121; in remix, 80, 85

OMFG Campaign, 87–88, 121
Organization for Transformative Works
(OTW), 4, 131
Ostroff, Dawn, 85–86
overflow, 23, 71. *See also* flow
Oxygen Network, 35, 59, 61

Pivot cable network, 180n28
paratexts, 6, 12, 13, 27, 55, 61, 65, 66,
177n6. *See also* transmedia extensions
Parents Television Council (PTC), 50,
87–90
Pemberley Digital, 15
Pew Research Center, 3, 31
performance: collective, 13, 27, 38–48,
56, 60, 61, 134, 139, 144, 156, 174; of

masculinity, 45, 56, 92, 139–140, 170;
of self, 38–40, 47, 49, 56, 61, 91–92,
144–145, 163, 165, 167–170, 187n41;
on Twitter, 138–144. See also musical
numbers
PFLAG, 72
Pinterest, 161
piracy: digital, 78–81, 84, 123; defense
of, 132–134
Polyvore, 4
Powers That Be, The, 145, 151
Prensky, Mark, 7
Pretty Little Liars, 13, 14, 83, 90, 94, 95,
105–113, 115; title sequence, 109–110,
116; and social media, 112–113
private eye, 53, 91, 95, 96, 100, 104, 124,
125, 139
private investigator, female, 14, 78, 93,
96, 104
professionalism, 14; in fan discourse,
159–160; in vlogging, 168, 170
prosumers, 22

"quality" television, 37, 132, 186n45
queerness: and conformity, 64; and
fandom, 9, 11, 141, 143, 144, 172–
175, 190n21; and identification, 11;
and representation, 44–50, 52, 53,
64, 69–73; usage of term, 179n15,
203n3; and visibility, 52

Rabinowitz, Paula, 91
race: in Glee, 13, 26, 30, 36, 37, 49, 56,
72; in millennial noir, 99; in fan fiction, 73, 189n28
racism, 25
Random Acts, 149–150
Rapp, Anthony, 173
read/write culture, 57, 85
Rebecca, 107–109, 193n17

remix, 58, 65, 66, 67, 79, 80, 84, 116,
118, 119, 120, 121, 165
Remix (Lessig), 85
remix culture, 57–59. See also read/write
culture
remix video, 5, 57, 65, 67, 79–81, 84,
120, 121,132–133. See also fan remix
video; vidding; vids
response videos, 74–75, 167; as labor,
136; and feels culture, 158
Revenge, 13, 14, 90, 91, 94, 95, 102–105,
115, 116
role playing games, 22, 195n21, 201n18;
Gleeful Little Liars, 127–129, The Lizzie
Bennet Diaries as, 161
romance: cross-cultural, 49; heteronormative, 36, 39, 47; fan investment in,
62, 67, 68, 73; and feels culture, 165;
and millennial noir, 80, 86, 102, 121;
queer, 46–49, 64, 71
Rood, John, 16
Ross, Sharon, 36, 118

Sandvoss, Cornell, 10
satire, 133; in Gishwhes, 152; in Glee, 38,
45, 83; in fandom, 132–133, 135,
140–145, 149; StarKids and, 202n2;
on Supernatural, 147–148
Schuester, Will, 42, 56
Second Life, 117
self-reflexivity, 51, 67, 118–119, 146–148,
185n25
seriality, 7; in Glee, 13, 27, 36–37, 40,
43, 48, 63, 65, 67, 69; in millennial
noir, 91, 93, 104; in television, 42, 43,
192n1
sexual orientation, 26, 44, 75
sexual violence: in fan work, 125, 126,
127; in millennial noir, 94, 98, 99,
112

shared authorship, 14, 136, 138. *See also* authorship: collective

Sherlock, 162, 171, 174, 201n20

slash, 11, 34, 62, 146

social media, 1, 190n1; and *Pretty Little Liars*, 110–112; and stardom, 141, 197n16; and StarKids, 202–203n2

social networking, 17, 18, 65, 79, 86, 100, 141, 183

source text: respect for, 131–132; response to, 65, 123, 125, 126, 127; shared, 157; transformation of, 162–163

Spreadable Media, 9–10

spectacle: in fan work, 72, 75, 188n14; in *Glee*, 38, 41, 43–46, 50–54, 56, 63, 64, 66

Squaresville, 15, 166–169

squee, 168

stardom: in *The Glee Project*, 60; transmedia, 135–140

StarKids, 171, 175, 178, 199n1, 202–203n2. *See also* Team StarKid

Strauss, Neil, 3, 4, 7, 12, 14, 15, 16, 17, 22, 27, 29, 30, 31, 32, 33, 34, 36, 39, 52, 56, 73, 86

streaming video, 85, 86, 87

Supernatural, 14, 171; as cult TV, 146; "The French Mistake," 146–148; masculinity in, 147; as millennial noir, 139, 140, 192n1; Misha Collins and, 14, 138, 141, 145, 149; representation of fandom, 146–147; satire, 147

superfans, 177n4

Supreme Court of the United States, 131

tags: emotion oriented, 158; at Leaky-Con, 172–173; tagfic, 158; tagmeta, 158; on Tumblr, 158. *See also* hashtags

Team StarKid, 172, 173, 202n2. *See also* StarKids

teen community, 27, 36. *See also* millennial collective

teen sex, 37, 66, 87. *See also* millennials and sexuality

Textual Poachers, 9, 11, 12, 33, 34, 175, 176; critiques of, 184n23; as intervention, 33

Thorne, Emily, 95, 103, 104, 105, 116

Transformative Works and Cultures (TWC), 11, 177–178n7

transformative authorship, 66, 158, 176. *See also* fan authorship

transmedia: definitions of, 196n4; extensions, 12, 19, 20, 21, 112, 114, 117–119, 116, 122; fan authored, 201n18; in *The Lizzie Bennet Diaries*, 161–162; stardom, 135, 138–141; storytelling, 14, 19

transformativity, 14, 54, 57, 93, 131, 156, 160, 168, 172, 176

transformative work, 131. *See also* fan fiction; fan art; fan remix video

Tumblr, 1, 4, 15, 65, 67, 128, 132, 136, 140, 152; citation for, 189; dashboard, 156; and feels culture, 156–158, 165; and Harry Potter fandom, 154; interface, 158; "Reblog if you are a wizard or a witch," post, 154–157, 159; reblogging, 155; tagging, 155; as transmedia, 161, 162, 164, 168

Twitpic, 135, 137, 158

Twitter: interface limits, 141; Mad Men Twitter Network, 201n18; Misha Collins on, 14, 135–142; *Pretty Little Liars*'s use of, 110–113; and Tumblr, 158; in transmedia context, 1, 15, 161; verified accounts, 142

Of Related Interest

Playing Fans: Negotiating Fandom and Media in the Digital Age
  by Paul Booth

The Fan Fiction Studies Reader
  by Karen Hellekson and Kristina Busse

Fangasm: Supernatural Fangirls
  by Katherine Larsen and Lynn S. Zubernis

What Is Your Quest? From Adventure Games to Interactive Books
  by Anastasia Salter